W9-BWS-873

Of Little Comfort

Of Little Comfort

*War Widows, Fallen Soldiers,
and the Remaking of the
Nation after the Great War*

Erika Kuhlman

Montante Family Library
D'Youville College

JAN 17 2013

NEW YORK UNIVERSITY PRESS
New York and London

NEW YORK UNIVERSITY PRESS
New York and London
www.nyupress.org

© 2012 by New York University
All rights reserved

References to Internet websites (URLs) were accurate at the time of writing.
Neither the author nor New York University Press is responsible for URLs
that may have expired or changed since the manuscript was prepared.

Library of Congress Cataloging-in-Publication Data

Kuhlman, Erika A., 1961–
Of little comfort : war widows, fallen soldiers, and
the remaking of the nation after the Great War / Erika Kuhlman.
p. cm.
Includes bibliographical references and index.
ISBN-13: 978-0-8147-4839-8 (cloth : acid-free paper)
ISBN-13: 978-0-8147-4840-4 (ebook)
ISBN-13: 978-0-8147-4905-0 (ebook)
1. World War, 1914–1918—Women. 2. War widows—Government policy—
United States—History—20th century. 3. War widows—Government policy—
Germany—History—20th century. 4. War widows—Government policy—
Western countries—History—20th century. 5. World War, 1914–1918—
Social aspects—United States. 6. World War, 1914–1918—Social aspects—
Germany. 7. Nationalism—History—20th century. 8. Transnationalism—
History—20th century. 9. United States—Social conditions—1918–1932.
10. Germany—Social conditions—1918–1933. I. Title.
D639.W7K84   2012
940.3′1—dc23   2011040565

New York University Press books are printed on acid-free paper,
and their binding materials are chosen for strength and durability.
We strive to use environmentally responsible suppliers and materials
to the greatest extent possible in publishing our books.

Manufactured in the United States of America
10 9 8 7 6 5 4 3 2 1

D
639
.W7
K84
2012

In memory of my grandparents,
Margareta Geiss and Richard Geiss

Contents

Acknowledgments

The idea for this book came to me while I read and lovingly fingered the pages of Helene Hurwitz-Stranz's anthology of war widows' memoirs, which she titled *Kriegerwitwen gestalten ihr Schicksal: Lebenskämpfe deutscher Kriegerwitwen nach eigenen Darstellungen* (Warrior Widows Create Their Fate: The Life Struggles of German Warrior Widows in Their Own Words). My reading took place in 2009 at the New York Public Library, the only institution in the United States whose holdings include the book. Hurwitz-Stranz wrote the introduction and edited the collection, which was published in 1931 in the old Gothic or *Fraktur* typeface. Challenging reading and translating, to say the least, but well worth the extra effort. Robert Weldon Whalen introduced Hurwitz-Stranz's work to contemporary readers in his 1984 book *Bitter Wounds*, about German society in the postwar years. My initial interest in *Kriegerwitwen gestalten ihr Schicksal* lay in Martha Harnoss's essay, which concludes the anthology, in which she outlined women's roles in rebuilding the defeated nation. I first read Harnoss's prose and perused the rest of the anthology in 2007 in the Berlin *Staatsbibliothek* (National Library), paying less attention to the gold mine that lay within the book's actual text. But the widows' words never left me, and soon I found myself imagining what other war widows might have written about their experiences both as soldiers' wives and as survivors of one of the world's most shameful butcheries ever to have taken place.

My thanks go out to Sion Harrington, archivist at the North Carolina State Archives, for his thoughtful assistance in finding materials that I hope I have put to good use here. At Idaho State University, I thank archivist Karen Kearns and Professor Pamela Park for their help in gathering and translating evidence, and Marissa Lawrence and Lori Barber for their assistance with the index. The Idaho State University Oboler Library's interlibrary loan staff retrieved countless books and manuscripts for me at the precise moments I needed them. Idaho State University also provided financial support through a grant awarded to humanities and social sciences scholars. The Idaho

Humanities Council, too, made this work possible through its fellowship program. My thoughtful friends Harry Phillips and Kimberly Jensen read parts of the manuscript and provided helpful advice as well. Thanks to Jamie Hively for her careful criticisms of my German translations. The comments of an anonymous reviewer helped me improve the analysis I offer in these pages manyfold.

Finally, I send heartfelt thanks to all those at New York University Press: to copyeditor Eric Newman for his sharp eyes, to Despina Papazoglou Gimbel and Gabrielle Begue for their assistance, and especially to Deborah Gershenowitz. Thank you for believing in this book.

An Army of Widows

In April 1919, the popular German magazine *Simplicissimus* published illustrator Josef Wackerle's watercolor titled *Die Witwen* (The Widows). The image shows two figures draped in black gowns and veils standing on a balcony overlooking a vast, empty sky and village rooftops below. "They are fighting over our conquered land," remarks the pregnant widow to her companion, "and yet we don't even know where our husbands' buried bodies lie."[1] By "they" Wackerle undoubtedly meant the diplomats who were squabbling over Germany's borders and colonies at the postwar treaty negotiations underway in Paris. While elites from the winning nations reconfigured the losing country's geographic "body," the widows felt powerless to reclaim and care for the physical bodies of their dead soldier-husbands. The defeated German nation and more than a million of its inhabitants lost both ground and lives to the ravages of the Great War. The widows' helplessness in the face of their bereavement matched Germany's inability to preserve the integrity of its own borders, rendering the vanquished state both defeated and weak, according to Wackerle: in other words, a gendered nation.[2] The cloaked mourner speaking in the watercolor may have sounded wistful, but her comment may also have betrayed a sense of angry, unfulfilled expectation. If so, her sentiments matched those of the 10,000 widows, orphans, and maimed veterans who had marched down the streets of Berlin on a gloomy December day in 1918 demanding compensation from their government for their losses.[3] Either way, Wackerle seemed to be in a sorrowful state when he worked on his painting. Perhaps the only bit of hope the artist could conceive lay in the pregnant widow's womb. New life undoubtedly symbolized fresh hopes. The expectant war widows made by Wackerle, and those fashioned by artist Käthe Kollwitz, embodied the powerful emotions of grief, despair, and hope in the same dark figures. Germans surviving the Great War could not have predicted how quickly the next bloodbath, and the nation-states that fought it, would threaten the lives of the subsequent generation.

„Sie streiten sich um erobertes Land — und wir wissen nicht, wo unsre Männer begraben liegen."

Josef Wackerle, *Die Witwen, Simplicissimus* 24, no. 3 (15 April 1919): 45. Copyright: Wackerle-Archive, EKS.

The relationship between a widow and the nation in which she lived has rarely been a topic of interest to historians. A brief survey of the literature indicates that many histories of female mourners have been published only recently and are based primarily on legal records in the medieval and early modern periods, or they explore their symbolic meaning in religious and secular literature.[4] Earlier in human history, widows had been considered little more than a dead man's wife: an object of pity because of her dependence on her now-deceased provider, or, considering her proximity to death, akin to a powerful pox to be avoided.[5] In many cultures widows were literally veiled and secluded from outsiders' prying eyes. The bereaved woman lost her status as *femme covert* (a woman whose legal rights were subsumed by her spouse upon marriage) and gained, at least theoretically, some independence as she and her children stood as heirs to her husband's property. But because of gender-based restrictions on education, occupations, and civil rights, there was often little she could do in her newly liberated state.[6] Unyielding in the limitations placed on the fairer sex, society had as its sole interest ensuring that the man's family did not fall destitute. A widow's singular interaction with her government—apart from signing her marriage certificate—may have taken place at the reading of her husband's will, and in this, of course, her experiences were not unlike those of most of her countrymen; most of the working-class soldiers who filled First World War trenches may not have had many dealings with their nation-state prior to August 1914, either. But in Germany, assembling politically was prohibited for women prior to 1908, whereas men of all classes had that privilege (as well as the right to vote, if they were over the age of twenty-five).[7] Given women's truncated ties to the nation-state, how do we come to the Great War and Josef Wackerle's comparison between the warring nation and the army of widows that fallen soldiers left behind?

Estimates suggest that of the 9 million uniformed men killed in the First World War, around 3 million had been married.[8] In France, 600,000 wives wore black; in Italy and England, the figure stood at around 200,000 each. In the United States the number of widows topped at around 33,000.[9] About 1.8 million German soldiers died in the Great War; of these, nearly one-third were married, resulting in widowhood for close to 600,000 women.[10] Calculating the numbers of fallen soldiers and the needs of their surviving dependents during and after the conflict directed a spotlight on war widows and their circumstances never seen before (although government leaders shifted the focus to what they saw as more pressing problems). Warfare in the early part of the twentieth century, altered by industrialization, produced these staggering statistics and ensured that war widows would become political actors in search of restitution from their governments for their losses.

Sigmund Freud declared in 1915 that the pervasiveness of death constituted the most significant aspect of the Great War.[11] The war accelerated some newer, twentieth-century attitudes and practices related to death, while interrupting others. In pre-industrial societies, most bodies were buried by families near homes or in village cemeteries. Mourners interpreted death as a return of the body and the soul to their natural and spiritual states. Death touched lives more frequently before the advent of modern medicine. As nation-states formed, industrialized, and urbanized, control over death moved from families, and especially from females, to professional undertakers and corporate-owned funeral homes. But old customs persisted, and Wackerle's widows understandably fretted over exactly where their dead husbands' bodies lay; people embraced some change, while warily eyeing other aspects of modern society. Just as control over death began to shift to impersonal entities, both sexes began demanding more personal satisfaction in life through their work and through companionate marriage. In addition, individuals began seeking greater meaning in death. At the same time, the Victorian era had produced improvements in health and medicine and a downturn in infant mortality, so death increasingly became associated with old age, rather than with young life. Expectations of longer lives made the deaths of young warriors that much harder to bear.[12] Death on Great War battlefields compounded individuals' sense of lack of control over life's ending. This phenomenon was heightened among survivors who had the least ability to know how and where their loved ones had died, such as Wackerle's widows, and it was magnified by the overall scale of Great War fatalities. At the same time, the nation-state moved in to manage soldiers' deaths and to control survivors' responses to death. Government and military leaders offered war remembrance ceremonies designed to impose upon a soldier's mourners their own definitions of the meaning of his passing.

The meaning of a husband's death to his widow depended in part on her perception of marriage itself. Most of the widows profiled in this volume were born in the 1880s and 1890s, when expectations about courtship and marriage were heightened by the publication of a multitude of new women's magazines, some of which are featured in these pages. For middle- and upper-class women, companionate marriage had replaced older partnerships that were based more on economics and social status than on friendship and romance. While companionate unions might seem to imply an equal relationship between spouses, such was not necessarily the case. German feminists Marianne Weber and Lily Braun hoped that greater female independence would lead to the end of patriarchal forms of marriage, but the 1900 German Civil Code reaffirmed women's and wives' subordinate position in society.[13] However, companionate marriage did go hand-in-hand with the late nineteenth century's "New Woman" who sought liberty and equality for her gender.[14] In the United States, dating practices replaced by 1925 the middle- and upper-class ritual of men "calling" on young women at their parents' homes. Courting outside parental control provided individuals with greater freedom to choose their own mates, as opposed to having family members make selections for them. For their part, working-class men and women socialized together unsupervised after quitting time.

Women's magazines reinforced courtship practices through articles on male–female relationships and through fashion and beauty product advertisements.[15] Readers of *Ladies' Home Journal* articles on romance could not help but harbor high expectations that the marriages they entered into, based on intense emotional and physical intimacy and love, would supply them with those qualities for the remainder of their lives.[16] Wives who lost their husbands in the World War had their hopes and dreams cut cruelly short. Widows writing in Helene Hurwitz-Stranz's anthology *Kriegerwitwen gestalten ihr Schicksal* (Warriors' Widows Create Their Fate) recalled their marriages as joyful events that the war intruded upon.[17] Given the emphasis placed on personal happiness and fulfillment, and the World War's interruption of those ideals, nation-states had to work harder to draw citizens' attention away from individual loss and toward a hoped-for, collective victory in war.

Great War widows who lost their soldier-husbands in battle performed honored roles as living, patriotic symbols of self-sacrifice to the nation. They aided the nations in which they lived by providing part of the justification necessary to re-militarize after the guns were silenced, because most women (and men) believed that females required male protectors and defenders. Great War soldiers confirmed this when they stated that they fought in defense of their homes and their homelands.[18] Postwar campaigns to raise national birth rates, which had plunged during the conflict, intensified women's connection to their children as well as the perceived need to protect and support the domestic sphere. Individual war widows made claims upon state welfare for restitution, insisting on their status as citizens—elevated citizenship, given their sacrifices—relative to the nation-state. But at the same time, widows' individual and collective mourning interfered with their nations' ability to conjure the glory and honor that constituted another motivating factor keeping soldiers in uniform.[19] Given their bereavement, governments had to work harder to retain survivors' loyalty in the face of the enormous battlefield fatalities that became the defining legacy of the Great War. In addition, some widows perceived grief in transnational terms, as a factor uniting women across and above national boundaries. War widows perpetuated war—a defining characteristic of the nation-state—when they performed their gendered roles as women and mothers in need of male protection; they threw a wrench into the war machine when they felt betrayed by their governments, or when they perceived their losses collectively as humans, across national boundaries. Realizing those transnational commonalities required that widows move, at least imaginatively, beyond their connection to their dead husbands and away from the nation for which the husbands had fought and lost their lives. Widows mourned individually and at times transnationally, while the public roles they played collectively in commemorative ceremonies as war widows pushed them closer to their nation-states.

This book focuses on the war and postwar experiences of people living in the United States and in Germany based on letters, diaries, popular-magazine articles, and correspondence between widows and their governments. The final two chapters necessarily broaden this scope to include widows hailing from the British Empire and France, because chapter 4 analyzes the transnational aspects of war widowhood, while chapter 5 reveals commonalities among western European nations regarding postwar campaigns to boost birth rates to compensate for wartime deficits. The choice of Germany and the United States is two-fold: First, the two countries share an intertwined past, and second, they allow for a comparison between a victorious and a vanquished nation in this particular conflict.

Germany and the United States share a history that also diverges at certain points. Both have an "exceptionalist" slant to their historical perception of themselves (*Sonderweg* in German), and both have a strong nation-centered historical tradition. Both industrialized rapidly and joined the imperialist race relatively late in the game.[20] Germany's international relations differed from those fashioned in the United States, however, primarily because of its central location among other competitive European power-houses. Each experienced nation-building conflicts in the mid–nineteenth century that resulted in a (more) centralized federal government in both countries. Germany contributed more than 5 million immigrants to the United States between 1820 and 1910.[21]

Comparing Germany and the United States not only provides a view of war widows hailing from nations on opposing sides; it also allows for an "Old World" and "New World" perspective on the war itself and on wartime and postwar experiences. Scholarship on modernity and the war is legion, but in these works soldiers' stories typically eclipse analyses of women's involvement in the conflict.[22] Europeans' perception of the United States as encapsulating modernity included their impressions of the New Woman, a short-hair- and -skirt-wearing, smoking and drinking active embodiment of liberty cut free from the suffocating propriety of her mother's Victorian generation. Although they tended to be dismissed as frivolous, in the United States younger women involved in the suffrage movement played key roles in obtaining the vote in 1920, an aspect of civic rights and duties also granted by Germany's 1918 November Revolution, and in both cases women's war work and support for the conflict resulted in at least a modicum of greater equality with and independence from men.[23] The Great War as total war had provided women with an entrée into society as industrial laborers, munitions makers, and general war supporters. Liberated females posed a threat to established norms and practices, including patriarchal control of both governments and the wearing of mourning clothes by women upon the death of a relative.

In addition, German women found American women fascinating. During the 1920s, U.S. (as opposed to French) modernity became the dominant paradigm of mass culture in urban Germany, including film, fashion, and the New Woman.[24] German and U.S. members of the international suffrage and international peace movements influenced each other a great deal, judging by their ongoing correspondence beginning in the Wilhelmine period and continuing throughout the Weimar Republic. Their mutual concern for social justice in both nations resulted in a "transatlantic dialogue" between German and U.S. leaders of these organizations.[25] The notion of social justice included restitution for widows who lost their husbands to the Great War on both sides of the Atlantic, although because the United States' participation in the conflict was much shorter, the German government served the needs of far more war widows than did the United States.

Great War widowhood drew upon the interpretations and meanings of widowhood, and war widowhood, in the past. The significance of widowhood becomes clearer through a comparison between the widow and her male counterpart, the widower. Husbands who lost their wives remarried quickly and more often than widows, signifying the importance of wives' unpaid labor in households. Widowerhood, therefore, tended to be relatively short and little noticed. Being a widower rarely changed a man's status in society, whereas a widow's place has typically been ambiguous. Widows remained in a precarious position for the rest of their lives, particularly if they shunned or could not find new suitors. This explains, in part, the historian's difficulty in detecting the widow's significance. Without a new man on whom to depend, an aggrieved female was still perceived as her husband's wife, even though he no longer lived. The wearing of black prolonged at least visually mourners' symbolic connection to death, although they were still alive. Lingering widowhood could also jeopardize communities, as women without male protection disrupted social order and stability. The bereaved stood as easy targets of blame for social ills. Widows figured prominently among all those accused of witchcraft in the seventeenth century.[26] Mourners choosing remarriage, however, faced religious and in some cases legal punishment: Widows were damned if they did and damned if they did not remarry. In the Middle Ages, the Catholic Church blessed the subsequent nuptials of widowers but not those of widows, clinging to St. Paul's notion that for females remaining widowed was a better option than remarriage.[27] The extent to which a widow could determine her own destiny reflected the constraints, both legal and cultural, placed upon all women, because nearly all women married at some point in their lives and because females generally outlived males.[28]

In most of the world's societies up until the aftermath of the Great War, widows displayed the significance of their new solitary and somber state by donning special clothing or by altering the appearance of their skin or hair. By wearing mourning clothes, widows took the first step in performing widowhood. Mary, Queen of Scots, for example, adopted a white peaked widow's cap for her frequent bouts of sorrow in the late sixteenth century. Three hundred years later, that most famous of perpetual mourners, Queen Victoria, popularized Mary's "widow's peak" in her headgear but extended it into a black mourning hood that hid her long tresses.[29] The period during which upper-class widows were expected to wear black varied, but in the nineteenth century a year in deep mourning was considered *de rigueur*. Widowers were free to remarry whenever they wanted, but their second mates were obliged to wear black out of respect for their predecessors.[30] Black indicated the widow's dark mood as well as her attempt to make herself appear unattractive to potential suitors whose attentions might compromise her allegiance to her late husband.

Along with the special trappings of widowhood came restrictions on widows' behavior. Some were cultural and represented a mourner's choice rather than a requirement. In this category we find practices such as the use of black-bordered stationery, the option of how long to wear "widows' weeds," and the refusal to be seen in public for a certain period of time. Seclusion afforded the widow's in-laws an opportunity to take the deceased's property for their own in some cultures. The Hebrew Bible commanded a brother of the deceased to marry his widow in a custom known as the levirate. If the dead man had fathered no male heir, his wife was compelled to comply with the practice.[31] In pre-revolutionary Russia, widows had the option of enter-

ing the convents of the Russian Orthodox Church, and elsewhere in prein-
dustrial Europe widows frequently sought refuge in nunneries where they
donned habits similar to widows' weeds.[32] Europe and North America witnessed the building of homes for needy widows beginning in the nineteenth
century, reflecting the shift of economic onus from the private to the public sphere with the advent of industrialization. Widows with children were
twice-burdened: first with the problem of economic security for themselves
and second with their duty to ensure the well-being of their offspring. A
mourner receiving an offer of remarriage had to take into consideration the
inevitable problems associated with adding a stepfather to her children.

Widows whose husbands died in battle distinguished themselves from all
other grieving females. War widows faced each of the challenges enumerated
above: how and whether to appear in public, the economic threats attendant
to losing a provider, the cultural stigma attached to remarriage, and how to
seek the best possible conditions for their children. But of all the ways to
categorize a widow's existence—younger or older; lower-, middle-, or upper-
class; mother or childless—only the war widow's experiences bound her as
tightly to her nation, with the exception of deceased national leaders whose
wives assumed their positions upon their deaths.

Women's relationship to war has also been fraught with ambiguity and
inconsistency. It is a history that intersects with war widowhood and with
the nation-state. Most armed conflicts in the eighteenth and nineteenth centuries were fought by and for the sake of the nation-state; the American Revolution established independence for thirteen of Britain's North American
colonies, the Civil War and Reconstruction reunited the fractured United
States, and the Franco-Prussian War brought about the unification of the
German nation-state. All of these wars occurred before women in Europe
and North America had many recognized civil rights. Women's position relative to men's has been subordinate in most of the world's societies, and it
has been kept inferior in part because of women's presumed inability to bear
arms. Arnold Ward, a member of the British House of Commons, for example, declared in 1917 that it was impossible to "separate the life of the nation
from the capacity to fight for it."[33] Females rarely played combatant roles, but
they supported conflicts in myriad ways: as camp-followers, nurses, bandage
rollers, arms makers, and maintainers of households. Aside from their helping roles, women patriots joined the cause through their pens, aligning their
prose with their nation's cause.[34] But their pacifist sisters shunned the nation's
armed endeavors, citing religious and moral reasons for rejecting the use of
weapons. Their rhetoric often upheld the notion that the female biological

function, as well as the female's presumed softer side, naturally led them to reject war.[35] Hoping to become heroes themselves, mothers reveled in the splendor that war bestowed upon their sons and argued, in the face of the pacifist position, that only through arms could the nation protect its children from harm. Other defenders of war positioned themselves as patriots in order to win the rights they lacked from the governments that could provide them, lashing women closer to the nation-state.[36]

Penelope, a character in Homer's classic epic poem *The Odyssey*, might have stood as the world's first literary war widow—except that the cunning warrior Odysseus survived the Trojan War, finally returned to his Ithacan kingdom, and reunited with his wife. But the "richly dowered" Penelope *behaved* like a war widow, even as she hoped and planned for her husband's eventual return. She made a laborious show of weaving her beloved's funeral shroud by day, only to unravel her work under cover of darkness, buying her spouse time and ensuring her chastity and loyalty to him—and preventing her and her husband's dishonor—as she waited for Odysseus to come home. In other cultures, too, a wife's devotion to her mate during war helped ensure victory, while her infidelity could result in death in enemy territory for her soldier-husband.[37] Penelope's suitors, like everyone else on the island of Ithaca, bided their time, waiting for the queen to fulfill her obligation and finish the funeral clothing.[38] Wives expected to care for their dead husbands' bodies, and Wackerle's two widows in his illustration lamented their inability to satisfy that obligation. One of the war widows featured in this volume, Elisabeth Macke, felt the same distraught emotion over her husband's neglected dead body. All of the tropes associated with Penelope—allegiance, steadfastness, and chastity—can be detected in the expectations placed upon the Great War widow. Odysseus's character traits—courage, cunning, and honor (similar to Penelope's except in the gender-defining chastity)—were rewarded aspects of twentieth-century warriors as well. But in the end Penelope had only to pass her husband's test of her loyalty, not mourn a death. Unlike a true war widow, the Ithacan queen did not have to struggle to maintain and celebrate the heroism of her husband, even while she sought restitution for his loss. In making demands of the state, wives experiencing war's sorrows, in Joy Damousi's words, "shape[d] an expression of grief which the myths of war sought to deny."[39] The history of Great War widows brings those war myths into sharp and often painful relief.

War widows are those wives who lost their soldier-husbands to armed conflict. Girlfriends or fiancées may have endured a terrible loss when their loved ones perished, and they may have worn somber clothing to signify their emotional response, but without a marriage certificate they could not choose where their men would be buried, nor could they collect war pensions from governments. Those privileges were restricted to legal next of kin. The suffering of women without a marriage certificate remained largely private, with important exceptions such as British nurse Vera Brittain's war poems and autobiography that lament the death of her soldier-fiancé.[40] Wives' losses fell along a continuum of significance and privilege. Married soldiers' valiant fighting and death in battle resulted in greater honor for their widows, as opposed to mourners whose warriors succumbed to disease in hospitals (legion during the 1918 influenza epidemic). In both cases, however, wives could gain restitution for their losses through pensions.

As the first industrialized war involving the world's major powers, the First World War was fought with more men than any conflict preceding. German soldiers were overwhelmingly young men drawn primarily from the working-class ranks of craftsmen and laborers. In the United States, too, historian Gerald E. Shenk argued that conscription protected the privileges associated with "property, patriarchy, and white supremacy."[41] Like their female counterparts, working-class German men may have felt little connection to their nation-state, except that unlike wives, mothers, and sisters, they were called to arms by the nation and by the prospect of *Heldentum*, or heroism. U.S. draftees registered excitement over the opportunity to leave their predictable, overly civilized lives behind.[42] With the exception of Russia, militaries accepted only male soldiers into their combat ranks, and generally only women displayed their grief publicly through mourning garb. Bereavement appeared, more than ever before, to be women's work. That is not to say that fathers and brothers did not lament the deaths of their sons or brothers, but by the early twentieth century most no longer wore black beyond the funeral.[43] Soldiers' bereavement for their comrades appeared in countless war poems and songs,[44] but warriors mourned in the field or in army hospitals, whereas most spouses and mothers grieved in their hometowns. While previously U.S. wives who had lost their husbands to war were called soldiers' widows, during the First World War the term "war widow" was used most often. The former indicated mourners' ties to a provider and protector, while the latter ratcheted up their connections to what was and still is perceived as a key national and historical event. In the German language, the word *Kriegerwitwe* (warrior widow) appeared more often than *Kriegswitwe* (war widow) or *Soldatenfrau* (soldier's wife), indicating women's position relative to their warrior-husbands and to the war itself.[45]

Unlike previous conflicts, the Great War brought little sense of the victory so anticipated by people in most of the warring nations, and, in addition, it brought instability and economic hardship in both defeated and victorious nations.[46] Given the continuum between the pity widowhood elicited and the privileges afforded to some powerful widows, the deplorable financial conditions of most Great War widows pushed the pendulum toward the negative side of the equation. War's glory—to which soldiers' wives were also heir—might have helped their legacy, but glory in the Great War was hard to come by.[47] Josef Wackerle's palpable sense of helplessness and defeat in his painting underscored this sad reality. War widows participated, albeit usually passively, in government- and military-sponsored remembrance ceremonies that conjured up the hoped-for images of military glory and honor meant to compensate for their forfeitures. Finally, the Great War has been defined as the first total war, meaning the "systematic, calculated incorporation of civilians into the category of participants."[48] Total war brought death, previously a private matter, more often into the public sphere. Once the presumed doyennes of domesticity, women now entered the public realm as the mourners-in-chief of fallen Great War soldiers.

The outbreak of war elicited ruminations on whether women should play public or private roles during the conflict. Soldier and writer Karl Jünger published a series of essays written by German women in response to the 1914 war declaration. In the book's preface, Jünger noted that German custom dictated that wives or potential wives should send their men to battle: to offer husbands, sons, brothers or fathers as their sacrifice to the Fatherland. Most German songwriters and poets, however, immortalized the deaths of German soldiers rather than women's forfeitures in their verse. Jünger's prose opened up an active space in wartime discourse for women, while at the same time subtly implicating them in Germany's losses.[49] More typically in Great War literature, females responded passively to wartime casualties. When soldiers lost their lives during the war, army officers penned the obligatory notice to their wives or mothers, repeating the familiar phrase "sacrificed on the altar of the Fatherland." This ritual prompted the jaded female voice heard in Leonhard Frank's antiwar novel *Der Mensch ist gut* (Humanity Is Good). After a young wife hears the news of her husband's death she repeats the phrase dully to herself: "Sacrificed on the altar of the Fatherland. Al-tar of the Father-land. She tasted the words with her tongue," wrote Frank, "gazed into the distance, tried to imagine the Altar of the Father-land. She couldn't do it."[50] Nearly all of the women contributing to Karl Jünger's book confirmed that in Germany women willingly offered up their men to the battlefields, while Frank, writing in 1918, imagined a disbelief in the notion of the nation's inherent goodness. Undoubtedly, the image of women surrendering their men (presumed to be their livelihood in the early twentieth century) meshed with the nation-state's drive to elicit its citizens' submission to the country's cause, tying women to the nation-state but also making them responsible for its deeds. But the official wartime rhetoric of women's offerings at the national altar did not always match the lived experience of millions of soldiers' wives.

The history of how war widows and their fallen soldier-husbands became icons of wartime sacrifice, duty, and mourning provides a window into the ways in which the nation-state created and used those symbols to achieve its own ends. In the presumed victorious nations, such as the United States, widows and mothers of dead soldiers organized to secure a platform from which their forfeitures and the nation's triumphs could be replayed over and over again. In the defeated nations, such as Germany, where more intense economic, political, and social turbulence marked the war and postwar years, warriors' and war widows' demands for restitution contradicted their nation's attempt to reverse its humiliating loss and shore up its survival. But the victorious and the vanquished shared certain aspects of war and postwar existence. In both the winning and losing nations, military front and home front were inextricably coupled in nations mobilized for violent destruction. Women built arms and men discharged them in battle. Widows and soldiers from presumably conquering nations and those from supposed defeated nations both surrendered to the power of the militarized nation-state, although male and female sacrifices were weighted unequally. Governments in nearly all the belligerent countries supported pro-natalist movements that encouraged women to have more children after the conflict ended. In literature and in life, widows and soldiers in warring nations were linked in wartime and postwar culture. While some mourners remained attached to their dead soldier-husbands, others disconnected themselves from the dead and continued to live their own lives.[51]

Scenes such as those depicted in Jünger's and Frank's prose, portraying women's honored calling, soldiers' sullen duty, and wives' dull surprise upon hearing dreaded news, were repeated over and over again in all mobilized societies during the First World War. Responses on the part of spouses to their losses took diverse forms in different places. Some merely donned the obligatory mourning clothes and breathed a sigh of resignation to their fate. Other widows took to the streets, demanding state restitution commensurate with their sacrifice to the Fatherland. "*Ein jämmerlicher Trost*" (of little comfort), complained a German soldier's wife about her government's restitution to its survivors, "[is a widow's pension] for a mother, who sees her children standing in front of the sweet-smelling bakeshop with hungry eyes . . . and who has to say to them: come, it won't work, we lost the war, we are poor!"[52] Some widows even fashioned careers out of their activism, erasing the supposed division between "public" and "private," male–female spheres. Perceiving a need for a male protector, others made hasty plans for another trip to the altar, this time to remarry rather than to offer a sacrifice. While losses affected individuals and families throughout the war and in its aftermath, mourning the dead (even the simple act of wearing black) also took place in societies and became in some ways and for some of the bereaved a political act.[53] Through the politics of mourning, widows carved out an active role for themselves in their societies at a time when women's political awakening in many belligerent countries, notably Germany, the United States, and Great Britain, was just beginning. Widows in Germany, the United States, France, Italy, and Australia formed organizations designed primarily to lobby governments for pensions equal to the losses they suffered.[54]

Widows and their fallen husbands helped create the culture of memory and mourning that engulfed the belligerent nations in the war's aftermath. As Franziska Seraphim has shown in her work on Japan following World War II, people's memories of the war as well as their visions of the future were conflicted and gendered—that is, war memories revealed the ambivalent connection between the war widow and the nation to which she sacrificed, while all combatant nations heaped honor and glory upon the image of the hero-soldier for his service to his country's cause, whether those objectives were fulfilled or not.[55] If widows symbolized weakness and loss, as Josef Wackerle's painting indicates, then soldiers continued to exude strength and courage, even in death. Below the grieving widows *Simplicissimus* printed "*Standrecht*" (martial law), a short essay written by Hans Bauer. Bauer described the tattered war posters still hanging in a schoolyard after the war has ended. In one picture, a soldier raises himself out of the blood and mire of battle, his heart shuddering with awe as he alone escapes the carnage. As a tribute to suffering and soldierly courage, *Simplicissimus* placed Bauer's essay together on the same page with Wackerle's image, in effect contrasting the widows' helpless resignation over the missing corpses of their husbands with the stalwart warrior's bodily refusal to lose. Bauer and other German Great War writers hoped to reclaim their nation's strength and manly honor after the national humiliations of the ceasefire and (as they interpreted it) the vindictive peace treaty.[56]

Recent studies of war widows have focused primarily on their impact on social welfare systems in belligerent countries.[57] But these studies neglect important questions about widows' roles in commemorative ceremonies, as victims of wartime atrocities such as the food blockade, their responses to pro-natal movements after the war ended, and the reaffirmation of patriarchy in the aftermath of the war. Elizabeth Domansky has argued that in Germany (but not in France or Great Britain) the supremacy of men as soldiering servants to the nation-state, rather than as husbands and fathers, replaced former patriarchal institutions. One of the ways that governments forced this change was by removing the locus of sexuality from the home and placing it in the nation. Women's reproductivity thus became an asset of the state, rather than of her family, tying her more closely to the nation (although still not offering her political equality).[58] In effect, this change obliterated the Victorian-era notion of separate public and private spheres.

Widows felt bound to their nations because they lost their husbands in the wars to which their nations were committed. But in total war the picture is more complicated. The process of mobilizing an entire nation to accept and then actively sustain combat required that national leaders be mindful of women's roles in society. If women's connection to the nation-state had been tenuous up until August 1914, after hostilities began leaders quickly found ways to include women in national service. German activists joined the *Nationaler Frauendienst* (National Women's Service) to help their government coordinate service and employment opportunities for females during the war. In Britain, women eagerly joined Voluntary Aid Detachment (VAD) nursing units, while their American counterparts (after April 1917) urged government and civil leaders to admit women to various semimilitary organizations including the Army Nurse Corps and the Women's Department of the Young Men's Christian Association.[59] In all the major belligerent nations, women in impressive numbers entered the workforce to serve in quasi-military units or as wage workers in munitions industries. Women did more than sacrifice their men; they also forfeited (in many cases) their lives, health, and time with their children.[60] Whether women's individual experiences added up to a deeply felt connection to the country they served is trickier to discern. Vera Brittain's earnest support for Great Britain's cause found expression in her service as a VAD nurse. The deaths of her brother and two close friends followed the loss of her fiancé. After the armistice, Brittain committed herself to pacifism, speaking out against the British saturation bombing of German cities during the Second World War.[61] Meanwhile, *Bund Deutscher Frauenvereine* (Federation of German Women's Associations) President Gertrud Bäumer's rhetoric lashed her organization closely to its nation during wartime. "Insofar as the women's movement is an organic institution, and wants to embody a new femininity in disposition and power," wrote Bäumer, ". . . it will inevitably be national, built from the blood and life of its own folk."[62] The BDF did not change its pro-war position throughout the conflict.

Personal losses undoubtedly hardened women's views of the war that had caused their grief, but negative attitudes toward war did not necessarily weaken their sense of national identity. Germany used its widows and soldiers to retain citizens' loyalty in the face of defeat, while victorious nations co-opted veterans' and women's auxiliary organizations—the producers of war memories—to help undergird their triumphs and extend a militarized society even after the war ended. American widows faced the same situation as the two figures painted by Wackerle, because most did not witness their husbands' overseas burials. The Gold Star Mothers Association (which included widows as well as soldiers' mothers) lobbied Congress to fund a pilgrimage to France to allow women to visit their men's graves. After Congress passed a bill in 1929 the U.S. War Department made provisions for the trip. The quartermaster arranged a journey to match the military life experienced by the dead loved one. The pilgrims were divided into separate "companies," paid visits to military hospitals and forts in addition to the cemeteries, and were even segregated by race, just as the American Expeditionary Forces had been. While the purpose of the journey was to offer the bereaved an opportunity to express their grief in front of their soldiers' graves, the pilgrimages also blurred the lines dividing military from civilian life.[63]

The nineteenth century has been characterized by some historians as the age of nationalism, a time when the powers assumed by the nation-state had peaked. In studying the origins of the nation, Benedict Anderson came to the conclusion that men built "imagined communities" held together by fictive associations of fraternity and ethnicity. If nations required imagined ties between men, then those bonds must need strengthening when societies are threatened, as they are during war.[64] During the Great War, fears took the form not only of invasion and destruction, but also of hunger and disease (for Germans, the latter was caused in part by Britain's ruinous economic blockade) that severely compromised the home front's ability to sustain the military front. The nation-state used these threats to prompt its citizens' continued participation in the war, even though ironically, at the same time, those same threats weakened their ability to participate.[65] This study views the nation itself, as well as the categories of "victor" and "vanquished," as socially as well as militarily constructed and therefore as open to analysis and interpretation. It scrutinizes the ways in which the winning and losing nations were created and supported by those with an interest in either maintaining national triumph or in dispelling national defeat, and how widows interacted with those constructs either to support their continuance or to help break them apart.

Past scholarship on death and mourning after the First World War has primarily focused on the experiences of single nations, as well as on the soldier, rather than on his widow. Jay Winter's work on war mourning and memories in a comparative European context remains exceptional, and he provided an invaluable jumping-off point for historians interested in the social and cultural aspects of the after-effects of war.[66] George Mosse offered researchers a look at the German experience, while G. Kurt Piehler included a chapter on World War I in his work on U.S. war remembrance. All three authors include to varying degrees widows' experiences and perspectives.[67] This is not surprising, as war has been conceived as men's work, while women were among those who remained behind, a fallacy that serves to reinforce the notion of a separate, private world different from (and less significant than) the public one. Paul Fussell's eminent *The Great War and Modern Memory* and David Cannadine's work on the impact of the First World War on British attitudes and practices surrounding death both exploit the letters and diaries of primarily British officers.[68]

In addition, international or comparative histories of the Great War's aftermath typically include only treaty negotiations and international relations between nations' elite politicians—in other words, the men determining Germany's boundaries as discussed by the two widows in the *Simplicissimus* watercolor. Focusing on women enables the historian to delve into the experiences of ordinary citizens, at least more often, rather than those of literate elites. Because women have traditionally performed the mourning rituals that served to obscure war's glory, their histories, too, have been hidden.

Chapter 2 of this volume focuses on the experiences of German war widows. Previous scholarship has claimed that soldiers' isolation from the home front resulted in an alienation so deep that veterans could no longer communicate with loved ones who had not shared their experiences. British poet Robert Graves and writer Alan Hodge, for example, believed that since 1918 there were really two British nations: one inhabited by those who had seen the Great War and those, including government officials—and most women—who had not.[69] An ignorant home front and a misunderstood battlefield by those at home encouraged the view that women were to blame for wartime losses. Home front versus battlefront disconnections slid easily into claims of innocence and ignorance of Second World War atrocities as well.

But evidence demonstrates that some couples maintained close connections with each other through letter writing. Among the billions of letters sent to German men in the field were those penned by Elisabeth Macke and Johanna Boldt, two wives whose communications with their husbands reveal intense ties between soldier-husbands and their spouses. While no one who had not witnessed trench warfare personally could duplicate those experiences, people remaining at home could understand grief and hardship. Boldt and Macke both had their husbands' deaths confirmed by the German government months after the men had actually met their fates; Boldt received letters from her husband after having already been informed that he was dead. Like their soldier counterparts who stated that only those who had also experienced battle could understand them, bereaved wives confirmed that they felt their experiences were so upsetting that only other widows could comprehend them. In addition to the Macke and Boldt correspondence, German war widows recorded their memoirs in Hurwitz-Stranz's anthology. These widows' remembrances demonstrate dramatic degrees of separation between official German wartime rhetoric and the lived experiences of women who had actually lost their husbands.

The United States entered the conflict two-and-a-half years after Germany had declared war. Chapter 3 reveals the ways in which U.S. women drew upon their European sisters' experiences. While the second chapter relies on widows' memoirs of their wartime experiences, chapter 3 makes use of the prescriptive literature that helped set the stage and determine the tone of U.S. war widows' experiences. Because the conflict was into its third year by the time the United States intervened, American women first read about what their European counterparts lived, enabling them to imagine and prepare for the political roles they thought war widows could potentially play in their own nation. Writers of popular-magazine articles concluded that women could take advantage of wartime opportunities and extend their roles in American society. War widowhood, accordingly, could be harnessed not as a moment of sorrow but as a patriotic opportunity to help the nation secure the goals for which their dead soldier-husbands had fought. Rejecting the mourning dress of old and instead displaying a gold star on an armband demonstrated widows' active involvement in a triumphant event of fundamental importance to the nation-state. Gold star widows traveling to France to commemorate their husbands' deaths viewed these journeys as opportunities not only to mourn absent soldiers' graves but also to once again prove their commitment to the national cause. The pilgrimages amounted to a refutation of war's sorrows that served to reinforce the myths of war. The intent behind the government scheme of compensation awarded to soldiers' wives and widows amounted to the same denial. But for one aggrieved pilgrim, Nancy Payne Marsh, the alienation from the nation for which her husband had fought and died was so deep that she could not bring herself to display her gold star; Marsh took her place among those whose "expression of grief" disavowed the myths of war.

Chapter 4 explores the transnational impulses that prevailed among war widows' ruminations about their wartime experiences. When Elisabeth Macke compared her widowhood to that of all of the wives whose warrior-husbands had perished in the conflict, regardless of where their national loyalty lay, she expressed her thoughts and feelings in transnational terms. As noted earlier, wars in this period were ostensibly fought for the sake of the nation-state. And yet the very conflict that soldiers engaged in, and that women had allegedly sacrificed their men to, brought combatants from other countries together in ways that, for some, led to their estrangement from the nation for which the men had fought. Those waiting at home recorded the same sense of dissociation from military control over their war widowhood. In addition to questioning their relationship to the nation-state, people involved in distributing humanitarian relief to the victims of the conflict often did so regardless of where and to whom the aid was being sent. War widows and orphans stood as the presumed recipients of the aid. For some charitable workers, humanity, rather than particular nations, stood as the real victim of the first industrialized, mechanized war in human history.

In Germany and France, government and private organizations began encouraging women to have more babies, in part to replace the millions of men lost in the war but also as a response to the rise of feminism. Chapter 5 places the history of war widows in the context of some belligerent nations' postwar pro-natalist campaigns. Because the propaganda insisted that the mothers be married, for widows that implied another trip to the altar. Remarriage, however, interrupted the ability of war widows to retain the honorable mantle of having sacrificed to their nations. In some ways, it implied a betrayal not only to her dead husband but also to the nation for which he had fought and died. In Germany, where economic crises were routine during some periods, officials knew that remarriage could save a widow from destitution and, of course, from making claims upon government welfare. The drive to help re-populate the country strengthened, at least potentially, the bonds uniting women with their nations.

The book's epilogue offers readers a summary of the significance of the history of war widows and fallen soldiers of the Great War period, as well as a brief look at developments during the Second World War, Vietnam, and twenty-first-century conflicts. Widows' organizations evolved in international and transnational directions, disentangling the war widow from her ties to the nation-state. The impact of this phenomenon must be seen in the light of the growing segment of female combatants in twenty-first-century wars, as well as increasing disillusionment with competitive nationalism, often seen as a cause of war. Far from universal, however, war, as well as its consequences, continues to be interpreted as primarily a national project that demands and creates close bonds between citizens—male and female—and their nations.

2

Trostlose Stunden

German War Widows

Dressed in deep mourning attire and dabbing at her tears, Frau Hillemann, a railway manager's widow, sat in her pastor's study after her husband's funeral. In answering Reverend Farbig's question of whether she intended to move away from the small village where she lived with her twenty-year-old daughter, Luise, to the provincial capital, the widow replied, "Yes, it would be the best that we could do, since we have to be out of our apartment, and I can't find another. You see, Pastor," Frau Hillemann sighed, "it would be good if we could earn a little money, at least my daughter, and she would more likely find finishing work to do in the city than in the village." As Anica Helmar's 1906 short story "*Einsame Frauen*" (Solitary Women) develops, Frau Hillemann's daughter does indeed find *Handwerk*, or finishing work, in the textile industry, but the two fare poorly, and soon the widow goes begging to the welfare office only to return empty-handed.[1] A brief glance at the history of widowhood in post-unification Germany indicates that even before August 1914, widows spent many comfortless hours weighing their futures in a rapidly changing society and economy.[2] Germany had begun its transformation from agrarian to industrializing nation by the time of the Austrian Archduke's assassination. Workers like Luise Hillemann were relative newcomers to industrial labor. Peasants moved from rural Germany to industrial cities, still maintaining close cultural and physical ties to the countryside as they labored in large factories. Industrial growth separated two institutions fundamental to traditional German society: the family and the workplace. Women made up about 30 percent of the German workforce in the early years of the twentieth century.[3]

Although by August 1914 German society was transitioning from a feudal past to a modern nation, its culture remained in many ways a pre-modern one. Military values, including the assumption of male superiority and a reliance on authority and hierarchy, held fast despite great economic change.

Before the war, laborers were excluded from political decision making and denied social respect, in addition to being exploited at work. While all workers were marginalized, female laborers were doubly so, given overall male domination. One Reichstag member, for example, declared that independent thought and action should not be encouraged in women.[4] Marriage confirmed women's subordinate position because the concept of *Züchtigungsrecht* (the right to use corporal punishment) made a husband's beating of his wife a legal right. Upon widowhood, women's status reverted to that of unmarried women, and they had few rights. Legal scholar Paul Schüler opined that widows' social and economic position in nineteenth-century German society was so inferior that it would have been better for her if she had died when her husband did.[5] Because the liberal tradition of natural rights resonated only half-heartedly in Germany, early feminists relied on a "Germanic" balance between women's duties in the home and their rights to economic and social equality. The middle-class German women's movement downplayed female suffrage, focusing instead on women's contributions to society as mothers.[6] Motherhood retained its hallowed place during the Weimar Republic, making it more difficult for feminists, and feminist widows, to challenge the traditional place of women in German society after the Great War.[7]

The Imperial government had encouraged industrialization while still barring the passage to social and political equality. When war broke out in 1914, the juxtaposition of a ritualistic German military still mired in the nineteenth century with the twentieth-century industrial forces that would actually fight the war stood in stark relief in the commercial and newly industrial city of Hamburg. On July 31, half of a platoon of soldiers and a drummer suddenly appeared in the City Hall marketplace. The soldiers marched and the drummer drummed while an officer read aloud the war declaration. But no one seemed aware that this old Prussian ceremony meant that Germany was now at war, and the crowd dispersed as quickly as it had gathered.[8] The excitement with which young German men and women greeted the World War is now largely recognized as myth. In a response typical of most of the contributors to Helene Hurwitz-Stranz's anthology of war widows' recollections, when one soldier's wife learned in August 1914 that her husband would not be drafted first, she "was glad that I did not have to give him up so quickly. How could I be blamed for that? He was my love, my everything."[9] The bravery with which the men were expected to fight turned to disillusionment when the "invitation to manliness" turned out to be a summons to a gruesome death if not for oneself than for one's beloved comrades.[10] Modern warfare offered no chance to prove their heroism, because industrial production yielded mechanized destruction, and the adventure that soldiers expected would relieve them of the banality of industrialized civilization was negated by the mass slaughter imposed, not by the enemy but by machines.[11] First World War warfare resulted in massive deaths when soldiers clambered up from the trenches unprotected; the enemy mowed them down like a scythe shearing blades of grass.[12] Less well known are the expectations of women versus the reality that they suffered through, brought to them by an industrialized war apparatus that they helped create. Like their male counterparts, women, particularly those who became widows, learned not to expect much from their participation in "total" war.[13]

Histories of wars have typically paid scant attention to the home front, except as it directly affected events on battlefields. But the Great War made nearly all aspects of the domestic life an integral part of the battlefield. This development proved to the female population both a blessing—in that women participated more fully in society during the conflict—and a curse, for if they were previously perceived as innocent bystanders to the annihilation of war, they were now directly involved in its destruction, and (in the case of Germany and its allies) in their nation's defeat. German military leaders blamed the home front when it failed to "hold out" and adequately support soldiers on the battle lines.[14] In October 1918 *Simplicissimus* magazine featured an ominous sketch of a ghostly German soldier drawing back a curtain on a battle-scarred landscape. "This is what the homeland will look like," warns the helmeted warrior, "if faint-heartedness prevails" at home.[15] Rather than honored alongside fallen soldiers (who by the early 1920s were vaulted up on pedestals in war memorials), widows found their social standing downgraded as a result of the nation's loss.[16] At the end of the war the German Reichstag president belittled widows' forfeitures in favor of soldiers' sacrifices by stating that "we honor their [widows'] pain and mourn with them, but the Fatherland thanks them and is proud of so many heroic sons who have spilled their blood."[17]

The worshipful war remembrance rituals in Germany served to justify and rationalize the deaths of nearly 2 million men in a war that only bore the fruit of a shaky republic to replace the old monarchy. But like all nations involved in the Great War, Germany shifted the responsibility of mourning from individuals in private families to the state. Germany's National Day of Mourning served as both a benefit and a bother for war widows. Through the honoring of dead soldiers, widows had their social positions quietly revered as warriors' living proxies, but remembrance ceremonies also served to prolong the war, keep mourners stuck in a perpetual state of sorrow, and conceal their economic struggles, postponing the moment widows could reclaim their own lives.[18]

A complete history of German widowhood after the Great War is waiting to be told. Many efforts conspired to keep wives' experiences out of the pages of history, most notably the myth posed by Field Marshal Paul von Hindenburg that German hero-soldiers had successfully kept the war out of the Fatherland, the much-vaunted "stab-in-the-back" theory, and the notion that women did not make history. As late as 1996, a major scholar of German history, Geoff Eley, lamented the lack of attention to women in the writing of pre-1930 German history.[19]

Helene Hurwitz-Stranz first created historical figures out of German war widows in her 1931 anthology of widows' memories. Robert Weldon Whalen used her collection in his chapter "Widows and Orphans" in his path-breaking 1984 book *Bitter Wounds*. Karin Hausen breathed new life into the war widow in her essay "The German Nation's Obligations to the Heroes' Widows of World War I," published in the 1987 anthology *Behind the Lines*.[20] Whalen's and Hausen's works joined myriad histories of the German home front during and after the war written in the 1980s and 1990s, including the works of Belinda J. Davis, Volker Ullrich, Ute Daniel, Susanne Rouette, Karen Hagemann, and Stefanie Schüler-Springorum. Davis and Daniel drew different conclusions from women's wartime experiences. Davis interpreted lower-class women's participation in wartime food riots as constituting their politicization, while Daniel posited that the Great War had little liberating effect on women; female employment remained around the same as prewar levels, as women were reluctant to take jobs they knew were only temporary.[21] Whether or not women worked for wages, the collapse of the consumer goods market shattered their confidence in the state's ability to secure food for its citizens, and instead of relying on the government, women found illegitimate ways to feed their children. Daniel concluded that women's perception of their role in society remained unchanged after the war.

Histories of Great War warriors from all the principal combatant nations deal in some way with the notion of the hero-soldier, a concept that leaders found necessary to implement and perpetuate in order to militarize the millions of bodies that were required to fight an industrial war, and in turn to rationalize their deaths.[22] The fallen soldier's counterpart, the war widow, had a hand in creating and enabling the war hero image that resulted in her own subordination.[23] In addition, widows themselves lent credence to the preference given to mothers, helping to keep all women in their inferior social position relative to men. All this occurred in the context of a defeated nation's trying to rebuild itself, and the granting of female suffrage during the November Revolution. For despite their complicity in the commemoration of the fallen hero and the glorification of motherhood, a segment of German war widows participated publicly in the expansion of women's rights in postwar Germany. Mourning women became an integral instrument in the remaking of the nation, just as they had been a fundamental, though unrecognized, part of the national war making machine. Statistics taken in central Germany indicate that most war widows were also mothers.[24] As the primary caregivers for war orphans, widows helped shape the nation through their children even though as their children's sole support and nurturer they were hampered by how active they could be in public life. Those who were activists made their suffering known to the state, displacing the image of the allegedly passive female and the conventional notion that a woman without a man was somehow an incomplete human being.[25]

This chapter interweaves the love stories of two wives and their soldier-husbands with the ways in which widows acted collectively to attain a political voice in the early years of the Weimar Republic. The first part uses the letters written by Elisabeth Macke and August Macke, the German Expressionist artist, to make the case that, contrary to some historians' views, husbands and wives expressed their experiences and emotions quite thoroughly and honestly during long absences from each other.[26] No one can deny that returning soldiers often felt set apart from civilians as a result of their ordeal in the trenches, but evidence suggests that a plurality of responses stemmed from a variety of battlefront and home front experiences during the Great War, including frequent communication and understanding between soldier-husbands and wives.[27] The missives exchanged between Johanna and Julius Boldt also support the notion of the symbiosis between battlefront and home front, although Julius asked his brother never to communicate the war's abominations to either his wife or his mother. Johanna Boldt's success in operating Julius's grocery store during his absence refuted the conventional view expressed in women's periodicals of the day that women could not run a business.[28] Widows like Johanna who became *selbstständig*, or independent, were more likely to succeed economically and to fulfill what they saw as their primary obligation to secure a future for their orphaned children. The final section will demonstrate the politicization of war widows as activists in survivors' organizations.

Telling the history of the Great War from the widows' perspective upsets conventional wartime temporality. Great War histories usually recount the political conflicts resulting in war preparedness, the call to arms, the strategies conceived and battle plans carried out, and finally the peace feelers sent out that ultimately resulted in the November armistice. A widow's war began with her spouse's departure, continued in the letters she received from her husband followed by his death announcement, and ended, practically speaking, with a trip to the welfare office and (often much later) a pension check that served as government compensation for her loss.[29] After the war, widows' organizations published calls designed to lure the aggrieved out of their individual sorrow and make them feel part of the rebuilding of the German nation.[30]

As Martha Hanna has noted, warring nations suddenly became letter-writing nations in August 1914. Villages and urban neighborhoods were transformed into war news exchange depots. Hanna makes use of the missives exchanged between French soldier Paul Pireaud and his wife, Marie, who ran the family's farm in southern France, in her book *Your Death Would Be Mine: Paul and Marie Pireaud in the Great War.* French writers composed more than 10 billion letters during the war, while British soldiers sent home an average of 12.5 million communications weekly. Germans posted 28 *billion* cards, letters, and packages between 1914 and 1918. Letters from those in battle made civilians very knowledgeable about trench warfare, despite military attempts at censorship.[31] Wives "did not live with death as their menfolk at the front did," Hanna contends. "But their understanding of the war was more vivid and more visceral than we might suspect."[32] What we suspected, based on Great War historians and literary critics such as Eric J. Leed and Paul Fussell, was that those remaining at home knew next to nothing about what soldiers experienced. Leed, for example, explained that "what men learned in the war set them irrevocably apart from those others who stood outside of it." Leed quotes the English poet Siegfried Sassoon, who claimed that the majority at home possessed "not sufficient imagination" to understand what warfare was like.[33] "But even if those at home had wanted to know the realities of the war," asserted Fussell, "they couldn't have without experiencing them; its conditions were too novel, its industrialized ghastliness too unprecedented."[34] In contrast, civilians who sought details of the ways in which their soldier-relatives died in battle were gratified when they made inquiries of the British Red Cross Wounded and Missing Enquiry Bureau, as illustrated in Eric F. Schneider's study. Helen B. McCartney's work has helped overturn the separation thesis as well. Turning her attention to children, Mona Siegel concluded that French schoolchildren were able to create meanings out of the conflict, even though many of them had been born after 1918.[35]

Philosophers have debated the relationship between knowledge and experience, and some have concluded that knowing what an experience is like *is* to possess the ability to recognize, imagine, and to predict behaviors.[36] Thomas Nagel identified a continuum along which one person can imagine the experiences of another depending on what similar encounters the imagining person has had.[37] Less than enthusiastic about these claims is Frank Jackson, who stated that "imagination is a faculty that those who *lack* knowledge need to fall back on."[38] Feminist philosophers have shown that in a male-dominated world—in addition to questioning women's ability to reason at all—men have been very vocal about their understanding of what it feels like to be female. The German writer Moritz Bromme, for example, insisted that he knew what childbirth was like; in contrast, Sassoon claimed that women could not understand men's military lives.[39] Women's presumed passive natures may have persuaded some that females could not grasp aggressive soldiering.[40] But the letters composed by August Macke, as well as those written by Paul Pireaud, indicate that some men did feel that their wives could imagine what war was like and that those remaining at home could and did comprehend combatants' battlefield experiences. For wives, receiving letters enabled them to trace their husbands' soldiering lives across the chasms of space and time that separated them.

For soldiers' wives, war came to an abrupt end with a terse death announcement, but for Macke and Boldt, who both lost their husbands early on in the conflict, the story is not so simple. August died in battle on September 26, 1914, and Julius succumbed to typhus in a Siberian prisoner-of-war camp on April 16, 1915. Yet neither woman had her soldier-husband's death confirmed until months later: Elisabeth the following February and Johanna that summer.[41] After the first indication that their men had been wounded or taken prisoner and official confirmation that they had succumbed, the incessant rumors that circulated (particularly about a warrior as well known as August Macke) turned widows' lives into miserable existences. Wives tried with sheer will power to bring their husbands home, even while they dreaded the worst while caring for their children (whose questions must have been painful to deal with, especially if the children were young) as best they could while they pined for news. As wives waited for letters and widows for news, Great War soldiers dallied in trenches for the "big push" that they hoped (mostly in vain) would deplete the enemy and gain territory for their forces. War for those at home and on the front lines meant comfortless hours of fruitless waiting. Once they received official word, mourners faced more delays in finding out where and how their spouses' bodies were laid to rest. For the first time, nations fighting in the Great War harnessed the bureaucratic powers of the modern industrial nation-state by putting unprecedented numbers of humans (5 million German soldiers by August 1914) and equipment on battlefields to kill the enemy.[42] But the swaths of stalemated trenches at the front and the endless hours of waiting for letters, death notices, and pensions at home demonstrated the inefficiencies of the military and its government. Private relief organizations such as the Red Cross searched hospitals and convalescent homes hoping to help relatives know the fate of their men sooner rather than later.[43]

While waiting made minutes seem like hours, soldiers' wives inked their frustrations across writing paper, communicating a vast collage of emotions in a single letter, similar to what one might feel after reading an entire history of the Great War. Telegrams could be sent for urgent news, and packages dispatched when those away from home needed a warmer overcoat or special treats from home. Because of heightened passions—the excitement of a possible homecoming, the anguish of missed responses to letters, and anger followed by hopelessness when bad news arrived—the effect of Johanna and Julius Boldt's correspondence from August 1914 to January 1915 is one of temporal compression, rather than expansion.[44] For Elisabeth and Johanna, the war consumed their correspondence after their husbands left home and receded as the details of their husbands' deaths and burials slowly became clear. For much of the German population, the presumed titillations of August 1914 gave way to the realities of total war with its infinite hours of delay and, ultimately, a disgust and distaste for the war that at least some had anticipated with such storied fervor.

Johanna Boldt's husband, Julius, enlisted as a private with the 84th Infantry, while August Macke served as a staff sergeant in the 160th Infantry. During the war, statistics were kept on the widows of the Fourth Army Corps from an area in central Germany. A majority of women surveyed were less than thirty years old, had young children, and had been widowed early in the war—all traits shared by Johanna and Elisabeth. Most lived in spare circumstances (widows aged with each year of the war, because the military began calling up older men). A majority of their husbands (65 to 70 percent) had been industrial workers making around 1,500 marks a year.[45] Johanna and Elisabeth enjoyed incomes in excess of that of most of their widowed comrades in central Germany.[46] Boldt's and Macke's experiences represent the multiple ways in which wives' connections to their soldier-husbands, and the deaths of their spouses in battle, drastically altered the lives of the 600,000 German women widowed during the Great War. Together, Johanna's and Elisabeth's correspondence with their husbands offers evidence to counter Leed's claims of the alienation and estrangement soldiers felt from the home front, Karin Hausen's argument that there remained an "unbridgeable" separation between men and women's wartime experiences, and Catherine Rollet's claim that "in times of war, the emotions of private life tend to become more closely hidden than in ordinary times."[47] That is not to say that Great War warriors returned easily and seamlessly to their former lives. On the contrary, as chapter 4 of this volume argues, many soldiers felt alienated from the traditions and values for which they had presumably been fighting. Wives, too, diverged from conventional female roles when they worked for wages for the first time. If men fighting in the trenches were thrown into inconceivable situations, the same can be said for women experiencing battle. To use the same terms as Leed did when he described Great War soldiers, women who were raped may have learned something from the war that "set them irrevocably apart from those others who stood outside of it" (but because rape victims have rarely left a written record, historians cannot know with certainty).[48] Great War alienation, however, did not necessarily include estrangement between husbands and wives.

Part of the notion of separation derived from the ways in which war literature and illustrations divided soldiers from those who were not there; another part related to the presumed value placed on a soldier's comrades as opposed to his family. C. Paul Vincent argued that wartime propaganda produced "twisted animosities, profound disillusionment, and an unnecessarily wide gulf between the soldier and his civilian counterpart."[49] William Faulkner's 1926 novel *Soldiers' Pay* featured a soldier's alienation from his former self. Lieutenant Mahon's scar, the result of a battle wound, severs his face in two. One half represents his current bare existence and the other his former life that he is striving to retain.[50] The persistence of stifling Victorian-era manners and mores was to blame for the inability of former soldiers and their lovers to achieve intimacy, according to J. L. Carr's splendid novella *A Month in the Country*.[51] One popular French picture postcard featured a cradle rocking in the center; gazing into it are the presumed baby's mother, grandmother, and grandfather. The backdrop is a French village, set off by a tricolored map of France. The caption reminded soldiers that they were defending those who could not defend themselves.[52] The feelings of estrangement that divided soldiers from their homes persisted after the war in Australia, where veterans insisted that women—wives and mothers—should be barred from Anzac Day remembrance ceremonies.[53]

But these bits of evidence do not tell the whole story. Some women, such as telephone operator Hilde Hammer, encouraged their loved ones to write the details of their experiences as soldiers. Adolf Schärf, her fiancé, obliged, providing detailed accounts of his life at the front. In this missive, he compared his feelings for her with those for his comrades-in-arms:

> The essence of camaraderie depletes one's self by sanding the rough edges of character with restrictions. Whoever sang in the soldiers' songs that a comrade was a friend was mistaken. The word friend doesn't belong in the military language and the service regulations that comradeship and friendship are synonymous are also wrong. Friend, for the military, is superfluous. Friendship stretches over life, but comradeship is only during one's service time. I have found no friends in the military. I have also lost my old friends. You are my sole friend now. I hope that you can also be a good comrade.[54]

French postcards depicted another way in which the two fronts were intertwined. A soldier and his wife use a military tank for their tryst, eliciting shocked looks from the German army; the caption says, "Everything for Victory," including lovemaking and its hoped-for outcome: another soldier for the French Army.[55] Pro-natalists in Germany forged an alliance with the military to discourage prostitution and encourage sex for procreative purposes. Interpreting wives' and soldiers' wartime relationships as a great chasm supports the theory, noted previously, that those at home could not understand warfare. But that notion held further, more destructive consequences besides mere alienation between individuals. The effect of these time-honored and much-invested-in home/front division interpretations among those living at the time and in histories written since has been to rationalize and justify the glorification of soldiers and the concomitant "veiling" of widows' lives. Soldiers were confident that those at home did not appreciate their sacrifices, making it all too easy for Germans to blame the home front for their defeat.[56] Finally, the myth of a home front ignorant of battle slid seamlessly into the notion (in the next worldwide bloodbath) that ordinary Germans did not know about the horrors of the Holocaust.[57] Arguably, U.S. civilians, too, kept themselves shielded from the impact of the atomic bomb that ended the Second World War.[58]

Instead, the two-way correspondence of these two couples indicates strong connections and understanding between battlefields and the *Schoss*, or the family fold.[59] Ties between spouses help explain widows' preference for their identities as mothers, rather than wives, because a widow could not without discomfort glorify her dead husband's martial deeds or defend the battles that had destroyed him. For example, one soldier's wife who had been working in an armaments factory suddenly quit when her husband died in the war. She explained that when her spouse donned his uniform, she had picked up his tools at the same factory and performed his work for him, representing him there for one-and-a-half years. But when he died, she could no longer do the work, though she confessed that she needed a job to support her child.[60] Rather than revere their soldiering, widows could raise their husbands' offspring and thereby fulfill the state's directive to honor the fallen by infusing in children a sense of respect and love of the Fatherland.[61] This act of paying tribute to the fallen through surviving children defended the prewar social order of family and Fatherland and, ultimately, resulted in little social or political betterment for German women.[62] But motherhood did allow widows to stake a claim in the future of the nation for which their dead husbands had fought. After a military loss, the idea of national renewal converged seamlessly with the goal of regenerating the population through its youth.

Elisabeth Macke, born in 1888 to Carl and Sophie Gerhardt, grew up in an upper-class household in Bonn. Her father had purchased in 1872 the pharmacy where he had been an apprentice. He later began manufacturing chemicals in his factory. He bought the buildings adjacent to his factory, including his own residence and later a house for August and Elisabeth. August Macke, the son of a building contractor and engineer born in Meschede, near Düsseldorf in 1887, grew up in Köln and Bonn. The family struggled financially and in Bonn August's mother, Maria Florentine Adolph Macke, ran a boarding house to make ends meet. Thanks to the father of a classmate in Bonn's *Realgymnasium*, August attended an art academy in Düsseldorf in addition to receiving further schooling in Bonn, where he met Elisabeth Gerhardt in 1903. He continued his art education at Düsseldorf's School of Applied Arts. Elisabeth's uncle, the Berlin manufacturer, financier, and art collector Bernhard Koehler, financed Macke's study of French Impressionism in Paris, as well as the artist's other travels for the rest of his short life. Macke and Elisabeth Gerhardt married in 1909. August was drafted in August 1914 and served as a deputy sergeant in the German 8th Army Corps. The couple and their circle of artistic friends all seemed stunned by their circumstances. "Who would have thought that we would experience such things," Elisabeth wrote to her friend Maria Marc, wife of Expressionist artist Franz Marc, "the peaceful times at Thunersee lies as though years behind me . . . as though we were in heaven."[63]

Although Sergeant August Macke wrote to his wife about his experiences in battle that "it is all so dismal that I don't want to write about it anymore," and later "I don't want to tell the details," and "it's good that you at home are spared from the war," he nevertheless described the combat he saw, including the first battle of the Marne for which he received the Iron Cross, in clear detail. Five days before his death August wrote to Elisabeth from Somme-Pié and included in his letter the Iron Cross, asking her to store it in her jewelry case. He then recalled the battle that he had fought a few days before. The company that August led entrenched itself to prevent the French from encircling them. Like many junior officers in the German army, Macke had deftly taken over his sergeant's position when wounds sent him to a field hospital. Lacking tools, he and his troops used cookware to dig the trench.[64] The burrow dug, the men then hunkered down, awaiting further instruction. Those who ventured out too soon either dodged or took bullets. Next, the enemy struck with grenades, sending the company's supplies sky-high, yet they still did not surrender their position. Suddenly, the unit received orders to retreat. Macke hauled severely wounded soldiers strapped to flattened tents through the muddy trench, delivering them to waiting orderlies. "For 14 days," he explained to Elisabeth,

> we fight and rest from such battles and trenches and observe, through binoculars, how the wounded French on the battlefields raise themselves up, scream, and lay down once more. Now and then we go too far out on a limb and offer the poor boys some water. Since yesterday it is quiet, and we can sleep . . . I must go soon. We have heard that our division will see quieter days, but who knows. . . . To you, my love, a heartfelt kiss from your August.

August Macke died on September 26, 1914, at Perthes-lès-Hurlus, France.[65]

For soldiers' wives, the appearance of the postal carrier could either bring elation or stop the heart. Some of the widows leaving their memoirs in Helene Hurwitz-Stranz's anthology recorded that the instant they received their husband's death notice were moments that they could not describe to others.[66] Sometimes black-bordered news came in the form of a letter. "Mrs. Schmidt, your good and loving husband and father George Schmidt died in battle on August 29 at Hohenstein," wrote one soldier to his comrade's wife. "I, his friend Gustav Schulz, had the honor of burying him on Sunday. When I return [to Germany] I can provide you with more information."[67] In more brutal cases, families saw that the envelopes they had sent were marked simply "Returned! Fallen on the field of Honour!"[68] Equally heart-wrenching were the letters from husbands that widows continued to receive even after the beloved had already passed away.[69] Wives did not necessarily hear of the death immediately, and for some the news came in agonizing twists and turns.[70] Elisabeth waited for word from her husband's comrade, whom August had entrusted to report to his wife in the case of his death. In October 1914, she began receiving back her letters sent to him, simply marked "wounded: field hospital unknown." As she complained to her friend Maria, "What I hear is all so unclear, and always from people who were not there [when August was wounded]."[71] Given his location outlined in previous correspondence, Elisabeth became certain that her husband had been taken prisoner by the French. Unable to ascertain which hospital he may have been sent to, Elisabeth visited August's company commander—also wounded—at a hospital in Bonn, but when the sergeant had left his unit, August was still unharmed.

Paranoia struck as she felt during her hospital visit that others there may have known something but did not want to tell her once they realized she was Macke's wife. Her last missive from August had been dated September 24, in which the artist had written that his company had dwindled to fifty-nine men. Two different newspapers reported that it was not the French but the English who had captured Macke and sent him to an English prisoner-of-war camp. One news reporter, Wilhelm Schmidtbonn, wrote admiringly that August's "young, brave wife always believed that he would be preserved: I suggest that she should receive an Iron Cross!" Elisabeth shunned his outburst, because she had had no premonition that August would return from the war unhurt, and yet upon reading such reports, she began to hope that he was not dead and instead only lay so badly wounded that he could not answer her letters. Then, in mid-October, she received a telegram stating that he had died in battle on September 26. Another letter from a captain, dated October 12, opened with a description of the bravery with which August drove his troops to overrun the enemy, and then detailed how he had taken an "enormous" number of French soldiers prisoner. Next, the captain reported that bullets hit Macke in the leg, and probably in the head while he was tending to a number of his men who had also been wounded. "The battle continued and in the evening," admitted the captain at the end of his letter, "I was met with the news that your husband had died."[72] Franz Marc, also an army officer, penned Macke's obituary ten days later, declaring that he had died a hero's death.[73] The valiant death trope, designed to console the widow, did not always work as planned.[74]

Despite these confirmations, rumors about August Macke continued to circulate, and doubt plagued Elisabeth. "Definite certainty [about his death]

I don't have," she confided to Franz Marc, "and yet in my heart-of-hearts I have no more hope. Who decided that this horrid war should so disturb our happiness and rip the life and work from a person as young and happy as August?"[75] On November 8 she wrote to Franz, "If it is true that he died in the hands of the French, then no one found him or buried him. None of his belongings have been returned to me. Whether he still lives, that is the big question." Later that month, she explained, "Soon all hope is gone and yet I don't let it [lack of hope] suffocate me: sometimes it returns like a lightning strike in my eyes, a feeling, I don't know where it comes from, but it beguiles me so."[76]

As late as February 1915 Elisabeth's feelings were still unsettled. Schmidt-bonn reported from Soissons on February 1 that August was still alive.[77] The crux of Elisabeth's uncertainty lay in the absence of August's corpse. On February 6 she wrote to Franz, "I've had enough strength this whole time, not to sink," she declared, "but all this back-and-forth [between hope and despair] robs me of that strength. Everything that I heard from August about how he should be buried makes me doubtful again [that he is dead]. And yet I believe that he indeed died in the hands of the enemy, but who knows, whether he has found a final resting place."[78] Finally, on February 20, she received official notice from the Ministry of War that her husband was dead. Sometime later, two soldiers knocked on her door. They showed her a drawing of where August's buried body lay in France, but Elisabeth doubted their veracity. "I believe," she wrote, "that the authorities do this to keep the relatives quiet."[79] As Ute Daniel has explained, women's wartime experiences left them suspicious and embittered about a government in which they could not yet participate.[80] Not all Great War families' experiences matched Elisabeth's, however. Some relatives receiving information from the British Red Cross had their questions answered, although they did not always appreciate the frank descriptions they were given.[81]

Elisabeth's *Zerissenheit*, or inner disturbance, over not knowing where August's body lay is understandable in the context of wives' expectation that they would care for their loved ones' graves. The Munich-based magazine *Kriegerwitwe*, for example, explained to its readers the comfort that widows felt as they cared for the memory of their soldier-husbands by tending to their final resting places.[82] As late as April 4, 1915, Elisabeth still fretted over her ignorance of the whereabouts of Macke's body. "And yet the first and last thoughts I have in the day," she told her diary, "are on the poor, cold body that lies who knows where."[83] Macke's grave lies in Souain, France military cemetery, where he was buried with several of his comrades. His name appears on the war memorial in the cemetery along with his rank and death date.[84]

Elisabeth confided to Franz Marc that her gloom lifted only when she heard her children's gentle breathing in their sleep.[85] To his wife's surprise, August Macke had bequeathed Elisabeth, his two sons, and his other possessions to his childhood friend Lothar Erdmann in the evening before leaving for war. Elisabeth and Lothar Erdmann married in September 1916. Unlike many German war widows, Elisabeth had never had, nor wanted, apparently, the opportunity to fend for herself; she had married August at age twenty-one and, with two small boys in tow, wed Lothar at twenty-eight. (Elisabeth married another First World War soldier in Erdmann. Later, when his political beliefs caught the attention of the Nazi government, armed thugs forced him to board a train bound for Sachsenhausen concentration camp, where he complained of the treatment of a fellow prisoner. As a result of his protests, and despite his status as a Prussian officer in the Great War, camp guards tortured him to death in 1939.) Her memoir contains no mention of pensions, or of seeking work or outside care for her children. Elisabeth's mother had sent the family monthly checks during Lothar Erdmann's occasional bouts of unemployment in the interwar years. Elisabeth Erdmann-Macke died in Berlin in 1978.[86]

Johanna's and Elisabeth's experiences of the war as soldiers' wives were limited because their men both died in the war's early stages. Thousands of German soldiers and their families lived through the war's later turbulent stages more intimately than those whose men were no longer at the front. Prior to 1916, Germans could persuade themselves that their soldiers were helping their country defend itself against an aggressive enemy that sought Germany's destruction.[87] The 1916 butcheries at Verdun and the Somme led to the formation of the Fatherland Party of Admiral Tirpitz and Wolfgang Kapp, and its aggressive aims drifted far afield from any defensive war. Some high-ranking officers began calling for a compromise peace based on status quo after the German army suffered miserable losses in 1916, rejecting the nationalistic goals they believed would prolong the war, but the German High Command chose a different path.[88] In any case, the defensive war myth lived on. Field Marshal Hindenburg announced to his soldiers on the day after the signing of the armistice that "you have kept the enemy from crossing our frontiers and you have saved your country from the horrors of war," an assertion that mythologized an untouched home front, contributed to the "stab in the back" legend, and helped drive widows' fate into the dustbin of history. Women activists and writers also lent a hand in upholding the defensive war fable.[89] *Bund Deutscher Frauenvereine* (Federation of German Women's Associations, or BDF) Chairwoman Gertrud Bäumer used even stronger language than Hindenburg's. "The German women have seen in this war the necessity of defending the existence of the Fatherland," proclaimed the future Reichstag member, "in a world configured by the dominating forces that have imposed their will upon our fatherland." In the same breath, Bäumer absolved all self-sacrificing women from accusations of guilt. "With this unanimous conviction they [members of the BDF] have served the cause of national defense, and they kept all the wishes and hopes for themselves that might have weakened their strength or crippled their willpower at bay." In the same BDF manifesto, co-founder Helene Lange, too, claimed that Germany had fought against the "inexhaustible weapons of the whole world" and could only defend itself against brutal power. The Bavarian widows' organization joined the chorus denying accusations of weakness in the face of defeat. "War survivors are not to blame for the outcome of this war. They could not have given more."[90]

In addition to the Macke correspondence, a multitude of other letters between German soldiers and their wives collected by editors Bernd Ulrich and Benjamin Ziemann demonstrate the strong emotional bonds between the fronts as well as the trauma suffered not only by soldiers in the trenches but by their loved ones at home.[91] The notion that only soldiers suffered adds fuel to the home/front division interpretation, a version of war that suited the popular perception of the nineteenth-century "separate sphere" ideology, wherein men direct a constantly changing public realm whereas women, chained to the kitchen and beset by "the boredom native to domesticity," remained unchanged.[92] The humor magazine *Simplicissimus* publicized the perceived frivolity of the home front with drawings of languid young women idle without their men; after the November Revolution, the publication portrayed the same women treating their newly won right to vote with yawning disdain.[93] The magazine accused women of being bored and flippant while their nation was at war. Another drawing shows a brightly smiling young woman cheering at the news that the German Army had just captured Przemyśl, Poland. "Hooray," she giggles idiotically, "I wish I could be captured so quickly!"[94] Soldiers also enabled the sharp home/front division when they idealized the infamous triad of German domesticity, *Kinder-Küche-Kirche* (children, kitchen, and church) to preserve some sense of continuity with his past life and of a unified identity while at the front.[95] This coincided with the notion that soldiers fought to defend the home and homeland while women were expected to safeguard the cultural values that the home embodied. Yet that formula presented a paradox: If men marched off to battle to defend the family home and homeland, a tradition in German society upheld by First World War propagandists, then their absence undermined domestic life, because men were still considered the primary breadwinners.[96]

But presumptions about such home/front divisions obscured a reality that many Germans lived. The German High Command's policies, for example, undermined the divide in 1916 by demanding military service of men up to age sixty and by stating that women—even widows with children—who did not work in some capacity for the war effort should not expect to eat.[97] Furthermore, not all soldiers interpreted women's existences as bored domestics. "You live and feel so much and so completely with all of us on the front," wrote Franz Marc to Elisabeth Macke, "that every soldier would like to thank you and shake your hand, even if he doesn't know anything about your agony, that your life forever in the fate of the war is interwoven."[98] The perception of the home front as a quiet, banal haven has already been disabused by scholars such as Belinda J. Davis and Ute Daniel. Daniel, for example, confirmed that the "trenches ran through the German housewife's kitchen."[99] Germany was unique in that its soldiers actually sent food *home* to their families, not only in packages but also in trunks, because of the blockade.[100]

But women's participation in creating the myth of the unaffected home front has not been fully explored. When a women's journal published Else Lüders's proclamation that no difference existed at all between prewar and wartime widows, and Alice Salomon's comment that "the only conditions distinguishing war widows from other widows are their massive numbers and the guilt the survivors feel," these comments reinforced the conventional wisdom. Rather than demand restitution for their loss, or an explanation of how and why their warriors died, or even express their grief, survivors, according to Salomon, should simply show the same loyalty to the Fatherland that their dead soldiers had exhibited.[101] Readers at the time, though, may have swallowed such comments with caution, because wartime censorship, or the threat of it, undoubtedly prevented editors from discharging more honest prose.

By 1920, however, a Bavarian widows' organization issued a call for action against the German state. "Like the old German saying: help yourself, so God will help you; through the power of a united organization [widows] will be heard by the government." The author admitted that the war wounded had already raised their voices in protest: Now it was time for women to do so, despite the fact that taking to the streets went against women's nature. War widows demanding justice, according to the organization, could spare the Fatherland from the ignominy and demoralization of defeat.[102]

Johanna Boldt's letters to her husband, Julius, informed him daily of events on the western front (her husband was stationed in the east), in Hamburg where the couple lived, and in her family and the family business. Although Julius's absence deeply upset Johanna's mental and emotional state and at times threatened to upend the well-being of his shop, overall, according to her daughter's biography, Johanna became a champion businesswoman, proving to be a very capable breadwinner and employer while her husband wore his uniform. Whether her capabilities threatened Julius's sense of his obligations as provider and protector we will never know, because Johanna burned most of his letters to her after he died. However, her position as *de facto* owner/operator of the Boldt family business did appear to threaten her brother-in-law, August Boldt.

Johanna Boldt was born in Hamburg in 1891 to a couple who were new-comers to the fast-growing city. With access to the North Sea, Hamburg connected merchants with opportunities to sell foreign wheat, coffee, and tobacco to German markets, and coal and iron ore to German industrialists. In turn, German goods were shipped to Africa, Latin America, China, and Japan.[103] Johanna's parents, Fritz and Bertha Hannemann, arrived in Hamburg in 1887. Fritz Hannemann's service in the Prussian military landed him a job as a bailiff, and he and his wife embodied thrift, industriousness, and order, characteristics highly valued in Hamburg society.[104] The newly arrived Hannemanns rented an apartment in the Eimsbüttel district and soon had three children. Like other middle-class Hamburgers, young Johanna belonged to a couple of social clubs, a hiking group, and a musical association. At the singing society she met her future husband, Julius Boldt.

The illegitimate son of a maid and a crane operator, Boldt stood to gain the most by his parents' move to Hamburg, and by his biographer's account, he did just that. After an apprenticeship in a grocery store, Boldt commenced the military service required of young German men. He took a job as a clerk in a *Kolonialwaren* (colonial goods store) upon his discharge. After several years of earning and saving, he opened his own shop. Boldt posed proudly at the doorway of his business, which included "two picture windows and four employees," a feather in his cap that elicited respect from his clientele and in his district of Hamburg called Hoheluft.[105] In addition, Boldt stood ready to defend his country. Like most bourgeois Germans in the *Kaiserreich*, he exemplified patriotic fervor. He celebrated *Sedantag*, the day commemorating the 1870 German capture of Napoleon III, with the other voices in his men's choral group by singing "The Watch on the Rhine." As the children of newcomers to Hamburg, both Johanna and Julius, born in the late nineteenth century, considered themselves loyal Germans first and Hamburgers second. Indeed, if Hamburg's strong cultural and economic ties to England were known to Johanna, they did not trouble her as she relished German submarine victories over the British.[106] Julius, for his part, understood his military duty as a welcome opportunity to serve the kaiser and to participate in a war that "many millions of men" felt lucky and honored to join.[107]

Johanna released storms of emotion—excited expectation, abiding love, raging jealousy, and deep despair—in her letters. She happily anticipated and carefully tracked German troops' progress toward a march down Paris's famed *Champs-Élysées*. She described to Julius the festivities Hamburgers reveled in when Germany appeared victorious. But as the war dragged on, her ebullient missives sometimes became crowded with accusations and recriminations. Long absences wreaked havoc upon wartime marriages. She saw soldiers drilling in Hamburg and wondered why it seemed that only *she* had to be without her spouse. Johanna sometimes blamed Julius for not getting any leave time, and, when Julius's unit traveled and she did not hear from him for long periods of time, she worried that he so enjoyed his warrior's life that peace would make him uneasy.[108] Johanna did not see the letter that Julius had written to his brother August on August 30, 1914. In this missive, Julius confided that "*der Krieg ist etwas sehr, sehr schreckliches*" (the war is something very, very abominable) and that August should tell neither Johanna nor their mother about it. Because Johanna burned nearly all of Julius's letters to her, we do not know if he ever described his experiences to his wife.[109] On August 31 she assured Julius that his patriotism and unshaken courage were praiseworthy but that he should "think also a bit of your wife and child. I mean by this, that it would comfort me if you were to be in a less dangerous position. You assured me that you would defend the fatherland with weapon in your hand, but the enemy's bullet won't ask about that."[110] Like Elisabeth, she let Julius know that she harbored a wish that a wound would send him home.[111] Part of her unease may have stemmed from the sudden appearance of mourning clothes in storefront windows, which clearly rattled her. "Comfortless, isn't it? But business is business," she chattered, sounding blasé. But later that evening she added these words to her letter. "Do you know, Schatzel, what I want? To rest my head on your breast and cry, until everything is quiet within."[112]

Aside from emotions, Johanna included practical matters in nearly every letter she wrote to her husband. As the wife of an enlisted man, Johanna Boldt received a soldier's allowance, called Family Aid. Such aid was looked upon with suspicion because it gave women money independent of their husbands, and accusations of decadence swirled around the beneficiaries. Many women, according to author and women's rights advocate Anna Pappritz, viewed Family Aid as a "veritable salvation" from their economic subjugation to their husbands. The amount Boldt received rose to 12 marks per month after the birth of the Boldts' second child, Ursel, on September 19, 1914. Johanna's Uncle Klaus worked at City Hall examining the claims regarding Family Aid that came across his desk. "That I receive support," she assured Julius, "no one else knows."[113] But after inspection of her income, her right to support was denied, and she had to repay some of the amount that she'd received.[114]

At the same time, Johanna's brother-in-law August Boldt began prodding her to hire a clerk to oversee the *Kolonialwaren* business. Johanna reported to Julius the heated exchange she'd had with August: "'Hire a clerk, in the interests of the store.' August meant that an industrious clerk would be an improvement," she complained, "[he] cannot grasp the fact that such a suggestion makes me writhe in opposition. He doesn't know me, he cannot see my inner being, doesn't know what 'your' shop is to me." She then explained to Julius just what the *Kolonialwaren* shop did mean to her:

Only when I am at the store working busily am I quiet, that means, I forget all cares and afflictions. If I were to hire such a clerk, I would become superfluous. . . . And you must not think that we don't do our work; on the contrary, we make sure all is done right. To overcharge ourselves by hiring a clerk is certainly not needed. August means that such a man would have more knowledge, could deal with customers and can understand them better.

Johanna then shifted to a self-effacing tactic.

That I cannot enhance the business, I know. I am or should be happy, to simply maintain it. August says . . . that it is your belief, that women don't belong in a grocery store. I told him that things are not as he says. Every woman should be proud [Johanna proclaimed] when she can help her husband. [August] doesn't want to hear any of that. Incidentally, I hear it often in the store: "How nice, that you can preside over the business." . . . I would be more unhappy [staying] at home than at the store, where there's life and where my brooding can be redirected. My mother helps out with my motherly duties. I do everything and want much more to do—only the business should not be taken from me. *It is mine.*

August Boldt chose the days just after Johanna had given birth to the couple's second child to make his demand.[115] He seemed to take advantage of a German law that required women to endure a six-week rest period after giving birth; Germany stood at the helm of protective legislation for working women, though these laws were suspended during the war.[116]

In the end, Johanna shunned his advice and retained full control of the shop. Despite her great confidence and obvious talents, however, Johanna in no way saw herself as a promoter of women's rights. "We [women] put ourselves gladly under the leadership of a man," she had carefully confessed to Julius *before* she launched into her tirade about her conflict with August. "Women are owed the protection of men," she declared, "and are created for that purpose."[117]

According to Robert L. Nelson, the rise of businesswomen back home threatened soldiers in the field.[118] Men fought to defend their homes, and presumably that would include the livelihood that supported it. Catherine Rollet noted similar contradictions in which soldiers couldn't afford to pay their mortgages with their military allowance, as opposed to their civilian incomes.[119] Because Johanna kept only a few letters from Julius after his capture and transport to the Siberian prisoner-of-war camp at Krasnoyarsk, Julius's response to her spat with August is not extant. She received official word of Julius's death in the summer of 1915. Cruelly, during the course of the following year, Johanna also received three cards from Red Cross agents in Hamburg, informing her that her husband was dead: one each in January, in July, and in August.[120]

According to Johanna and Julius's firstborn daughter and biographer, Edith Hagener, Julius's death caused the world to come crashing down around his widow, and Johanna responded by staying in her darkened bedroom. A photograph of the war widow appears in Hagener's biography showing Boldt wearing the trappings of "deep" mourning: a black hat, veil, and dress. During this period Johanna's mother instructed her two granddaughters to creep about on tiptoes and not disturb their mother. Later, when Johanna recovered from a bout with influenza, she leased and then sold the *Kolonialwaren*. According to Edith, Johanna and her parents (whose loyalty to the *Kaiserreich* remained steadfast throughout the war and the November Revolution) believed that the workers' councils that had formed in Germany in the immediate aftermath of the war would rob them, and so Johanna held the proceeds from the sale in trust. She began receiving widow's and orphans' pensions monthly.[121]

Johanna did not let her bitterness over her loss or the formation of the Weimar Republic interfere with her own sense of self-worth, however. She developed a yearning to be *selbstständig*, or independent, and she could do this only by earning money. So, in the winter of 1919–20 she found a job as a bookkeeper for a small firm for remuneration that was "far under the pay scale." When, as a war widow with two children, she pleaded for full wages, her supervisor asked rhetorically what Johanna's children had to do with him. A few years later, she pedaled her bicycle fifteen kilometers every day to her job as a clerk in a large firm outside the city. Her boss paid her according to scale in this case, although women's wages were below men's. Working for money, no matter how paltry, gave Johanna a new lease on life. In her free time she earned a swimming teacher's license and her driver's license. To further polish her new prospects, she began wearing sporty, flirty clothes, a move that created a sensation among her acquaintances. In 1925, with the help of a Jewish couple whom she befriended, Johanna became the owner of a stationery store. In 1930 she gave up her *Selbstständigkeit* and her business in favor of marriage to a civil servant. According to Edith Hagener, Johanna's second husband could not wed a woman who earned an income, as "double-earners" were not allowed to serve in government. Although her spouse was not a Nazi Party member, Johanna surrendered all contact with her Jewish benefactors after 1933 (the couple fled to South America in 1936). Johanna Boldt died in 1962.[122]

Boldt's life as a New Woman made her daughter uncomfortable, however. Remaining widowed granted women an autonomy that they may not have had before, particularly if they had gone right from their fathers' homes to their marriage beds (as both Johanna and Elisabeth had done). Widows' courting and remarrying may have reinforced the notion that a woman without a man was somehow incomplete, and yet it also implied a certain amount of individual choice. "To court and to remarry," wrote Drew Gilpin Faust about U.S. Confederate widows during the Civil War, "was to assert one's claims to happiness as prior to one's dedication to self-sacrifice and self-abnegation." These last two traits epitomized German womanhood.[123] Widowhood as a result of war undoubtedly added a somber layer of dedication to the selflessness that daughter Edith seemed to have expected her mother to play out, perhaps even until her own death. This may explain Hagener's fears of the independent adult Johanna chose to become, and the dismissive tone she adopts when recording her mother's second marriage. Elisabeth, of course, also exchanged wedding vows again, but the extent to which she desired remarriage, given August Macke's bequest of her to Lothar Erdmann, is not clear. In any case, it seems that Johanna embraced her independence for fifteen years, until she married her civil servant, while Elisabeth did not.

In making new vows, Johanna and Elisabeth were less representative of typical German war widows. Richard Bessel records that only about one-third of war widows remarried in the immediate postwar period, and after 1930 finding a new life partner became more difficult.[124] Mourners recording their memoirs in Helene Hurwitz-Stranz's anthology of war widows' lives indicated the economic and emotional factors they pondered when faced with a marriage proposal.[125] Robert Weldon Whalen surmised that the bereaved may have relished their independence enough to forgo new vows—if they could achieve it.

In their dedication to their children, however, Boldt and Macke joined other mourners who left remembrances of their war experiences. "My child was all that made my life worth living," declared one woman, although in the same breath she acknowledged that she felt burdened and alone as sole provider for young lives.[126] Such declarations dovetailed with the emphasis German society placed on women's motherly sacrifice of self to others. Women's periodicals joined the chorus of voices elevating mothers'—as opposed to widows'—forfeitures to the war. Else Lüders penned a tirade against the inequities suffered by mothers who had lost sons in the war. The economist and social worker argued that society owed mothers a larger pension than that granted to widows, because the Fatherland brought its hardest victimhood to mothers. "Wives are younger and more elastic" than mothers, reasoned Lüders; and besides, a groom could be replaced, but a son could not. Furthermore, widows could take comfort in their children, whereas mothers were left with nothing.[127] In traditional German culture, the death of a son meant that a woman's purpose in life had been taken from her. For proud middle-class *Bürgers* such as the Boldts, a son signified an heir. "How glad I would have been," Johanna admitted to Julius upon the birth of his second daughter, "to have gifted you with a boy."[128] In the short story that opens this chapter, the widow Frau Hillemann wistfully remembers her only son, who had been the "highlight" of her life.[129] The importance conferred on male over female children contributed to the emphasis women themselves placed on motherhood versus widowhood in postwar German society.

Women's periodicals and survivors' organizations stressed over and over again that the best way for women to honor their dead warrior-husbands was through the raising of strong and worthy citizens, promoting women's value as mothers.[130] A widow who worked for wages in a factory or a shop or in another woman's house threatened that obligation to her dead spouse.[131] But the contested question of who had paid the higher price in the war—soldiers or widows, mothers or orphans—became part of the larger question of women's roles in and value to German society. Great War soldiers felt certain that their sacrifices were unappreciated by those remaining at home because they were not understood, and some maligned women for their perceived unwillingness to surrender more. Critics of Family Aid claimed that wives were in no way connected to the sacrifices their soldier-husbands were making.[132] Meanwhile, widows were certain that soldiers didn't understand *their* suffering.[133] Feminist and *Die Frauenbewegung* editor Minna Cauer noted women's need to feel honored during war, and she argued that women, too, gave of themselves to society but that their forfeitures went unnoticed because females remained homebound. Cauer asserted that the forfeitures women made in childbirth equaled what warriors gave up on battlefields. Men and women serve the nation differently, she reasoned, but equally; men's defense of the realm cannot be likened to bearing children, which constituted women's duty to country. With this statement, Cauer repeated an oft-heard analogy, first uttered by Social Democratic Party (SPD) member August Bebel (and derided by his colleagues) in 1895. By 1915 losses from the war had lent credence to the notion. Social Democrat Alfred Grotjahn suggested that reproduction marked the only female offering equal to that of men's military service to German society.[134] Scottish physician Caleb Saleeby remarked that England should support pregnant wives, because they were doing equal service to the nation by giving birth to a new generation of recruits.[135] But German society was not ready for public acknowledgment of women's equality relative to men. Cauer anticipated that her argument would fall on deaf ears because her essay's main point was that *only* if women performed a "service year" to complement young men's required military duty, *then* female equality could at long last be secured.[136] German women's magazines did not publish statements such as U.S. physician Ester Pohl Lovejoy's comment that women suffered more in war because (unlike soldiers who fight gloriously for their ideals) women "must live and be confiscated with the goods and the chattels."[137]

One of the questions women's historians have asked is whether armed conflicts have tended to emancipate women from their inferior position in society, or whether wars leave women in essentially the same position as before.[138] While several countries granted female suffrage after the war, direct cause and effect between wartime service and enfranchisement has been more difficult to establish. Women "filling in" for absent males surely cast doubt upon the old axiom that women did not belong in public.[139] The Berlin women who protested Germany's food policies won public praise as political actors, according to Belinda Davis, and made officials aware of the connection between subsistence and sacrifice to the nation, and furthermore defined the state's obligations vis-à-vis the citizen.[140] When soldiers' wives like Johanna Boldt succeeded in conducting their husbands' businesses during the war, they—and their children—were more likely not only to survive but also to thrive economically, reducing their dependence on pensions that covered only grocery bills.[141] For Johanna, as well as the widows anthologized in Helene Hurwitz-Stranz's book, work served to free women from their reliance on men.[142]

Most German women depended on men for their livelihood at some point in their lives, but many also experienced wage earning. Katharine Anthony reported in 1915 that there were about 10 million married women in Germany. The average marriage lasted for only two decades, and nearly half of all women over the age of fifty needed a job to earn a living.[143] Of Germany's 10 million wives, 2.8 million worked for wages. Of the 2.4 million German widows, around 1 million earned their daily bread. All those involved in the interface between widows and work—politicians, social workers, feminists, and widows themselves—agreed that women who had worked for wages before they married stood the best chance in the job market.[144] Like all female wartime wage earners, widows faced the possibility that their jobs would revert to returning soldiers, although some employers granted special consideration to war widows, surely a sign of the honor that Minna Cauer claimed all women sought.[145] In contrast, however, Johanna's first employer showed her no such mercy when it came to obtaining a higher wage. Women's paychecks for work typically performed by men were, as Boldt discovered, 25 to 35 percent lower than men's.[146] In addition to interfering with women's perceived obligation as caregivers to children, working for low wages threatened to alter middle-class women's social status, always of concern in German society. Catholic German Women's Federation leader Hedwig Dransfeld reported that war widows were determined to uphold their social rank.[147]

Eric J. Leed argued that the war retained class structures and even amplified class antagonisms, despite perceptions of unity wrought by August 1914.[148] A widows' history of the war confirms the ways in which Germans kept their collective eyes fixed on class as a primary determinant of an individual's place in society. Edith Hagener's biography of Johanna and Julius Boldt is shot through with references to their (and to Johanna's parents') *bürgerlich* existence. Despite a 1920 law that disconnected the amount of widows' pensions from their husband's military rank, measly government restitution meant that war widows were among Germany's most impoverished population.[149] Given the significant numbers of war widows, combined with unemployed females and women working for subsistence-level wages, the war helped make being an unmarried female very nearly an economic class distinction.[150] Some mourners penned their frustrations about class inequities in postwar Germany in a war survivor's magazine. "The new war pension is of little comfort to me in the face of those whom I have seen sitting in their automobiles and carriages [and] who . . . spend thousands on wine and champagne while at the spa," wrote a captain's widow.[151] Women's magazines published several articles suggesting that survivors seek wages and food as farm laborers, where they could earn three times as much as the pension doled out to a private's widow, though less than that earned by an average skilled worker.[152] Wages and salaries increased during the war, but real incomes actually declined.[153] Contributors to Helene Hurwitz-Stranz's anthology of war widows' memoirs recorded the dire financial positions war widows experienced after the conflict ended.[154]

While many writers and welfare workers encouraged the bereaved to seek jobs, others corralled outgoing widows back into their proper deferential roles as mothers. According to Anna Lindemann, wartime activist and suffragist, war widows should re-dedicate themselves to the acceptable role women had played in prewar German society by sacrificing their own well-being for that of their children and for society as a whole. "War widows should help the German economy by fulfilling their honorable obligation to only accept as much welfare from the general public as absolutely necessary for herself and her dependents and earn [money to pay for] anything else she may want."[155] Writing in 1915, Lindemann predicted that if Germany prevailed in the war, the postwar prices of consumer goods would simply revert to prewar levels. Mourners could help bring about this return to "normalcy" by restraining their own needs. Lindemann's prose offered widows little room for the independence and individual self-fulfillment desired by Johanna Boldt.[156]

Although she suggested wage labor for those needing something beyond subsistence, Lindemann planted the seeds of doubt in widows' minds about whether toiling outside the home was appropriate. Instead, she suggested that soldiers' thoughts turned fondly to the quiet ways of homemakers as they waited in the trenches for the next "big push." As their men fought, wives should assess whether they could deal with the employees of their husbands' firms and whether they could lead the businesses or how they would handle the businesses' demise.[157] In either case, warned the suffragist, women who did operate their men's establishments often discovered that they would have to be closed anyway.[158] And what should working-class widows do if they desired goods for which their pensions proved inadequate? Lindemann cautioned laborers' widows that training for certain positions would cost them the well-being of their families. The solution lay in *Handwerk*, the kind of work that Frau Hillemann's daughter sought in the short story presented at the beginning of this chapter.[159] In addition, Lindemann forecast physical collapse for women who had never earned wages before.[160]

Lindemann's pamphlet, like women's periodicals, paid scant attention to a major employer of women during the war: armaments factories. Altogether, weapons plants employed 3 million women by mid-1917 and around 6 million by the end of the war. Female munitions workers earned fat paychecks and a full stomach in exchange for heavy physical labor that threatened the health and lives of some workers. Female laborers complained of hauling 70 to 80 pounds of shells at a time in weapons plants. Women munitions workers whose hair had turned a garish green from the chemicals they handled were a common sight in Hamburg.[161] An explosion at the munitions factory in Albertstadt, a Dresden suburb, killed 200 workers, both men and women, on December 28, 1916. Overall, estimates show that at least two-thirds of civilian deaths directly attributed to the war in Germany were women.[162] The German government suspended protective legislation during the war and then reinstituted it afterward as a means of reducing the female work force.[163] There were few complaints about such unequal treatment from women's periodicals. Female SPD members and the bourgeois women's movement all agreed that women should take their place behind men for available work.[164] Josephine Levy-Rathenau, founder of the magazine *Women's Work and Training*, heralded wage labor as a step toward female equality, but her speech before German welfare leaders proved exceptional. By February 1918 social workers regarded employing war widows to be "dutiful thanks to the dead soldiers, whose survivors, widows, and orphans must carry on," indicating that widows' work merely constituted another opportunity to honor dead soldiers rather than promote female equality.[165]

Whether or not they perceived work as liberating or as a step toward a more egalitarian society, widows pounded the pavement for jobs because they had to. Charitable organizations helped soften the blow, but paltry pensions ensured that they would seek wage work; labor and welfare were bound up with each other.[166] Widows who became political actors did so most often through their roles as welfare recipients and as members or leaders of war survivors' organizations. Widows' activism brought them valuable political and organizational skills that they used to demand justice from the society to which they had sacrificed their husbands. Those who belonged to female-only groups took notice of the lack of opportunity to belong to any sort of organization, and they found that in groups that excluded men they could comfortably voice their opinions.[167] Widows and veterans acting in concert further demonstrated the unity of home and battlefronts (similar cooperation occurred between widows and war-wounded veterans in Italy).[168] Both viewed a livable pension as their right; Helene Hurwitz-Stranz's contributors viewed war widows and war victims as allies in the fight for survivors' rights to gain equitable compensation from their government.[169]

When Germany collapsed militarily in November 1918, the nation faced a deluge of returning soldiers—some seriously injured, most looking for work—crossing the Rhine River all at once as per armistice agreements. The Weimar government instituted various job training and loan programs to veterans, but these proved insufficient. The war pension represented the most important form of government benefit to the survivor, but it did not compensate adequately for veterans' or widows' sacrifices. As early as December 1918, veterans and war widows organized to demand fair restitution. In a grim recall of the presumed cheering throngs of August 1914, on December 22, 1918, some 10,000 maimed and blinded ex-soldiers and widows marched to the War Ministry in Berlin demanding something more than the perfunctory "thanks of the Fatherland" for their service.[170] By 1921 there were seven war victims' groups representing about 1.4 million members.[171] Widows' participation in these organizations varied. While they fought alongside ex-soldiers for greater government benefits, they remained subordinate to the veterans and male survivors.

Prior to 1920, widows' pensions were determined by soldiers' rank. After 1920, the National Pension Law mandated that widows receive 30 percent of a veterans' full pension. Orphans and dependent parents also qualified for benefits. Those ineligible for government allowances included wives of husbands whose causes of death were unconnected to their military service, who had gone missing during service, or who had committed suicide.[172] Whether a widow received benefits was determined by the pension courts upon receipt of the widow's application. An enormous bureaucracy, perhaps rivaling the military itself, emerged as widows sought relief. Workloads at these courts were "out of control" as widows waited—sometimes for years—for a decision regarding their applications.[173]

Soldiers' wives had grown unpopular during the war as recipients of special dispensation, such as reduced rent and Family Aid.[174] When wives became widows, they applied to the government of a society that had already shown hostility toward them. Membership in a survivors' organization could be interpreted as a public protest against the nation for which widows' husbands had fought. Women's magazines warned complaining widows that their problems were nothing compared with the tribulations of those in the field.[175] But Helene Simon, co-author of *Maternal Care and Intellectual Activity*, left little doubt as to the appropriate action for widows to take. Writing in *Die Frau*, Simon articulated her sense of the nation's obligation to the war widow precisely: The nation-state and the community were creditors who owed their debtors—the war widow and war orphan—for their losses.[176]

Through the pages of women's periodicals, in survivors' journals, or on the streets, female activists demonstrated their ability to take control of their own fate and help determine the fate of their nations. Women served on executive committees locally (though seldom regionally or nationally) and in the membership of larger survivors' groups including the *Reichsbund*, the *Recishverband*, and the *Zentralverband*. All of the elected officers of the Bavarian War Survivors' Organization were female in 1920.[177] In 1921 a group of war victims met with the *Reichspräsident* and other government officials. Half of those in attendance were women. President Friedrich Ebert refused to raise benefits, blaming Treaty of Versailles reparations requirements that he claimed kept his hands tied. The *Reichsbund*, the most popular war survivors' organization, linked civilians suffering from wartime trauma with combat veterans, arguing specifically that war-induced neurosis appeared in *both* veterans and in civilians. Female leaders in the SPD made similar claims, arguing that combatants were not the only ones coping with psychological stress in the aftermath of war, favoring a broader definition of "war victim" that included economic stresses related to wartime losses. Working-class women suffered doubly from neuroses generated by war memories, in addition to the stress of working and caring for their families. This phenomenon had already been explored in a 1916 article entitled "Women Psychoses in Connection with the War," published in a German psychiatric journal. When a woman killed her children and herself in 1926, the *Reichsbund* blamed the act on the strain of the woman's caring for her war-invalid husband and their four children.[178]

Widows requested access to job training programs, similar to what was offered to war orphans; rather than positioning themselves as nurturers of children, in this case widows demanded equal treatment relative to them. One war widow anthologized in Hurwitz-Stranz's book managed to find work and care for her children simultaneously. She became active in the SPD, she wrote, in order to fulfill her duties as an equal citizen. Next, she became the recording clerk of her local workers' council. Her constituency elected her to city council, and she took her seat on the Board of Directors of the regional welfare office as well. In the latter position, she was able to fulfill her ideal of fighting for the rights of war victims.[179] Helene Hurwitz-Stranz perceived her own job as observer on the National Pension Court as enabling her to help shape the fate of her nation. Court observers influenced decisions regarding whether and how much money widows and other survivors received from their governments. This work, she recalled triumphantly, enabled her to substantiate the government's offer to war victims of the "thanks of the Fatherland."[180]

Despite Hurwitz-Stranz and other widows' successes, however, survivors' groups also fought for men's privileged position in society. Women's primary concern should be the education of their children, according to the leader of the Rhineland branch of the *Zentralverband*. The Ludwigshafen branch of the *Reichsbund* passed a resolution to protest against the continued employment of women. "Many young men and women dissipate in an irresponsible manner the money which they steal from the war victims in so shameless a manner," the group asserted. At a meeting of more than 700 regional *Reichsbund* groups, members insisted on welfare reform and on the firing of all women not dependent on gainful employment in favor of injured war veterans. Instead of work, the members asserted, widows should rely on their pensions and be resigned to their fate as wards of the state.[181] Henriette Brey, writing in *Die Kriegerwitwe*, complained that while men feel henpecked in marriage, the tables turn when women try to participate in mixed-sex organizations. "[In meetings] we are only permitted to participate by saying, 'we are also here!'"[182]

In a defeated nation such as Germany, war widowhood took on added burdens related to the continuing economic blockade of Germany, the punishing peace settlement (as most Germans perceived it) that included the infamous "war guilt clause," and the payment of war reparations. From an economic standpoint, it was hard to imagine how German widows could have fared much worse. Given Paul Schüler's perception that unmarried women's position in German society was so poor that widows would be better off if they died with their husbands, these developments in the history of widowhood during the Great War may not seem that surprising. But the connection between women and events of national importance, such as the war and the revolution that followed, enabled (or perhaps forced) widows to see themselves as much more than merely the wife of a dead man. Taken in its entirety, Hurwitz-Stranz's volume of war widows' recollections stands as a monument to survivors who perceived their experiences as collective rather than as solely individual, and who vowed to change the society in which they lived for the better. Meanwhile, newspaper and popular-magazine authors writing in the United States before U.S. intervention in the war were encouraging their readers to develop romantic, idealized, and unrealistic images of war widows that suited a modern, industrial war. They took as their model the modern, liberated New Woman that Johanna Boldt strove to become.

3

The War Widows' Romance

Victory and Loss in the United States

When German forces launched the siege of Verdun in February 1916, they hoped to blast their way through the stalemated front and force General Joseph Joffre's French Army to shrink back in defeat. But the French, though ill prepared, responded in kind, and after five bloody months the assault changed nothing, except that it cost more than half a million French and German lives. The German Expressionist artist Franz Marc, close friend to August and Elisabeth Macke—who had confessed to Elisabeth only five months earlier that despite his revulsion of the war, he still yearned to be a better soldier—was among those who lost their lives at Verdun, in his case from a shrapnel wound.[1] After a year and a half of fighting, the war seemed to be nothing more than a devouring maw, swirling away young lives, resources, and money.

Again hoping to break the ubiquitous impasse, German ambassador to the United States Johann von Bernstorff announced the reintroduction of Germany's policy of unrestricted submarine warfare on January 31, 1917. President Woodrow Wilson severed all diplomatic ties with Germany in response, turning Bernstorff out of his Washington, D.C., abode on a cold February day. Theobald von Bethmann-Hollweg, the German chancellor, bided his time in Berlin until winter released battlefields from its frosty grip while the American public waited for the expected war declaration. Wilson first reversed himself on the preparedness question in 1915, and then later on the issue of war itself, even though he had won a second term as the man who "kept us out of war." Pacifism as a reform had surged in popularity during the Progressive era, even as military-preparedness parades, led by the well-heeled National Security League, vied for public attention.[2] The Zimmermann telegram episode followed in early March 1917, inflaming U.S. public opinion further against Germany; the next step came on April 2, when the president delivered his war message to Congress.[3]

Women in voluminous black skirts and veils in city streets had become a common sight in Europe well before 1917. Nearly a quarter of a million men fell in battle in the month of October 1914 alone. The French lost 300,000 men in the last five months of 1914, averaging 2,000 deaths *per day*.[4] As if to familiarize New Yorkers with what lay in store for them, the February 18, 1917, edition of the *Syracuse Herald* offered prefatory remarks on the significance and meanings of "modern" war widowhood during the Great War, before the nation entered the fray. And it was a rather excited introduction at that. Newspaperwoman Ethel Thurston used her article titled "The Romance of the War Widow" to reveal to readers what the allied countries were experiencing during the present conflict. "The great novel of the war," penned Thurston, "the story 'yet to come' that one hears so much about, may not be, after all, the story of the soldier who gave his life on the battlefield. It may be the romance of the widow of that soldier." Thurston went on to assess the positive character traits of the bereaved that the war had produced thus far. Soldiers' widows, she gushed,

> have not lived up to traditions. . . . They have wept, but they have not been the helpless, forlorn creatures that one associates with widow's weeds. They have not lived in harmony with the pathos of the poet's imagination. They do not pine away their lives in cloistered seclusion—hope, faith, energy all gone. There has been a certain militancy about the widows of the war. They have shown a strength over sorrow. They have grieved but have not allowed their grief to conquer them. As the true soldier fights his way through blood, his own and his comrade's, so the widow has fought her way through tears to genuine achievement.

The widow's combative manner allowed her to continue the work begun by her husband in the field of battle, while still remaining at the home front. Thurston linked this new widowhood to changes that had taken place for women both before and during the World War. Females had entered occupations previously closed off to them. Their success in these new occupations granted them the self-confidence they needed to put shoulders to the wheel in tandem with their warrior partners. Thurston saw in the war a potential for greatness and glory, not just for U.S. soldiers, but for the American woman.

Indeed, the real romance of the war widow derived not so much from widows' labor as from the promise of heroism offered by the war itself. This, too, was now available to the fairer sex. In Thurston's mind, the World War had changed not only the "mien of grief" but also the spirit of battle. Onlookers saw not the "dashing brilliancy" of wars past but "a war of endurance" that required the patience necessary to hold out longer than the enemy. "Victory," explained Thurston correctly, "will go to the side better able to replace its fallen men and better able to keep its army supplied with the necessary food and ammunition." The deadlocked course of the war thus far had convinced Thurston of that. Therefore, belligerent societies required women to do men's jobs: sweep streets, conduct streetcars, and make ammunition. War widows proved to be best suited to play these roles, particularly in the armaments industry. What could be more romantic, mused Thurston, than a grieving wife building the weapons that would ensure that her husband had not died in vain?[5] Lucy Stone Terrill Keller, a prolific *Saturday Evening Post* romance writer, became Captain Walter S. Keller's widow on September 17, 1918. Keller did exactly as Thurston suggested when she volunteered as a Young Men's Christian Association canteen worker overseas. The widow was placed with the company to which her deceased husband had been attached when he fell under enemy fire.[6] In addition to voluntary war work, gas mask manufacturers eagerly selected females to labor at their plants, particularly if they had husbands, brothers, or sons fighting overseas. The company theorized that such employees would perform with more than the usual care the delicate task of repeatedly testing the masks.[7]

Romance or sentimental novels had reached their zenith of popularity in the United States after the Civil War. In the late nineteenth and early twentieth centuries, a host of diverse romance venues blossomed. Weekly story papers and dime novels began appearing in newspapers and bookstores, including serialized story paper romances. Authors such as Elinor Glyn, E. M. Hull, and Ethel M. Dell each boasted bestselling romance novels in the early 1900s.[8] Lucy Stone Terrill penned stories with titles such as *The Old Beau* (1913), *Inherited Tenderness* (1933), and *Autumn Boy Friend* (1934). In addition, Terrill saw her *Saturday Evening Post* story "Face," about a soldier's guilt in his buddy's wartime death and his attempt to clear his conscience by marrying his deceased comrade's widow, made into a film called *Unguarded Women* (1924). The popularity of the romance as a literary genre lay in its ability to simplify moral ambiguity, according to critic Northrop Frye.[9] While historically romance as a literary genre has been associated with women, during the war, male soldiers at times adopted that mantle as well. The *American Jewish News* reported that the death of David Davidson "revealed one of the real romances of the war—a story of self-sacrifice that cannot fail to thrill one." Davidson's married brother had answered New York City's first draft call, but the unmarried Davidson brother persuaded the draft board that he should go in his brother's stead. The twenty-six-year-old artist succumbed to wounds on November 7, 1918. The newspaper interpreted Davidson's sacrifice as chivalrous—because it preserved the life of a man upon whom a woman depended—and the reporter assumed that readers would also uniformly view his death that way.[10] Ethel Thurston touted women's war work as a romantic response to armed conflict. If she saw any moral quandary in widows' fashioning the weapons that would, in turn, make mourners out of other soldiers' wives, she left it out of her essay. By obscuring those who stood as targets for U.S.-made bullets, Thurston maintained a clear-cut boundary separating friend from foe, and "us" from "them."

By profiling "romantic" widows, Thurston suggested that the honor attached to their bravery in the face of their lamentations could be what lay ahead for U.S. women as well.[11] In celebrating what had befallen upper-class women, however, Thurston ignored the plight of poverty experienced by most Great War widows in the countries her article discussed: Wives wearing black in France and Britain tended to be on the low end of the economic scale. In all the combatant countries, war widows dependent on state support faced deprivation at best and poverty at worst. Such an admission might have left U.S. women less than enthusiastic about their wartime prospects, despite Thurston's giddy promise of feminine heroism.[12] In addition, Thurston's article failed to mention the difficulties widows faced when they had small children to care for. The working widows Thurston featured could seek wage labor more easily because they were not obliged to arrange for childcare.

The U.S. Veterans Administration reported that 105,488 soldiers died as a result of the World War; 33, 337 of those servicemen left widows.[13] Entering the conflict late had enabled the United States to train not only for the mobilization of its army (still woefully underprepared) but for that of its civilian society as well.[14] The prescriptive literature that appeared in newspapers and magazines helped U.S. wives rehearse the roles that they would play both as spouses and as widows of military men when President Wilson issued his war declaration in 1917. Representations of war widows' experiences in Europe helped their U.S. sisters formulate their own unique responses to wartime loss, including the invention of the gold star armband that, for some, replaced traditional mourning practices supposedly still entrenched in the archaic place known by Americans as "over there."

While patriotic women wholeheartedly embraced the notion that they might have to make the supreme forfeiture in war, as their European counterparts had done, they were also charged with readying their men to be crusaders and redeemers of the Old World, reflecting the American exceptionalism presumed to be driving U.S. foreign policy during World War I.[15] The U.S. government–issued gold star badges offered to war widows and mothers became symbolic of the supreme sacrifice made by individual women to the national war effort (and complemented the soldier's image as crusader fighting for the nation's cause).[16] In addition, the Adjutant General's Office distributed Victory Medals to mothers and widows on the "pilgrimages" they made to visit their dead relatives' graves in France.[17] Insignia and medals helped fashion the myth of unity among a disparate population viewed by female reformers as well as those in government as necessary to win the war. While Gold Star widows and mothers embarked on pilgrimages and marched in Armistice Day remembrance ceremonies designed to "prove the victory," the traditional, individual expressions of grief—the wearing of black funeral garb and widows' seclusion—became disavowed and subsumed under the banner of collective national glory. "Death," as Lisa M. Budreau wrote, "became an occasion for a gold star reward."[18]

The U.S. government's scheme of supporting wives and children financially while their servicemen fought overseas and the system by which widows and orphans were compensated upon the servicemen's death, were also designed to create a docile (but inspired) and united home front dedicated to a noble cause. Widows acted out their grief in public as part of their national duty during the most important event in a nation's history: a foreign war. Duties performed publicly had been prescribed for them by articles such as Ethel Thurston's, and some, such as Harriet Pierson, clearly reveled in that glory. But *privately* they struggled against that patriotic narrative as they filed claims to receive war pensions from federal and state governments in an effort to secure what they were owed. In the United States, unlike in Germany, there were no *public* displays of widows and maimed soldiers parading for their pensions in Washington, D.C. (the parades came later during the infamous 1932 Bonus Army March when the U.S. military turned tear gas onto World War veterans marching for their bonus payments during the Great Depression).[19] As in Germany, there was little glory for U.S. widows when they made their claims, and some interactions can best be described as humiliating. Some widows could discern no righteousness in the war's alleged purpose before the United States had even entered the war. Resentful war widows expressed disillusionment when the U.S. government did not live up to promises regarding the care of soldiers' bodies upon their deaths in battle or protect widows from economic impoverishment. Citizenship requires a feeling of mutual obligation between a citizen and her government, a sentiment that unfulfilled promises ruptured.[20]

In addition to newspapers such as the *Syracuse Herald*, popular-magazine editors warned U.S. readers well in advance of a war declaration that they would likely be changing how they grieve. The U.S. opinion journal *The Literary Digest* published an essay similar to Thurston's piece in early 1916, but the *Digest* article added a religious undertone to the subject of grief that meshed with Americans' sense of themselves as morally righteous, and it did so without the emphasis on the modern war widows' gusto, or on their potential for munitions factory work. Editors published the comforting words of the Reverend Archibald Alexander, whose essay "The New Mien of Grief" directed the bereaved to not only endure their grief but to "efface as far as possible the signs of wo [*sic*]." Like Thurston, Alexander elevated mourners' bearing of their sorrow to the presumed level of heroism exhibited by their counterparts in the trenches. "We speak of the courage and sacrifice of our men," cautioned the English clergyman, "and we can not [*sic*] speak too highly or too gratefully about that. But there is something else that runs it very close, if it does not exceed it, and that is the quiet heroism and endurance of many of those who have been bereaved." The minister praised the "marvelous spirit of self-restraint" and self-control exhibited by survivors. "They are not shirking any of the duties of life. They are claiming no exemptions on the ground of their sorrow, and they excuse themselves from no duty merely because it would hurt. They wear their hurt gently like a flower in the breast."[21]

Alexander alluded to the Biblical character Joseph in the Book of Genesis—who hid his grief when his brother Benjamin failed to recognize him—to persuade his readers to mimic the bravery displayed by mourners. The *Literary Digest* editors seemed convinced that such courage would soon be required of the U.S. home front. Alexander's inspiration came not only from the Bible but also from a young British wife whose husband had chosen to return to battle rather than retreat to the comforts of his home.

Despite attempting to equate the valor of the soldier with that of those who smiled through their tears, Alexander left no doubt that it was only the warrior who could achieve eternal life: and only through commemoration of him could survivors share a modicum of what their loved ones had earned. "If death is ever glorious, it is when it comes to the soldier fighting for a pure and worthy cause. . . . and it is not death to fall so [on the field of honor]. Rather it is the finding of life larger and more glorious still. It is that that marks the war-mourners of to-day as a caste royal and apart."[22] U.S. readers learned in advance of their own participation in the war that only through commemoration of a military death could survivors achieve the same luster. The reverend encouraged all mourners, whether wives, mothers, or fathers, to commemorate the glory of the fallen and derive from that the strength they needed to perform their duties with a "cheerful bearing." Thurston, too, touted war widows' ability to overcome their grief, but she encouraged them to pursue the war work that she believed lent widows' lives special meaning as dead soldiers' living proxies, reflecting an even more active period of bereavement than Alexander was willing to suggest. Both writers sought to extend the deeds of the dead through those they left behind. Obscuring grief for the sake of patriotic duty assured the government that it would have citizens' consent for its war effort.

But not all Americans appeared flush with anticipation at what the war might bring them. While writers like Thurston dodged the moral gray area inherent in a call to arms under the guise of romance, cartoonist M. Trapp questioned the morality of the United States' military preparedness in the face of its official declaration of neutrality. Like Alexander, she, too, used the sacred to inveigh against the profane. The image she drew reflected the thoughts of many of those dubious of war's benefits, and she used a war widow to shed a decidedly unromantic light on battle. In addition, she seemed to anticipate John Dewey's assessment of Wilson's war footing as "the immense moral wrench involved in our passage from friendly neutrality to participation in war."[23]

Trapp's drawing featured a mother seated with a crucifix on her lap, surrounded by three children; two are sleeping while the other one is kneeling with clasped hands. The family appeared on the steps of the White House in Washington, D.C. President Wilson stands perched on the steps above, one hand in his coat pocket while the other is outstretched toward the widow; a fat-cat munitions magnate lingers behind him, holding a satchel marked "wages of Judas Iscariot." Meanwhile, surrounding the scene is a long line of maimed warriors stretched around the backside of the steps leading to the White House (in wheelchairs, with broken arms, missing legs), each wearing a different uniform—some officers, others enlisted—symbolizing the vast geographic scope of World War victims. An angel floats in the sky above. The president is listening to the widow, but the dialogue accompanying the broadside indicates that Wilson's ties to munitions makers will not let him make the correct moral choice. The war widow's eyes are downcast, but her visage is thoughtful, rather than meek like that of her children. She reminds Wilson that he could stop the war with the stroke of his pen by ordering an embargo on all war supplies "as all other neutral nations have done." Repeat-

M. Trapp, "Delegation of war-widows, war-orphans, and maimed war-heroes at the White House, Washington, D.C., 1916." Detail of image #72238. Courtesy Wisconsin Historical Society.

ing a phrase Wilson used regarding affairs in Mexico in 1914, the mother pleads with him to consider the world's "higher humanity" and warns him that if he betrays his Christian impulse (there were Presbyterian ministers in Wilson's family on both maternal and paternal sides), the United States will lose "its fair name for honor, humanity, and justice."[24]

This sense of betrayal tinged with shame resonated among many Americans during the World War, and those who felt wronged directed their wrath not only at Wilson but at impersonal corporate forces. While there is no evidence that a confrontation ever took place between war-maimed soldiers, widows, and Woodrow Wilson, Trapp's sentiments matched those of the laborers who staged more than 4,000 strikes during the first year of war to protest munitions companies reaping higher and higher profits.[25] Elizabeth Grimm, U.S.-born widow of the German-born engineer Carl Robert Grimm, living in Germany, declared that "the entire conduct of the U.S. has been underhanded, *un neutral* and cowardly. One must ask where are the *men* of Revolutionary days. If the U.S. would . . . send milk and various other harmless and helpful articles, she would aid humanity, but bullets, cannons, grenades etc. 'I ask for bread and ye send me bullets.'"[26] The corporatization of American society and culture against which both Trapp and Grimm railed also affected mourning rituals. Whereas in the early nineteenth century grief united a family around a set of sacred rituals that were meant to transfer the soul of the dead from the profanity of this world back to the original state of nature, by the late nineteenth century death moved away from family control and into the hands of commercial undertakers and funeral parlors.[27]

The image of Woodrow Wilson first as a Christ-like figure betrayed by capitalists and then as deceiving the nation himself undoubtedly resonated well in a nation awash in the redemptive potential of U.S. exceptionalism. Trapp's cartoon leaves no doubt that the righteous step for the president to take would be to enforce neutrality, rather than partake in the profiteering of the munitions industry. The widow proclaims that the United States cannot "take exception" to its time-honored principle of neutrality without endangering its reputation. But Wilson did take exception, the broadside suggests, and he sold his soul for pieces of silver, for the sake of munitions makers' profits, and for the military preparedness movement. In doing so, according to Trapp, the United States lost its identity as the "city on the hill." But some war widows, such as Theresa Johnson, believed in President Wilson's exceptionalist idealism; about her husband's battlefield death Johnson exulted, "I am proud that my husband was one of many Americans who gave their lives for those principles which we Americans love so well and helped to make the world safe for democracy."[28] Trapp and other U.S. pacifists, anti-imperialists, and isolationists hoped for a redeemer who would save the world from war's carnage by using the United States' neutral position to stop the war, while Wilson and his supporters imagined that U.S. intervention would save the world from Prussian militarism and for American-style democracy. Both believed that the United States embodied the potential to save the rest of the world.

U.S. soldiers and the government they served helped create the crusader and redeemer roles for themselves, and war widows later verified this role when they took their pilgrimages to France to honor their dead husbands. Historian G. Kurt Piehler interpreted the American Battle Monuments Commission's choice to adorn military cemeteries with crosses as reflecting the agreement among Americans that the dead had given their lives to redeem the nation.[29] The military newspaper *Stars and Stripes* regarded the American occupiers of the Rhineland after the November Armistice as noble pacifists. "We go in among [German civilians] as conquerors . . . but we must go in among them with a humble and contrite heart . . . for we enter also as peace-makers, 'for they shall be called the children of God.'"[30] An American Telephone and Telegraph advertisement published in *The Outlook* included a description of the "Victorious Crusaders" that the nation had sent off to war, then repeated the "larger life" promise for homecoming soldiers proffered by Archibald Alexander.[31] Nancy K. Bristow uncovered the impetus among Progressive-era reformers, including women, to create crusaders among America's fighting forces.[32] Major Charles C. Pierce consoled war widow Harriet Pierson when her soldier-husband died, describing Ward Wright Pierson as "the one whom you gave to your country and the world for the saving of civilization," reminiscent of the same sense of moral clarity found in Ethel Thurston's endorsement of munitions work for war widows.

When the U.S. Congress passed Wilson's war declaration against Germany and its allies on April 6, 1917, those at home began to formulate their own response to the war. Ambivalence surfaced quickly about whether to discard the usual rituals and fashions of mourning during wartime or hold fast to traditional ways of displaying one's status as a grieving spouse or parent. In her work on late-nineteenth- and early-twentieth-century American funeral practices, Cynthia J. Mills concluded that death was one area in which the Victorian era retained its tenacious hold on "modern" American society.[33] But the Great War served to loosen those ties. Directed to adorn their sleeves with a gold star armband by the president, most of the aggrieved offering their opinions in U.S. newspapers and magazines desired the distinction the armband brought to the wives who had sacrificed their husbands to the nation's cause, rather than mourn their individual losses. Even embittered wives and mothers, demanding more specific information about where their husbands or sons were buried and how and why they had died, asked, in the same sour communication with the War Department, if they could please have memorial flags and Victory Medals as compensation for their husbands' or sons' lives. Mary Nevins, mother of Private Joseph Benedict Nevins, ordered her compensation from the Bureau of War Risk Insurance for herself and "the [other] Mothers of soldiers that gave there [*sic*] lives like dogs. And," she added, "I would like a Victory Medal."[34] When the U.S. government could not or would not fulfill its end of the reciprocal citizen–government relationship, grieving relatives sought something from the government that they blamed for the loss to aid in their bereavement.[35]

Newspaper society column writers, female reformers, war relief society activists, and the U.S. president all endeavored to create a distinction between deaths unrelated to the war and those suffered in the line of duty after April 1917. The purpose of the division was threefold: First, it helped to elevate, venerate, and re-create (from the Civil War period) the honor and glory of war as a noble, national cause. Second, it was used to predict the everlasting life that was believed to accompany a death inflicted by crusading for principle, as Archibald Alexander had suggested, and served as compensation for the soldier's sacrifice. Finally, it upheld the fiction of national unity during wartime. For all of these reasons, the investment on the part of the U.S. government in the gold star emblem paid off in numerous newspaper and magazine articles devoted to demonstrating that women indeed romanticized their roles as widows as Thurston had predicted but that, contrary to Thurston's proclamation, women sought at least some of the "dashing brilliancy" of war that the newspaperwoman thought would be subdued. Women acting as dead soldiers' living proxies at funeral and remembrance ceremonies served as representations of this honor; in addition, they did so in the public sphere, the Victorian era's presumed male-dominated orbit.[36] In perhaps the most stunning example of a war widow's interpretation of herself as her dead soldier-husband's proxy, Harriet Pierson wrote to the Quartermaster General's office twenty years after her husband's death to ask what arrangements she needed to make in order to have her own body buried at Arlington National Cemetery when she drew her final breath. Pierson's husband, the decorated Major Ward W. Pierson, found his final resting place at Meuse-Argonne American Cemetery in France after he succumbed to battle wounds on November 9, 1918, just two days before the signing of the armistice. The Quartermaster rejected her wish, stating that she would be eligible for burial at Arlington only if her husband had been buried there as well.[37]

Mourning dress, according to Geertje van Os, offered people a way to announce a change in their social role and their entrance into the social category of "widow."[38] One method used to differentiate deaths resulting from the war was the wearing of a black armband adorned with a five-pointed gold star. The emblem enabled wearers to feel attached to their dead serviceman, as it resembled more closely a military Medal of Honor worn by a decorated soldier than did a black dress. While the gold star served to elevate the wearer to the position of glorified soldier, some commentators hinted that the wearing of a black dress mirrored the accursed frivolousness and self-indulgence to which women were thought to be prone. Nineteenth-century male social commentators belittled the ludicrous "minutiae of mourning" that preoccupied their female counterparts.[39] During the Great War, women themselves began leveling criticism at female mourners who donned black, saying that it represented "a selfish attempt to hide one's pain in order to hold off intrusion."[40]

The debate over precisely what mourning attire, if any, women should wear began indirectly before U.S. intervention, with Ethel Thurston's article about romantic widowhood. Although she did not address the issue of clothes or funerals specifically, she did, like Archibald Alexander, suggest that outward displays of grief kept brief would constitute a welcome change. Coincidental with the arrival of the first shipload of U.S. doughboys on French shores in June 1917, a *Syracuse Herald* article praised French women for their "lighter" mourning practices. When *poilus* (French infantrymen) return from the front, explained the writer, they feel inspired when they see girls exerting their usual charms in attractive, flirty dresses, as opposed to finding women dressed in mourning or in the "plain, severe working uniform" that many female munitions laborers were sporting.[41] Labor leader James W. Sullivan contradicted the article as a whole when he announced after his trip abroad that "all France is in mourning." Sullivan, too, supported the abolition of black clothes, noting that the French working poor could ill afford to uphold such refined traditions.[42] No debate appeared in German women's magazines over *Trauerkleidung* (mourning dress). Judging by descriptions and photographs of widows' attire, mourners adhered largely to traditional dress and veils.[43] The heavy crepe material used in making mourning dresses common in the nineteenth century was expensive because manufacturers treated the silk gauze until it lost its sheen. But wearers preferred it because it represented the heavy heart of the aggrieved, and because its matte finish was thought to reflect the wearer's retirement from gaiety during the required two-year mourning period.[44]

Thomas F. Enright, Merle D. Hay, and James B. Gresham became the first U.S. soldiers to lose their lives at St. Mihiel Salient in eastern France in November 1917. Debate over the appropriateness of "widows' weeds" then began in earnest. Chicago reformer Louise De Koven Bowen, chair of the Women's Committee of the Illinois State Council of Defense, appealed to women to abolish the wearing of black upon the death of a U.S. soldier. She admonished members of her organization to uphold the "glory of death . . . rather than its sadness." Mourning's "lugubrious uniform" had become outdated in recent years anyway, stated a *New York Times* editorial, and a gold star emblem worn instead of black crepe would "show a higher appreciation of what death in the country's good cause" really was, "a manifestation of its glory rather than of a private grief [that] becomes the patriotic citizen." The writer suggested that the honor received by the fallen soldier could be transferred to his living proxy, and that the gold star would symbolize that transference.[45] The desire for public praise rather than private grief won many women over to Bowen's cause. Canadian mourners of Great War soldiers, too, adopted a purple sash.[46]

Of all the ruminations on the subject, the *Syracuse Herald* posted the most politically charged article about the fashion of mourning.[47] The unsigned editorial parroted the patriotic message heard in other columns, but it positioned the choices made by U.S. soldiers' widows and mothers as affecting the rest of the world. Bereaved Americans, opined the writer, did not forgo the customary reverence and respect shown for the departed at funerals, but they did shun needless displays of overwrought emotion (anthropologist David E. Stannard explained that in the nineteenth century, funerals in the United States were "elaborate, dramatic, and somber").[48] It was simply part of the "American character" to free oneself from outdated funeral rituals that were still insisted on in the Old World. Instead, in the hustle and bustle of everyday life in the United States, people went straight to funerals from work wearing the same clothes and same "natural and unaffected" demeanor. Men took the lead in shrugging off mourning rituals, confirmed the writer, but "even the American wife and mother" would do her patriotic part to refrain from outward lamentations (the black armband worn by President Calvin Coolidge on the occasion of his predecessor Warren G. Harding's death in 1923 cast doubt upon the writer's view that men were at the forefront of wardrobe change, although admittedly the frugal Coolidge was not known for setting fashion trends).[49]

By noting women's tag-along response to change in this manner, the columnist reified Victorian-era notions of rational, practical-minded men versus sentimental women. Because men were believed to live a more public life, Victorian mores held that they need not be as stringent in following mourning customs and could resume their normal routines after the funeral.[50] The writer distinguished the "American character" from that of other nations but

Chicago Daily News, "Gold Star Mothers, Grant Park Chicago, 1918." Image #DN-0070373. Courtesy Chicago History Museum. Note that the two women in black dresses are combining new and old mourning attire practices. *From left to right:* Mrs. Anna G. Dorian, Mrs. Amos E. Vaughan, Mrs. Lee W. Sosthein, Mrs. Oscar Vogl, and Mrs. Edgar J. Curtiss.

included a list of the United States' allies in the conflict and suggested that American women forgo the "satisfaction" of wearing black out of respect for the many more multitudes of aggrieved women in those countries. The British had acknowledged that national morale would suffer if all women who had suffered a loss were to wear traditional mourning garb.[51] One German writer, Else Lüders, found mourning a wartime death to be a sign of a lack of gratitude for soldiers' heroism on the part of the aggrieved.[52] The *Syracuse Herald* reporter supposed that women derived satisfaction when they received sympathy from others. Overall, he or she made refraining from traditional mourning rituals and fashions a national imperative, rather than an individual choice, during wartime. In Indianapolis, columnist Belinda Brewster praised the ways in which losses were creating unity among American women regardless of their "caste, creed, or previous condition of servitude."[53]

Essayist Frank Crane surveyed New York society women, the presumed leaders of American taste and etiquette, to gauge their attitudes toward changing notions of appropriate mourning behavior during wartime, and found that most echoed De Koven Bowen's sentiments. A badge of red, white, and blue, proclaimed Mrs. Rupert Hughes, reflected the only consolation for the grief-stricken woman. Maxine Elliott declared that "for me it is inconceivable that a woman should wear conventional mourning for her relations who died in a war." Instead, she should want to feel pride for having made such a noble sacrifice. In addition, Elliott noted the needless expense of purchasing a new set of black clothes (although presumably she and her social set could easily afford such an extravagance, even during war). According to Crane, only a minority of those surveyed felt that the decision to wear mourning should be a matter of personal choice.[54]

The growing power of the female consumer in the United States may have swayed some bereaved mothers and wives to either adopt or forgo traditional bereavement garb. A *New York Times* article praising French mourners, for example, encouraged readers not to simply retain the previous year's wardrobe instead of buying new fashions, because clamping one's purse tight against new purchases was throwing female workers in New York City's Garment District out of work. In addition, readers casting their eyes upon the numerous articles debating what aggrieved women should or should not wear undoubtedly noticed the advertisements for mourning frocks strategically placed alongside the editorials.[55]

In the writer's zeal to banish the wearing of black, the *Syracuse Herald* columnist instructed every American publication to demand the immediate discarding of customary mourning for the remainder of the war, for the wearing of crepe "will hinder, not help this country *in its part* in preventing the struggle from ending in a German peace."[56] Instead of announcing a new direction in fashion and social custom for its own sake, however, the writer asked only for temporary change because of the war. Unlike Thurston, who linked women's advancements both before and during the war with high expectations for women in the postwar world, this particular *Syracuse Herald* writer did not seize the opportunity created by the war to herald a new dawn for the New Women who were shedding their old customs or their traditional place in society. Instead, the article demanded that patriotic fervor eclipse the self-indulgence of women's everyday lives: The nation's noble cause should overcome individualism, especially in time of war. War work enabled women to shirk these qualities. Sir Robert Scott's widow, Lady Scott, remarked that war work resulted in "absolute freedom from the unrest that is the characteristic disease of our times." War work had the added benefit of "clear[ing] yourself of the disgrace of leisure." To encourage women to apply for work in munitions plants, newspapers featured ads asking women "Which Will Your Brother or Sweetheart See," a slacker lounging with a book or an industrious weapons maker?[57] Brewster, too, encouraged women to give up their "fluffy frocks" worn to bridge parties in favor of practical clothes that would take them to war relief meetings and Red Cross work. The tradition of wearing black to indicate bereavement persisted into the post-war era, although widows were released from their obligation to wear heavy crepe. Letter writers continued to use black-bordered stationery to communicate their bereavement.[58]

President Wilson weighed in on the mourning fashion debate in May 1918, further politicizing bereavement practices. By the time of his war declaration to the U.S. Congress, the commander-in-chief was undoubtedly cognizant of the need to create a home front ready and willing to sacrifice for the cause. He had received letters from women imploring him to instruct widows to adopt gold stars rather than black crepe. He finally responded to Anna Howard Shaw, chair of the Women's Committee of the U.S. Council of National Defense, agreeing with the idea of what he called the "service badge." Specifically, Wilson approved of the Women's Committee's decision to adopt a three-inch black band adorned with a "gilt star," to be worn on the left arm. The Women's Committee explained that this would "express better than mourning the feeling of the American people that such losses are a matter of glory rather than of prostrating grief and depression." The Committee referred anonymously to a letter it had received from a bereaved mother who wished to extend her "gallant son's expectation that I should regard his death as a happy promotion into higher service. Patriotism means such exalted living that dying is not the harder part."[59] Like Louise De Koven Bowen, Wilson thought that wearing black placed too much emphasis on loss.[60] "Depressing," "gloomy," and "overwrought" communicated the moods that writers and government officials used to complain about the grieving process during the Great War. "Think of the depressing effect upon the entire country when funeral ships begin to arrive and funeral trains pass through villages, towns, and cities," warned Gold Star mother Mabel Fonda Gareisson to persuade readers that soldiers' bodies should remain in France.[61] Like his commander-in-chief, one U.S. Military Intelligence officer criticized wreath laying on Armistice Day as "conveying the idea of mourning rather than patriotism."[62] For his part, Wilson declined to make his personal preference public because he did not want to risk his words' being interpreted as a forecast of high death tolls.

Nevertheless, the *New York Times* published Wilson's letter directing women to wear the gold star.[63] Wilson and the U.S. Military Intelligence officer's desire to dismiss grief differed from communications that relatives received from their government when they made inquiries regarding where their soldiers had been buried. Mrs. Gansloser had written to the Graves Registration Service (GRS), a branch of the Quartermaster General that dealt with overseas burials, asking where her son had been laid to rest. She received this enumerated request:

1. It would likely to involve further delay if we should write personal letters in each of the many cases of notification of relatives as to the present resting places of their noble dead who glorify that nations' roll of honor;
2. Will you therefore please accept this letter as being the best we can do, just now? And will you also accept the sympathy of those who have been working hard for many months to render worthy service to tens of thousands of sorrowing people, in the care of their dead?

In this missive, Charles C. Pierce, chief of the GRS, acknowledged war's sorrow and begged Mrs. Gansloser to have patience as she waited for the military to sort out the tremendous task of dealing with the World War dead. "Thousands of bodies have been transferred to larger and better cemeteries," explained Pierce in the same letter, "for reasons which were deemed imperative by the military authorities of all the Allied Nations, and the great task of improving these cemeteries is well under way." Gansloser's file does not indicate whether Pierce's response healed the rift in the reciprocal relationship between Mrs. Gansloser and her government.[64] Leaders of other at-war nations also wrung their hands over so many wartime deaths and their impact on public morale. Australians wore badges of mourning, while Canadian mothers received Silver Cross medals. Germany belatedly bestowed *Ehrenkreuz* (cross of honor) upon next-of-kin of Great War soldiers in 1934, although only if relatives applied for one. These symbols of honor and sacrifice drew women into the reciprocal citizen–government relationship, offering them a chance to feel part of the nation-state (even if belatedly, in Germany's case).[65]

The invention of the gold star armband, and the choice by many to wear it instead of traditional mourning attire, progressed directly to the creation of the Gold Star Widows and Mothers pilgrimages. These government-funded, all-expenses-paid voyages to France allowed widows of servicemen killed overseas to visit their husbands' graves and act out publicly the war widows' role that Thurston had prescribed for them before U.S. intervention began. The legislation to allocate resources for the trips became politicized as law-makers considered the cost of repatriating dead bodies back to the United States, as opposed to funding visitations. Sponsors of the legislation used the trips to cement ties with the United States' allies during the conflict in order to ameliorate the effects of the U.S. Senate's refusal to join the League of Nations.[66] Finally, the U.S. government's sponsorship of the pilgrimages was designed to reinvigorate nationalist sentiment and re-celebrate its perceived victory in the Great War. For despite the expectation of a sorrow-tinged voyage to cemeteries and gravesites in France, the pilgrimages at the same time celebrated American nationalism and its noble, victorious cause.

The *New York Times* reported on the pilgrims' arrival in France, stating that "although [the pilgrims were] plainly shaken with grief at first and with many of them sobbing, they soon recovered their composure, and pride for their soldier dead restored their spirits." Like the women lobbying for the gold star in place of black attire, the newspaper confirmed the "new mien of grief": stoic resignation and patriotism.[67] Other sources affirmed this shift in attitude from sorrowful to patriotic. In its 1930 Armistice Day edition, the *Chicago Tribune* published a cartoon suggesting to readers that they disavow any ambivalent feelings they might still harbor about wartime losses. The cartoon implied that the benefits of peace were ambivalent, whereas the joy of victory was visceral. Armistice Day 1918 "meant more than peace," explained the artist, against the backdrop of a line of doughboys, eying a white flag labeled "peace" warily; instead, "It meant Victory!" the cartoon assured readers in the next panel. In this view, soldiers tossed up their helmets in jubilation or in reverence before an oversized American flag.[68] Because the legislation tasked the Quartermaster General (QMG) with planning for and carrying out the pilgrimages, the journeys took on a military veneer that enhanced the national honor and glory theme that widows had chosen to adopt by the wearing of the gold star armband when their husbands died.[69] In this way, participating war widows contributed to their nation's perpetual state of war. Not all Gold Star Widows celebrated the militarization of their widowhood, however.

The pilgrimages were designed in part to provide a sense of national unity, but instead supporters had disparate notions of the meanings imparted by the voyages.[70] The American Battle Monuments Commission endorsed the unity theme when it insisted that all memorials be approved by them, a regulation that even the patriotic American Legion decried.[71] While the QMG arranged for survivors to be divided into "companies" and herded into military forts and hospitals during their tours, at least one senator and one of the most active Gold Star Mothers pilgrims referred to the journeys as peace pilgrimages.[72] Adding further to the disunity, widows were separated by race on board pilgrimage ships and in hotels.[73] Some African Americans responded to invitations to travel to France on segregated ships by noting that they preferred "to remain at home and retain our honor and self-respect," rather than visit their loved ones' graves under such circumstances.[74] One Gold Star mother asked the Quartermaster General's Office if kosher meals would be offered to the "mothers of Jewish boys." No, replied the QMG, because Jewish boys had eaten the same army rations as their non-Jewish comrades.[75]

Shortly after the November 1918 armistice, the QMG office began soliciting choices of the next-of-kin in the matter of where their soldiers' bodies should find their final resting places: either burial in a man's hometown, in a national cemetery, in Arlington National Cemetery (if qualified), or in one of the newly constructed national cemeteries in France, Belgium, and England (all at government expense). Great Britain did not repatriate its soldiers' bodies; France brought the bodies of its soldiers (when they could be identified) to waiting family members via train. In addition to having lost the war, Germany lost all rights to repatriate the bodies of its soldiers lying in France or Belgium.[76] Women, like most African Americans, may have felt little or no connection to the politics of U.S. intervention in the World War, because most females were still disenfranchised in April 1917 and because Jim Crow laws prevented African Americans from voting. Such circumstances may have encouraged families to disengage the bodies of their loved ones from a foreign war they had neither endorsed nor rejected and return them to their homes.[77] On the other hand, the counsel of revered national figures such as former President Theodore Roosevelt and General John J. Pershing convinced many widows that their husbands should remain where they had "fallen," in France.

Two organizations vied for survivors' attention: The Bring Home the Soldier Dead League advocated "a tomb in America for every American Soldier," while the Gold Star Mothers and Widows maintained that warriors' deaths were spiritual, and that their final resting place should be where they fell in noble battle.[78] Still, 70 percent of relatives wanted the remains of their loved ones returned to the United States despite the high cost, indicating an overall desire to mourn individually rather than participate collectively in national war remembrance ceremonies.[79]

Widows, mothers, and other survivors corresponded with the QMG to let their preferences be known. Like German widows Elisabeth Macke and

Johanna Boldt, both of whom waited months for concrete evidence of their husbands' deaths, U.S. war widows choosing to repatriate sometimes had to wait for years before their spouses' bodies could be returned from overseas. Kentucky war widow Grace Brooks, for example, wrote dozens of letters to the QMG, complaining about the two-and-a-half years she was forced to wait for the remains of her dead soldier to be returned to the couple's home at Dry Creek. When news reached her that her husband's body had been exhumed and reburied at an American cemetery in France, she cried to Secretary of War Newton Baker, "Does this mean that our dear boys are not to be brought home for final burial? That was the promise made before our dear boys left—that their remains would be brot [sic] back."[80] Brooks recalled the War Department's declaration in April 1917 that fallen soldiers' bodies would either be buried in their homes or in national cemeteries.[81] In similar fashion, German war widow Maria Geiger wrote to Kaiser Wilhelm asking for his help in sending the body of her husband back to his home in Leutkirchen, Württemberg. "Thus, Your Excellency, I would like to beg most humbly if Your Excellency could be of help in transferring my husband's corpse back home, for we would love to bury our unforgettable husband and father in the homeland." There is no evidence that Geiger's request was granted.[82]

By the mid-1920s newly enfranchised female activists geared up for their campaign to enact legislation that would permit the pilgrimages to take place. Women's organizations, such as the American Legion Women's Auxiliary, the Gold Star Mothers and Widows, and the American War Mothers, all cut their political teeth by testifying during debate in Congress over whether to fund Gold Star pilgrimages. By the mid-1920s, these groups were fearful that their men's sacrifices, as well as their own, had been forgotten by the American public, and individual members expected something in return for their forfeitures.[83]

Widows such as Elizabeth Hamm, however, shirked the politicization of the pilgrimages and remained at home, despite their fervent devotion to their dead soldier-husbands' military exploits. "I have never availed myself of the offer made by the U.S. government to visit the cemetery . . . because I wholly disapprove of this expenditure of public money. The legacy of suffering and financial anxiety that a war widow must carry," Hamm assured the QMG, "cannot be assuaged by such measures, and the burden of taxation upon the country should not have had this additional item laid upon it. There are better monuments to be raised to our dead right here and now, in a constructive disinterested foreign policy . . . free from the possible taint of political interest."[84] Like Hamm, some British war widows considered any sort of government compensation to them, including pensions, to be "blood money" that stained the patriotism of their husbands' memories.[85]

Congressional testimony privileged mothers over widows, primarily on the basis of mothers' blood ties to their sons. As Mathilda Burling stated bluntly, "It was our flesh and blood that enriched the foreign soil." More to the point: ". . . it was the mothers who had won the war." Only "mothers of the blood" could be considered genuine bearers of the nation's heroes, and adoptive parents were forced to resign their memberships from the American War Mothers.[86] In addition, mothers charged that widows "were not worthy of the trip," and that they conceived of the pilgrimages as a "junket" rather than a trip to honor the dead. General Pershing had urged dough-boys to write home to their mothers on Mother's Day to demonstrate their affection to the patriotic women left at home who were cheering them on to victory, building up the pedestal upon which mothers presided in American life.[87] The preference shown to mothers stemmed from the United States' early national period, when notions of "republican motherhood" held that women's sole connection to the newly founded nation lay in instilling republican ideals in their children.[88] Other nations also lent mothers preferential treatment. Joy Damousi's work on Australian mourners explained how mothers achieved special status over widows. Sidonie Wronsky, Berlin educator and editor of the *German Journal of Social Welfare*, rationalized the German system of postwar social welfare for war survivors as an outgrowth of the recognition of the biological and sociological bond between mother and child.[89]

Testimony on pilgrimage legislation indicates that legislators and Gold Star Mothers conceived of U.S. soldiers as "boys," rather than as men. Too much attention from mothers, however, was seen by some as "undercutting the virility" soldiers needed to fight the war.[90] In any case, President Coolidge signed legislation authorizing both mothers and widows to board ships bound for France. Lisa M. Budreau has written that mothers stood at the pinnacle of the remembrance pyramid after the Great War, but widows received preferential treatment when it came to decisions as to where the body should rest, who should receive government compensation for the loss of a breadwinning male, and to whom the government should offer vocational training as further compensation. All of the aforementioned privileges depended on the mourner's decision to remain a widow, however.

The U.S. Congress enacted legislation in 1929 that authorized pilgrimages to U.S. cemeteries in Europe "by mothers and widows of members of military and naval forces of the United Sates who died in the service at any time between April 5, 1917, and July 1, 1921, and whose remains are now interred in such cemeteries." Congress later extended eligibility for voyages to mothers and widows of servicemen who were buried at sea and those whose places of burial were unknown. Widows who had remarried were not permitted, nor were those who had opted to repatriate their husbands' bodies. The QMG found that 17,389 women were eligible to become pilgrims. More than 6,000 women had traveled to France by the time the program ended in October 1933.[91]

Nancy Payne Marsh, widow of the Reverend Lieutenant Arthur H. Marsh, boarded the SS *Washington* in 1933, joining the final pilgrimage to France to visit her husband's grave. But the militarized pomp and circumstance surrounding the pilgrimages seemed to leave her blood cold. On board the ship, she refused to wear her Gold Star badge and ripped the emblem off of her deck chair. She encouraged other pilgrims to also remove their "dog tags."[92] Part of her resentment may have come from the murky details she had received about her husband's illness and subsequent death. Marsh had died of bronchial pneumonia at a hospital in Vittel, France. She heard of his death from two different sources: First, the Red Cross sent her a telegram attributing his death to pneumonia, and second, Marsh's Episcopal Church had announced in a newsletter that his death had occurred while he was ministering to soldiers in battle. Trying to determine the true nature of her husband's final days, Nancy Marsh put the question to the War Department in December 1918. By the following February she knew the truth: An army chaplain who had presided over Marsh's burial explained that he had been gassed and had died of the effects at an American hospital.

Marsh's letters to the War Department indicate her indecision about whether to leave her husband's body in France or to bring him home. One factor that could help her make up her mind, she wrote, would be if she could be buried in France next to him. As of September 1919, however, the War Department had not yet established a firm policy for dealing with dead American soldiers buried overseas. In responding to her request, the QMG encouraged her to leave his body with his comrades. Marsh's eloquent letters, filled with her quandary and her intense love for her husband, called into question the notion that only the "blood" connection between mother and son deserved a pilgrimage.[93]

By spring 1921, Marsh confirmed that she would keep Arthur's body in France. But her attitude toward the government that had called her husband to serve had changed. Had her husband not been killed by gas-induced pneumonia and remained overseas longer, she noted sarcastically, his company commander might have made him an undertaker, given the sheer numbers of dead men that the war had produced. Marsh was not the only one to express her disillusionment with the U.S. military. The allure of the Gold Star Mother had faded by the time the pilgrims left U.S. shores, according to Lisa M. Budreau. A 1933 John Ford film, titled *Pilgrimage*, revealed an overbearing Gold Star Mother in a less-than-favorable light. Philip Stevenson's sardonic 1935 *Esquire* article depicted a group of self-righteous Gold Star Mothers as obnoxious cows. For many Americans, satire and irony, modern sensibilities that replaced older forms of honor and glory, eclipsed by the mid-1930s the government's earnest attempt at comforting wives and mothers. Emotional responses to the war generally had grown thin by then.[94]

The gilded edges surrounding the Gold Star Mothers may have faded with time, but the glory surrounding their heroic warriors soldiered on, aided by some of the widows the men left behind. War widows, including Harriet Pierson, Laura Evelyn Sorenson, and Theresa Johnson, venerated their husbands' wartime deaths, interpreting them as the sacrifice of an individual to the glory of nation and the nobility of war.[95] These war widows deemed their government's compensation, in the form of high praise, pilgrimages to France, and Medals of Honor, for their men and for themselves as their soldiers' living proxies, to be sufficient to maintain the reciprocal citizen–government relationship. Widows such as Nancy Payne Marsh shirked their status as a Gold Star Widow and the honor attached to it, finding it inadequate compensation for the loss of their husbands' lives. Other mourners, such as Elsie MacKenzie, betrayed their wistful hopes that their husbands had indeed died heroic deaths, even though they admitted that they had not been told any of the details of their soldiers' deaths.[96]

Civil War veteran General George W. Wingate understood survivors' irritation with government bureaucracies in determining the true nature of their relatives' deaths. Wingate founded the Victory Hall Association (VHA) in New York City in 1919 to collect subscriptions for the funding of a memorial to New York City's dead World War soldiers in part to relieve survivors' frustrations. Wingate placed advertisements in local newspapers that asked for the details of warriors' final days.[97] He also wrote to relatives of men and women who had died in service overseas based on lists he had received from the War Department. "The official records on individual cases contain only a meager account of the individual hero of the deceased members in the World War," lamented Wingate, "and it is because of that that we are writing the parents for such details as they may have."[98] Wingate received more than 8,000 letters, primarily from widows, mothers, fathers, sisters, and brothers, explaining their soldiers' deaths using the language of praise and honor that Wingate himself used when soliciting responses. "It is our purpose," explained the general, "to preserve a record that . . . will detail all the incidents surrounding the culmination of that service in heroic death . . . of all who gave gallant service and life itself to their country."[99]

Despite the confirmation of warriors' heroism appearing in nearly all of the Victory Hall Association records, an undercurrent of ruptured citizen-government relations persisted throughout Wingate's correspondence with survivors. Widow Edna Beatty, for example, informed Wingate that she had been told that her husband had been hit by a German explosive shell while standing outside his dugout, knocking him down and breaking his leg. "But no one could make me ever believe," wrote Beatty, "that my husband died of a broken leg. In my estimation it was far more serious, but this was all I was permitted to know."[100] Edgar M. Guckenheimer's father penned a letter that stands out as the most breathtakingly distrustful of all VHA correspondents. The elder Guckenheimer, a Greenwich Village shopkeeper, had written the War Department to learn the details of his son's death. He had never received more than the perfunctory telegram. After making inquiries among his son's comrades, he received a missive from a German soldier describing Edgar's tragedy, which Guckenheimer believed resulted from the neglect of his company's officers. "You can see," Guckenheimer told the VHA, "that my son was not killed in action as stated by Washington officials, but was murdered through the carelessness and incompetence of the officers in charge of his company or regiment."[101] For survivors such as Beatty and Guckenheimer who let their loved ones' bodies remain overseas there was no closure—no funeral, no headstone, and no veneration.[102] In addition, the VHA read letters from survivors who expressed their frustration over their inability to receive government compensation for the loss of their breadwinners.[103] Wingate's organization consoled families in their bereavement, when at times the federal government tried to cover it up.

The body of a dead American soldier occasionally became a contested symbol of the honor and glory imparted to it by the U.S. government and by private organizations. Sara Manning Kephart, widow of James Watson Kephart, tangled with a woman calling herself Ethel M. Kephart who also claimed to be James's wife. Ethel Kephart wanted the soldier's body returned to Pennsylvania, but Sara refused to recognize her wishes. Divorce proceedings had not been finalized before James's death, and the QMG allowed Sara, rather than Ethel, to make the pilgrimage to visit Kephart's grave. Roy B. Martin's parents wrote heartfelt letters to the QMG, asking that it repatriate their son's body so that he could rest at home in West Virginia, but Martin's widow, Juanita Martin, had her choice honored over parental preference.[104]

Not all parties involved held widows' rights in such high regard, however. Sergeant Frank Downer's body lay beneath the soil at the American Cemetery at Oise-Aisne, France. Carl A. Swallow honored Downer by naming his local Monongahela, Pennsylvania, American Legion Post after his fallen comrade. In April 1927, Swallow began a lengthy correspondence with Assistant Secretary of War Hanford MacNider. In its quest to erect a bronze slab in honor of Downer at the cemetery in France, the Frank Downer American Legion Post #302 overlooked legislation that mandated that only next-of-kin could order any kind of graveside monument to mark burial places overseas. The law was designed to create uniform U.S. military cemeteries in foreign countries and represent a vision of wartime society as unified in its dedication to the ideals of freedom and democracy.[105] Swallow responded tersely to MacNider's recitation of the rules, revealing a rupture in citizen–government reciprocity. "It raises a question of doubt in our minds when we are not permitted to honor and revere the memory of Downer," wrote Swallow. "It may interest you to know that this Post was named for Downer because we loved the man both as a citizen and as a soldier and his spirit is always with us in peace as in battle." In answer to MacNider's comments regarding the right of the next-of-kin to decorate a soldier's grave, Swallow wrote: "Mrs. Downer, Sgt Downer's widow[,] cannot be approached upon the subject. She has remarried and the chances are this subject will henceforth and forever be furtherst [sic] thing from her thoughts. Should we forget so easily if everyone else sees fit to do so," proclaimed Swallow accusatorily, implying that Downer's wife had already blithely erased her husband from her mind. Emma Julia Downer, however, had not remarried and had taken a pilgrimage to France to honor her dead husband's grave. Swallow's juxtaposition of his comrades' love and reverence of Downer with his widow's presumed dishonor of him, in the form of remarriage, illustrates the notion that women's devotion to their husbands was only temporary, and easily replaced with a new marriage, whereas soldiers' dedication to their fallen comrades remained timeless.[106] Gold Star mothers employed this same idea when they accused mourning wives of seeking a journey to France merely to enjoy a "junket."

The American Legion involved itself in another case in which a war widow had remarried, demonstrating its interference in the matter of war widows' subsequent marriages. Private William Howard Bratten died of tuberculosis in 1919 after his discharge from the U.S. Army. His widow, Florence M. Bratten, remarried in May 1923. Florence Bratten lost her right to receive bonus payments from the state of Illinois upon her remarriage, but her son by her first marriage, William Harold Bratten, stood next in line to receive the payments. Shortly after Florence's second marriage took place, Thomas C. Dooner, American Legion Post #199 member and deputy sheriff of Edwardsville, Illinois, informed the Illinois Service Recognition Board (SRB) of the wedding. J. A. Jaworski, assistant chief clerk of the SRB, confirmed that the second marriage invalidated Florence's claims and stated that Private Bratten's child was henceforth the legal beneficiary. Therefore, wrote Jaworski, an application should be filed for the child of the deceased veteran by a duly appointed guardian, with a letter of authority of guardianship attached to the document. Jaworski enclosed the correct beneficiary forms for execution. Dooner did Jaworski's bidding, and the Edwardsville National Bank of Springfield, Illinois, became the child's legal guardian. In announcing to the SRB that the bank had become the son's legal guardian, Dooner noted that "naturally the mother of this child does not take kindly to the idea of having someone other than herself to handle the finances of this child." He asked Jaworski to send him Florence M. Bratten's SRB file. Jaworski declined to take this step, but he did send the application that would enable the state of Illinois to send bonus payments to the Edwardsville National Bank. The records do not include Florence M. Bratten's response to the procedure.[107]

Unlike the pilgrimages, war widows found no glory or honor in securing their financial futures and perpetuating their dependent status through government pension systems. Like the pilgrimages, however, the U.S. government's attempts at protecting the home front from the upheavals of war became riddled with contradiction and disillusionment. Officials endeavored to create the deepest breach between home front and battlefront that it possibly could. Lawmakers used federal funds to support and protect soldiers' wives and their children to ensure home front tranquility, even as government bureaucrats, relief societies, and businessmen lured women's active participation in the armament industry and other paid labor forces, as Ethel Thurston had predicted it would. The U.S. government designed a system called Allotments and Allowances, administered by the newly endowed Bureau of War Risk Insurance (BWRI), to pay soldiers' wives to retain their positions as homemakers and mothers. The Allotments represented a portion of the husband-soldier's pay, while the Allowances signified the U.S. government's addition to the wife's income. The German government also offered wives a separation allowance (so did Great Britain and France), but German spouses received their checks from municipal governments (where Johanna Boldt collected hers), and soldiers fighting for Germany did not see a deduction from their paychecks going to their wives, as did U.S. and Canadian servicemen.[108] According to K. Walter Hickel's 1999 study of the BWRI, only the United States and Canadian governments paid their soldiers enough to make deductions feasible. The BWRI provided money for a soldier's immediate family regardless of need. Wives without children received $30 monthly, and for households including children up to $65 was available.[109] Not all spouses received their Allotments and Allowances, however. Walter B. Drebelbis, for example, enlisted under an alias for the purpose of skirting the deduction from his military pay that would have gone to his wife. Upon Drebelbis's death, his widow, Dorothy B. Drebelbis, helped confirm the soldier's real identity with dental records and ensured that she would receive compensation by certifying the couple's marriage license. Despite her husband's duplicity, Drebelbis made a pilgrimage to visit his grave in France.[110]

An ocean separated the United States from the trenches of western Europe—German and French citizens did not have that luxury—and the U.S. government stood ready to take advantage of that distance. As one U.S. government official boasted, "Never in history was a war fought with so few hardships and privations in the homes of men called forth to war."[111] Thomas B. Love gloated that the Allotments and Allowances scheme marked the "most liberal provision ever made by any government in the history *of the world* for its fighting forces in time of war."[112] With declarations such as these, women were represented in the exceptionalist view of the United States' war effort. Wives and mothers who shrugged off their mourning garb and donned instead the Gold Star emblem reinforced the notion that while Europeans suffered terribly, the U.S. home front remained untouched by war's sorrows and privations.

As Hickel noted, Allotments and Allowances helped preserve family life as Americans understood it: male breadwinner, female dependent. Officials administering the system worked to preserve the male prerogative of provider and the woman's obligation as housewife and mother. But white employers living in the South revealed their racialist assumptions of this paradigm when they complained of the shortage of black female laborers that the system created in southern states; in other words, they thought that only white women ought to stay home to care for homes and families.[113] Supporters of the legislation that instituted the BWRI argued that a hasty end to the conflict would further the goal of preserving the American household. If soldiers knew that their dependents were well cared for at home, remarked congressmen during debate on the October 1917 War Risk Insurance Act (WRIA), then the fighting spirit "over there" would remain high. Representative Sam Rayburn of Texas proclaimed that the Act would "end the war successfully and at the earliest possible moment."[114] Rayburn admitted that "there is not much enthusiasm for this war" in homes including a mother and a wife dependent on a man's wages.[115]

If lawmakers believed that they could successfully keep the war at bay stateside, they could not deny that it came home to families who lost their loved ones. Once newspapers began announcing fatalities, the campaign to replace traditional mourning attire with the gold star of honor waged by journalists, reformers, and the U.S. president amounted to a denial of war's sorrow: Soldiers died and widows (and mothers) cried. The system of compensation to widows, also part of the WRIA, represented a veil that further obscured war's tragedies. Called compensation rather than pension, the term was designed to detach the corrupt nature of Civil War pensions (the word was reinstated in a 1938 bill related to war pensions). Compensation offered widows and other dependents an income to take the place of their breadwinner's lost wages.

Unlike the testimony surrounding the legislation to fund the pilgrimages, the WRIA gave widows precedence over mothers of soldiers because compensation was paid to widows and their children automatically, regardless of need, "in view of the fact that the statute recognized the moral and legal obligation of a man to support his wife and children."[116] Compensation to either parent of the dead soldier depended on need, which had to be proven. However, a wife's claim to compensation ended upon her remarriage, an uncommon occurrence except when the widow was a young woman.[117] In the case of a new union, lawmakers reasoned, her new husband took over her first husband's obligation to support her and her children. Compensation was tied neither to soldiers' rank nor to the deceased man's civilian income. "It is based on a new principle, namely that of the family need, on the theory that under the conscription law the family is conscripted when the bread winner is taken away."[118] German feminists argued that birthing babies constituted women's service to nation equal to men's military service; in the United States, wives did not have to offer anything, because in drafting their husbands the U.S. military drafted them as well. Widows received $25 if they were childless; they could claim as much as $52.50 for children, depending on the number. Compensation amounted to anywhere from $5 to $12.50 *less* per month than what widows had received in Allotments and Allowances while their husbands still drew their soldiers' pay. The BWRI director claimed that the compensation offered to survivors was generous, but an investigation of Illinois widows calls that assertion into question.

Aside from the goals of preserving gender roles and a strong fighting force as an avenue to end the war quickly, the impetus for the WRIA came from industry and Progressive-era reform. Industry, according to Texas lawmaker Thomas B. Love, offered "an honest contract of employment [which] must include provisions for support of a man's dependents after his death. These things are essential to the living of the employe [*sic*]. Without them life is not worth living."[119] Samuel McCune Lindsay, Columbia University economics professor and a member of the American Association for Labor Legislation, noted that laws requiring compensation to a worker's family in case of death related to his or her job placed the financial burden of the loss on industry. In analogous fashion, Lindsay thought that the government should compensate families for deaths occurring in the line of duty and distribute the burden through taxation.[120] Beginning in 1914, the U.S. government began compensating the shipping industry for losses suffered in belligerent waters. Mothers' pensions, first instituted in the United States in 1911 in Illinois, built upon the same idea. Chicago Judge Henry Neil had declared that states should compensate poor mothers with an income so they could stay at home and care for their children, rather than be forced to relinquish offspring to state-supported institutions.[121]

While a widow's compensation was need-blind, the BWRI did attach certain strings to her award. The aggrieved had to apply for compensation from the BWRI office. No payment would be made for death or disability occurring later than one year after the man left the service, unless a medical examination at the time of his resignation or discharge or within one year thereafter proved that the soldier was then suffering from an injury or disease likely to cause death or disability later. None was paid for death inflicted as punishment for crime or military offense unless inflicted by the enemy. Widows needed to make their claims within five years after the death was recorded in the department in which the man was serving at the time of his death, or in case of death after discharge or resignation from service, within five years after death. The BWRI would accept only notification from the man's service unit as proof of his death. Finally, the BWRI deemed that a dishonorable discharge terminated the widow's right to compensation, tethering a wife inextricably to the conduct of the man she married (later legislation related to pensions questioned this regulation, although no change was made). Congressmen sparred with one another over whether widows of dishonorably discharged soldiers should be aided; one argued that "a man's wife ought to find out about him before she married him."[122] As of July 1, 1918, actuary S. H. Wolfe reported that 15,088 claims for compensation due to deaths in the service had been filed by widows or their representatives, of which 6,716 were disallowed as not adhering to the Act. Some 1,446 claims calling for monthly payments of $38,642 had been allowed, and the remaining claimants were waiting for investigation and adjustment.[123]

Allotments and Allowances and compensation proved to be more difficult to administer than predicted, and, ultimately, the system provided only a rocky road at best toward the goal of an untouched home front. Writing about Allotments and Allowances, Hickel argued that soldiers' wives took advantage of the direct purse strings the government gave them and acted independently in the public sphere, providing women a sense of national citizenship; seeing this in African American women unsettled southern white men.[124] Hickel claimed that the system "undermine[d] the privileged position of men within the family and the state."[125] While Allotments and Allowances provided women with an income apart from their male breadwinners' control, widows' connections to the nation-state were at times antagonistic, because the reciprocity required for citizenship to work was absent in many cases. Several *New York Times* articles critical of the BWRI reported that not only did it take months for a soldier's dependents to receive their portion of his income and the government's supplement, but the agency's delinquency caused the serviceman overseas much distress over his family's unmet needs. The agency responded that many soldiers did not fill out the form to generate a paycheck correctly, and if they were already overseas, it could in fact take months for corrections to be made.[126] For men enlisted or drafted in the first wave of troops deployed, this meant that their wives may not have received incomes until April 1918. Illinois widows reported having to wait a year and a half to receive their dead husbands' bonuses from the state.[127] So while supporters trumpeted the United States as the nation that cared the most for its fighting men and their families, in practice the bureaucracy did not reach its goal. Reports of BWRI failures do not indicate that women tangled with officials over absent paychecks: Instead, one soldier-husband merely reported that his dependent wife still waited for her check.[128] Furthermore, an Illinois study of widows' economic circumstances demonstrated that widows lived more poorly than they had before the war, so it is doubtful that they were satisfied with their newfound relationship to the nation-state, nor could they have acted independently in the public sphere as consumers, if they had little money to spend.[129]

The Illinois General Assembly enacted a statute in 1921 providing compensation to all men and their beneficiaries who had served in the World War. When all claims had been made upon this fund, there was an unexpended amount of $101,804. The General Assembly passed an additional law in 1929 "to provide relief for indigent widows and children of deceased World War veterans." The law directed the governor to appoint an advisory board of five people, representing the American Legion, the Women's Auxiliary of the American Legion, the United Spanish War Veterans Association, the Women's Relief Corps, and the Veterans of Foreign Wars. This board supervised expenditures, but the Department of Public Welfare determined families' eligibility.[130]

When the 1929 bill passed, the governor of Illinois recommended that the original five people supervising expenditures also be charged with investigating applications for relief under the law. This Advisory Committee set out the general policies regarding the applications. Illinois aid was not need-blind, as the WRIA had been, but like the WRIA it was granted regardless of cause of death (i.e., whether related to the man's service), because the widow of any man who had been a soldier was eligible. The state granted no aid until all of the present resources of the applicant had been exhausted. If a claimant's family could help, then the state required that it do so before it granted money to the applicant.[131] Funds could not be used to pay back debts. Claimants had to show that their deceased relative had lived in Illinois. As of July 1, 1931, the committee had received 308 applications for relief and granted aid to 157; it rejected 65, three widows withdrew their claims, and 83 were still pending. Most widows—34 out of 65—were denied aid because they were deemed "not indigent."[132]

Prevailing attitudes about women living without men were similar to those in Germany. Widows who were experiencing economic difficulties had spent their insurance money too quickly, according to the committee. One widow had used her insurance money to buy furniture for her boarding house. She did not keep any books, so the committee could not discern how much she had lost on her house, or how much it had at any time actually supplemented her meager savings. She had many outstanding debts, according to her application. The Committee urged her to find employment, and as conditions improved she could leave her son with her mother during the day. This particular widow did not seem to be sufficiently businesslike to warrant encouraging her to continue to take boarders, according to the committee. In another example, a widow used $918 of her $1,600 insurance payment to pay for her husband's funeral expenses. Penniless, she expressed dismay when the committee told her that she had been too extravagant. She felt that she would have "broken faith" with her husband had she not used the money for his funeral.[133] Natalia Greensfelder, author of the study of Illinois war widows, declared that women were simply not able to manage their money.[134]

Of the sixteen applications rejected for "technical reasons," two were deemed so because the husband in question was still alive; in three cases the committee discovered that the spouse was not a World War veteran; in three more cases, the veteran was not an Illinois resident. With the exception of one case listed as "unknown," these situations seemed relatively cut-and-dried. In seven instances, however, the widow was denied aid because her children were deemed "ineligible." In all seven cases, the committee discovered that the offspring had not been fathered by the veteran, but that the wives had remarried and were applying for aid for children from the second marriage. According to Greensfelder, the committee felt that although the law provided aid to the widow or the children of the deceased veteran, the legislation did not intend to support widows bringing up her children by another marriage.[135] Massachusetts widows giving birth to illegitimate children, or who took in male lodgers, or who were arrested for habitual intoxication lost their assistance as punishment for their presumed immoral behavior.[136]

In denying aid, the Illinois Advisory Committee waffled on whether the state did indeed wish to honor its deceased veterans, or whether the grants were based solely on the needs of this particular group of citizens. Because presumably a war widow had the right to procreate with another man after her first soldier-husband died, it would seem that if the state wished to help her, it would extend that aid to her under any circumstances. But in this case, the law appeared to discriminate against the war widow for remarrying and having birthed children with her subsequent husband. As far as the federal government and the state of Illinois were concerned, the war, and the honor and glory extended to soldiers and their widows who had fought in it, ended for the widow upon her remarriage. Was remarriage viewed as dishonoring the deceased veteran, as Drew Gilpin Faust's research in the U.S. Civil War indicates?

Upon making new vows, widows lost compensation, their ability to educate themselves with government aid under proposed legislation, their ability to take possession of deceased bodies, and their right to visit their late husbands' graves under the federal government–sponsored pilgrimages. Remarriage, in other words, carried with it severe penalties for war widows. Newly wedded women did not uniformly accept or acknowledge this reduction in their status, however. In some instances, war widows demonstrated their deep ties to their deceased soldier-husbands, even after remarriage. They also revealed a desire for the reciprocity that they expected when dealing with their government as citizens. Agnes M. Courter, widow of William J.

Courter, remained very devoted to her deceased warrior, despite her second nuptials. She enclosed to the Victory Hall Association a letter that she had received from Courter's comrade Captain Howard Bird, in which William's death was described. "For it [Bird's letter] has been a comfort and has opened my eyes to why he went when I often wished he could have stayed at home," explained his widow. "After reading Bird's letter you will realize (partly only) what he meant to me." Agnes M. Courter had taken new vows and became Agnes C. Dolan during the period of her correspondence with the VHA.[137] When Richard E. Cook's widow, Eva, remarried and became Eva R. Finn, she wrote to the Quartermaster General, informing the office of her changed status but saying that she still wished to make a pilgrimage to visit her late husband's grave. The response she received informed her that by law "the term 'widow' means a widow who has not remarried since the death of the member of the military or naval forces," and that therefore she was ineligible. The unlucky Finn subsequently sent another missive explaining that her second husband, Lieutenant Matthew E. Finn, an air corps pilot, had been killed in a crash in 1927, and she asked whether this might change her status regarding her eligibility to make a pilgrimage to visit Cook's grave. Another negative response arrived from the QMG. Finn persisted, however, particularly when the QMG then asked her whether Richard E. Cook had a living stepmother who might want to journey to France (prior correspondence had established that Cook's biological mother had long since passed away). Finn informed the QMG of Cook's stepmother's address but argued that, because Richard Cook and his stepmother had never met one another, "I therefore wish to ask for the pilgrimage for myself as the widow of Lt. Cook." Washington, D.C., sent her another refusal.[138]

Both the federal government and the Illinois state government placed a high priority on making sure that war widows applying for trips to France or for compensation from the state had not remarried. Illinois widows applying as survivors for their husbands' war bonuses were required to submit three affidavits from citizens confirming that "the claimant has not remarried since the death of above named veteran."[139] Newspapers reporting on the Gold Star Mothers and Widows' pilgrimages reminded readers that remarried widows were not allowed to make the trip.[140] Nuptials with a second husband indicated, to some parties, a lack of loyalty and honor on the part of the widow to her deceased warrior-husband that at the very least caused eyebrows to rise. In Germany, Helene Hurwitz-Stranz's anthology of war widows' memoirs includes the remembrances of aggrieved wives who had remarried (although the majority of the twenty contributors were still without husbands as of its publication in 1931). The title of the anthology, *War Widows Create Their Own Fate*, indicated Hurwitz-Stranz's conviction that war widows could, and did, define the term for themselves. Remarried memoirists who recorded their recollections of their first marriages and the war they lived through still identified themselves as war widows, despite their subsequent unions.

As was the case with their counterparts in Germany, U.S. war widows shunned excess scrutiny of their private lives that they encountered when they responded to the QMG's invitation to visit overseas graves, or when they applied for aid. Surviving wives believed that the state of Illinois wanted to grant money to them as their soldier-husbands' living proxies as a reward for the service that their husbands had rendered to their country and for their sacrifice of their life partner, and that therefore the usual social investigation should not accompany the grant.[141] In other words, while Illinois lawmakers viewed the money as "relief" (as did their counterparts in the federal government), the widow conceived of it as "reward."[142]

Whether the compensation was relief or reward, the applications indicated real need among war widows, in contrast to the rosy proclamations mouthed by supporters of the WRIA ("few hardships and privations in the homes of men called forth to war," and "most liberal provision ever made by any government"). Greensfelder wanted to determine the financial situation of war widows relative to their husbands' deaths. Was poverty the direct result of the veteran's death, or did it derive from some other cause? The sociology student used pre- and post-income levels of the families to determine the answer. She checked to see how many years the husband had been dead before the wife made application to the state. She took the date of the man's death as a basis, then looked at the number of years intervening between the date of his death and the date on the aid application. She discovered that in twenty-nine of seventy-three cases the veteran had been dead less than two years and that in ten instances he had been dead for a period of more than four years. In instances where the breadwinner had been deceased for many years, Greensfelder wondered how the widow had gotten along in the intervening years. She noted other sources of income, such as the earnings of the widow, mothers' pensions, other relief agencies, institutional care for family members, insurance money, relatives' assistance, and federal funds (undoubtedly federal compensation). Widows' earnings, mothers' pensions, and insurance money, respectively, occurred with the highest frequency. Unemployment (64 percent) constituted the greatest reason for seeking aid from this fund by the families of deceased World War veterans.[143] During the early twentieth century, widows constituted a disproportionate share of wage-earning women, yet historians know less about this group of workers than any other segment of the U.S. labor force. Nevertheless, American widows continued to depend on the munificence of relatives. For despite a growth in welfare programs during the late nineteenth and early twentieth centuries, the patriarchal family remained widows' primary means of support.[144]

The plight of Illinois widows illustrates the inadequacy of government programs to keep homemakers and mothers out of the work force. Greensfelder noted the inaccuracy of family income records, but generally she found in a majority of cases significant discrepancies between incomes when husbands were still alive versus after their deaths. "It is interesting to note that 28 of 57 of these families have been forced to live with a decrease in budget of $60 or even more, whereas 22 are lacking $90 a month, or even more." In Germany, too, war widows were considered to be economically worse off than if their husbands had lived.[145] Published in 1931, Greensfelder's study relied on records created just prior to the peak years of the Great Depression.[146]

Well before the economic downturn, however, the U.S. Congress intended to help needy widows and orphans nationwide. The Kenyon-Fess bill, introduced in 1921, proposed the reorganization and restructuring of certain government bureaucracies; in addition, it proposed to provide vocational training for war widows and orphans. As newspaperman Frederic J. Haskin described it, "the United States government is planning to help the wives and children of heroes fit themselves for jobs whereby they can earn their bread and butter." Some 12,000 widows and 6,000 orphans would have benefited from Kenyon-Fess, according to "conservative estimates" compiled by the War Department. The aggrieved had to prove that their husbands had died in the line of duty, and they became ineligible if they remarried, once again forfeiting their eligibility by not retaining their widowhood.[147] The American Legion supported this bill. Organized labor, under the leadership of the American Federation of Labor's Samuel Gompers, opposed it.[148] The legislation passed in the Senate but, although its prospects looked "excellent," it died in the House.[149] A bill providing for the vocational training of war widows apparently amounted to an admission that WRIA had failed in its purpose of keeping potential women wage earners in the home. In Australia, pensioned widows received the kind of vocational training Kenyon-Fess had hoped to provide, although only if they could prove that their children would not be adversely affected by either their mothers' schooling or by their employment afterward.[150] As S. J. Kleinberg has noted, in the United States as elsewhere most widows "carried the problems of widowhood with them to their own graves."[151]

As U.S. war widows fashioned their own response to the Great War, they relied upon the experiences of their European counterparts. They took advantage of their nation's initial declaration of neutrality in the conflict by imagining how their war widowhood might differ from that expressed overseas. Eager to be part of their nation's seminal event, they signed up for war work and expected to continue to aid their nation-state should calamity befall them. With an exceptionalist, modern spirit they donned the new, militarized emblem of mourning and carried out their widowhood duties, by all appearances, with an energetic spunk. Apart from the spotlight that Ethel Thurston's piece had directed on them collectively, however, many of them struggled individually with sorrow and resentment, and many also continued to depend on male protection to keep them from poverty. When they perceived that the U.S. government had deceived them when it refused to communicate with them honestly about their husbands' deaths, or when it did not provide adequate compensation for their loss, their ties to the nation-state were severed. Thurston's heady prose had not prepared them for betrayal, and even the shiniest gold star could not obscure their regret.

Widows' private struggles were heard in the halls of the U.S. Congress in 1938, though only indirectly. Their continued dependent status, secured through the passage of bills that extended their pensions, facilitated the coming of the next war, because soldiers could rest assured that the government would take care of their families while they fought. Committee on Pensions Chairman Allard H. Gasque repeated the need for a strong military that he felt compensation provided. "It is the young men of this Nation who love their country and who would be willing to sacrifice their lives for it at all times," surmised Gasque, "knowing full well that they will be taken care of after giving their services, and that their families after them will likewise be taken care of." Representative John M. Robsion of Kentucky blustered, "We have never lost a war, owing to fighting men's spirits which in turn was due to the U.S. government's generous provisions for its soldiers and their dependents." The insistence that women maintain their loyalty and their continued dependence on men resounded in the bill's requirement that "if at any time the widow should remarry the pension will stop." One witness promoted the legislation because it would allow an aggrieved wife to "keep her little brood around her, to protect and care for them . . . [and not] shunt them off into orphans' homes."[152]

During discussions over the bills, congressmen and witnesses outlined what they believed their nation needed: a strong military, a certain victory, and the resources necessary to protect its loyal women. All of those elements served to reinforce a reciprocal relationship between dutiful citizens and their protective government, and between a man and his wife. Women did not participate directly in society as citizens, because their relationship to their government was one-sided; they received only governmental protection and could offer only limited service to the military and could not ensure a victory. Lawmakers referring to females during debate mentioned them only as mothers protecting their offspring.

For some feminist pacifists, the disconnection between disenfranchised females and their nation-states before the war had been reinforced by the war, despite gaining suffrage in many nations. The overwhelming losses caused by the conflict, and the inhumane nature of combat during the war, caused some women (and men) in North America and Europe to disengage themselves from the nation-state in whose name the war had been fought. In rejecting the intense nationalism that they felt had brought about the war, these transnational thinkers upheld ties between victims of war regardless of nationality, and they fashioned themselves as the saviors of humankind when the war finally ended.

4

The Transnationalization of Soldiers, Widows, and War Relief

Soldiers' Pay, William Faulkner's 1926 novel about the fate of a Great War hero, is not a romance, although it has all the ingredients of one.[1] Military aviator Lieutenant Donald Mahon lies wounded after the enemy shoots down his airplane over Flanders Field. His fiancée and his father both assume he is dead, until the pilot reappears miraculously in his hometown in April 1919 with all the potential for the reverence due for battlefield bravery. In Mahon's pocket is a letter from his beloved, filled with expectations of chivalrous knights in battle undoubtedly heightened by the romantic aura surrounding the World War flying "ace."[2] Cadet Lowe, a fellow passenger riding the troop train headed for Mahon's hometown of Charlestown, Georgia, envies the lieutenant's facial battle scar for its heroic implication and, even when he discovers that the prodigal son is dying, wishes the disfigurement were his.[3] But the moral clarity that defines the romance novel requires decisive direction and action subsequently taken, and Mahon, blinded by his wound and very nearly on his deathbed, sits motionless and completely helpless. Faulkner's other characters in *Soldiers' Pay*—Mahon's father, an Episcopal Church rector; his buddies Joe Gilligan and Julian Lowe; his fiancée, Cecily Saunders; and war widow Margaret Powers—all confuse one another's identities, mistake symbols for reality, and mix up the past with the present.[4] Only the war widow, Margaret Powers, conducts her affairs with certitude, but she betrays no sense of her actions as morally righteous. The soldier she had spent three days with before marrying, Captain Richard Powers, died from a bullet purposely fired by one of his own men in the trenches of France. Margaret's thoughts soon turn to what she will do with her dead husband's insurance money: She will use it to tend to Lieutenant Mahon's needs.[5] But when Gilligan hears of her plans, he can't quite make sense of them.

"Funny?" [asks Margaret].

"Sure. Soldier dies and leaves you money, and you spend the money helping another soldier die comfortable. Ain't that funny?"

"I suppose so. . . . Everything is funny. Horribly funny."[6]

Having been robbed of a body over which to mourn in the case of Powers, she marries Mahon and presides, Persephone-like, over his death and burial.[7] Far from eliciting a hero's welcome, Mahon's homecoming provokes confusion and quandary instead of clarity. Faulkner's warriors, rather than being conventional romantic figures, are instead transnational and modern, according to literary critic David A. Davis.[8]

The term "transnational" refers to that which resides above or beyond the boundaries of the nation-state. In terms of historical scholarship it has been defined as a school of thought that takes as its starting point the interconnectivity of people around the globe and the flow of people and ideas across national boundaries; in the process, its adherents reexamine ties that continue to bind humans to citizenship within the nation-state. [9] U.S. war widows represented the nation-state when they journeyed overseas to pay homage to their soldier-husbands' graves. Their trips were sponsored by the U.S. government and they waved flags as they placed wreaths festooned with national symbols at military cemeteries. But when war widows grieved over dead husbands, they engaged in an activity—mourning—that looked very similar no matter where, no matter in what nation, that grieving took place. Officially orchestrated expressions of bereavement, such as moments of silence or Memorial Day parades, involved war widows performing scripted, national roles; privately, widows mourned husbands killed in international conflicts across and above national boundaries.

Elisabeth Macke penned her thoughts about loss early on in the war, when battles had gone largely in the German military's favor. "My heart cannot be joyous over the big victory. Among our enemies are hundreds who feel and think exactly as we do: they have had to abandon everything, wife and child and home, and are going off to be slaughtered. . . . When you think about it," continued Macke, "it is an abominable example of humanity that, given our sophisticated culture, such a war is still possible. Where is the humanity?" In addition to her concerns for the human race, Macke compared her own situation with that of other war wives and found commonality there as well. "And what happens to all the women who are in this circumstance [not knowing where/how their husbands are]?" As she waited for confirmation of her husband's death, Elisabeth's sense of herself as sharing the fate of other war wives persisted. "And all these hundreds of women, who alone with their children stand around the tree [of life], only to be alone all those years."[10] This sorrowful passage from the German novelist Leonhard Frank in his book *Der Mensch ist Gut* (Humanity Is Good) mirrors Macke's mood:

> So, how many women are there then [mused a war widow]? Two million, maybe, who sit in their rooms and, like me, think of their dead husbands. Look out the window, and think of their dead husbands. Do the dusting, take care of the kids, knit the socks, do the cooking, go to work, and think of their dead husbands, of their dead husbands. Go to bed at night, and think of their dead husbands.[11]

Macke and Frank understood war widows as individuals whose experiences were multiplied hundreds of times in the lives of others in all the war-torn nations.

The World War destabilized the regional constructions of place and identity for survivors such as Macke and for soldiers. U.S. recruits transferred first from their homes to national military training camps, where the army schooled them in the nature of the conflict and the United States' relationship with its allies.[12] Then they shipped overseas where they fought side-by-side with and against foreigners. European soldiers, too, lost their local dialects when they served in national armies.[13] Though not a soldier, the rootless Margaret Powers nevertheless connects to combat by virtue of her war work and by her two-time war widowhood. She tells Joe Gilligan that she left her boring and meaningless small-town existence in Alabama, moved to New York City, and then served at a Red Cross canteen where she met Richard Powers. Of the four traveling companions, only Donald Mahon has a home. For David A. Davis, the confused and confusing Faulkner characters represent a "modern, placeless identity."[14] The American-born Frederic Henry, Ernest Hemingway's ambulance driver in his classic 1929 World War I novel *A Farewell to Arms*, served with the Italian army and, having gone AWOL, wanders from Italy into Switzerland with his pregnant fiancée to escape arrest.[15] The end of the First World War marked a continuation of combatants' disassociation with their national, regional, and local identities.[16]

What were the national practices and ideals from which soldiers and their survivors felt alienated? The masculine obligation to protect women and the homeland, as well as a desire for military glory and heroism—all constituted men's and women's expectations for why and how nations and their citizens fight wars.[17] But on board the steamer bound for France, war widow Nancy

Payne Marsh rejected the militarization of war widowhood when she ripped up her Gold Star badge and tore off her military "dog tags." British bombardier Ronald Skirth refused to aim his gun at a French church during target practice and lost his corporal's stripe as a result.[18] Historian Mona Siegel found a disparity between the history of the Great War as told to French children through their schoolbooks and the paradigmatic commemorative discourse in France, which she interpreted as more pacifistic and internationalist in comparison with those of other nations. U.S. war veterans formed the patriotic American Legion to relive their wartime experiences, but French veterans wanted children to learn to hate war.[19]

If these examples demonstrate a rejection of warrior traditions, then to what degree did people really *want* a war to begin with? Gauging Europeans' enthusiasm for taking up arms remains a thorny undertaking for historians. L. L. Farrar Jr. doubts that Great War soldiers or civilians were ever as animated by the virulent nationalism that earlier historians have claimed. Outside of ruling classes, he believes that resignation, rather than aggressive nationalism, best describes responses to the guns of August.[20] Depicting a more somber acceptance of belligerency, rather than the "huzzah!" response assumed and perpetuated by many historians, makes the distancing from lethal forms of nationalism more understandable.

Along with overzealous militarism and imperialism, historians have perceived nationalism as one of the primary forces instigating the worldwide conflagration, and the desire to serve king and country drove volunteers such as Julius Boldt to enlist. Both German and British soldiers believed they were fighting in defense of their homelands and of their families.[21] Britain fought the war to reduce German naval power, France to break up the German Empire. German political and military elites fought to maintain their power, to distract popular attention from the social democratic elements within its borders, and to develop Germany's world power potential. For their part, Americans were told that they were fighting to promote democratic ideals and stop German militarism. Traditional gender roles—including the masculine protection of the feminine implied in national defense—motivated young men to visit their local recruiting offices and not a few women to insist that their men join up as well.[22] Chivalry and heroism continued to exert a strong magnetism on Great War participants, and these traits constituted part of the "innocent" past to which they yearned to return when the fighting stopped.[23] Among soldiers and civilians alike "the nearly overwhelming urge to return to something approximating 'normality'" after the war, explained Frans Coetzee and Marilyn Shevin-Coetzee, "bore witness to the very difficulty of doing so."[24]

Given the attractiveness of convention for some and the rejection of it for others, perhaps the most accurate statement that can be made is that the men and women who experienced the Great War vacillated on a continuum between intense loyalty to the nation and its warrior traditions and revulsion at the senseless destruction that those same nations wrought as they fought the first modern, industrialized war among the world's major powers. In addition, those survivors embodying a rejection of tradition, rather than representing alienation from their wives and families, demonstrated that modern, transnational forces resulting from the Great War eroded the national identities of the men—and the women—who fought it.[25] While the pull of nationalism remained intact during the interwar years, governments were obliged to work harder than ever to maintain it after the war through war memorials and remembrance ceremonies, some of which were themselves transnational in content and meaning.

Historian Jay Winter defined war remembrance as people or groups of people engaging in acts of remembering together.[26] Winter identified two different types of war remembrance, each shaped by the twentieth century's two World Wars. World War I helped define people's wartime identities, particularly their national identities. In the aftermath of that conflict, the nation-state sought to control war remembrance and ensure citizens' loyalty and their willingness to fight and sacrifice again in future wars. During the Second World War there arose a new "identity narrative," according to Winter: that of the subjective experience of witness and survivor, and Winter viewed the Holocaust as primarily responsible for bringing those perspectives into postwar public discourse.[27] But the publication of Helene Hurwitz-Stranz's anthology of war widows' memoirs, and U.S. war widows' correspondence with the New York City Victory Hall Association (VHA), the organization dedicated to honoring soldiers' individual lives apart from the nation they represented (discussed in the previous chapter), indicates that personal experiences had already gained traction during the First World War, and that individuals and their governments clashed over the meanings and interpretations of the war. As this chapter will demonstrate, the national identities supposedly heightened by the Great War proved to be far more transnational than previously expected.

U.S. government–sponsored propaganda promised that returning soldiers would "come back better men" because of their wartime service.[28] Such rhetoric slammed headfirst into soldiers' lived experience of the massive deaths and injuries caused by industrialized trench warfare. Those experiences were communicated to loved ones back home. Irony, as Paul Fussell reminded us, became the linchpin of modern memory.[29] Winter pointed out that historians no longer view war remembrance as confined to the soldiers who fought it; since the 1960s and 1970s it has included women and children as well. But VHA representatives had solicited widows and other survivors' remembrances long before.[30]

While war widows expressed their grief privately in transnational terms, war relief workers voiced their concern for all of humanity, regardless of nationality. The need for aid constituted one of the major reasons why nationalism lost preeminence in some survivors' minds, and war relief workers spoiled the traditional, heroic, national narrative of war when they reminded people of the ravages caused *by* war, although the U.S. government also tried to control relief efforts, just as it controlled public war remembrance and attempted to manipulate individuals' private war memories. Pity for and guilt over the human wreckage caused by battle and by the devastating British food blockade that served as the Allies' greatest weapon motivated relief workers to aid destitute widows and orphans, across and above national boundaries, and in some cases such activity lit the fires of pacifism within their hearts and minds as well.[31] In ways that U.S. newspaperwoman Ethel Thurston did not predict, the Great War fostered the transnationalization of war widowhood.

Nation-states gained citizens' loyalty during war in part through the invention of tradition. The three factors that are included among the reasons why men, women, and nations fought wars—heroism, chivalry, and national defense—are all connected to the concept of nationalism itself. The trope of the hero calls to mind a helpless female tied to a railroad track and a man of action who springs forth to save her, moments before the train speeds by. In the same way, the warrior soldiers forth to save the homeland (embodied as female, as in "Lady Britannia" and "Mother Russia," for example) and the women themselves, who keep the hearth fires burning at home.[32] In 1882 the French philosopher Ernest Renan defined the nation as a spiritual community formed on the basis of the memories of the willingness of citizens to sacrifice themselves on its behalf and the expectation of sacrifice necessary in the future. Both the heroism that accompanies wartime forfeiture and the suffering that follows loss are integral to the concept of the nation. Memories of the past play a critical role in the "invention of tradition" that helps fuse together disparate populations under the banner of nationalism and national identity.[33] U.S. Gold Star Widows upheld this understanding of the nation—through their 1928–29 lobbying efforts on behalf of pilgrimage legislation and on the journeys themselves—when they reminded their countrymen and -women of the victory that their sacrifices had won a decade before. The Great War itself can be defined as a struggle by elite leaders of the combatant nations to shape the collective memory and national identity with phrases like "the war to end all wars," "sacrificed on the altar of the Fatherland," and "to make the world safe for democracy."[34]

Nation-states took on greater authority as the conflict stalemated into a war of attrition by the end of 1914, requiring the unleashing of massive armies, resources, and women accompanied by deft censorship and propaganda machines. Total war blurred traditional gender divisions. Propaganda eroded people's understanding of individuals as responsible and rational beings.[35] Katherine Anne Porter fictionalized this aspect of the Great War in her 1939 novella *Pale Horse, Pale Rider*, about a newspaperwoman's struggle to maintain her dignity during the incessant and invidious Liberty Bond drives and Red Cross demands. "It's the skulking about, and the lying," Miranda confides to her soldier-boyfriend Adam. "It's what war does to the mind and the heart."[36]

Nation-states created wartime symbols and rituals to help ensure that citizens would make sacrifices for the good of the whole. (By contrast, Porter's character Adam sacrificed himself, too, but only for his lover.[37]) Invented traditions include a set of practices that present the symbols and rituals in order to inculcate values and norms of behavior, confirm a particular ideological purpose, and demonstrate connections between the present and the historic past.[38] The 1930–33 Gold Star Mothers and Widows pilgrimages were without precedent in U.S. history, and yet the rituals and ceremonies in which the travelers engaged duplicated the experiences of the heroic soldiers whose lives the pilgrimages were designed to honor.[39] The first worldwide conflict of the twentieth century, with all its technological advances and its matching spirit of modern, total war, still relied upon medieval notions of chivalry and comradeship. French boys learned to glorify war, know their duty, and "love [their] rifles" in pre-1914 classrooms.[40] Governments and their militaries created the "cult of the fallen soldier," especially in Germany but elsewhere, too, to secure citizens' fealty to the nation-state in the future. Commemorating the Unknown Soldier—another First World War invention—in England, the United States, Germany, and France served the same purpose.[41] Warring nations needed women to act in numerous civilian and quasi-military roles, so Liberty Gardens, along with Liberty Bonds, were invented to invite their active participation. Victory Medals and *Ehrenkreuzen* (crosses of honor) served to engage mourning women's loyalty to the nation long after their men had died and the guns had been silenced. Because the traditional veiled, retiring widow could not fulfill the new mandates of total war, in strode Ethel Thurston's working war widow, who sported another invention, the Gold Star armband, which replaced the somber black crepe. When female activists sought less conventional statuses for themselves in relation to the war, they faced veto (as when U.S. nurses' request for military rank was refused).[42]

If nationalism and the values and traditions the nation represents" are invented, or "imagined," as Benedict Anderson preferred, than they need to be reinvented when transnational experiences, such as the butchering of millions of human beings in a worldwide war, challenge them.[43] New York banker Benjamin Strong understood this when he wrote to a group of Jewish Liberty Bond donors in May 1918. "However severe must be the price of the war," acknowledged Strong, "we can at least take *some comfort* in the fact that it does bring out the best in the nation, leads us to understand what it means to be living here in this splendid country and builds up a national feeling which is a great asset and a very hopeful one for the future."[44]

One of the ways in which nations have sought to concretize national identities in the aftermath of great individual sacrifice is through the building of war memorials. Many of the commemorative monuments unveiled on Armistice Day or thereafter contained national symbols. The Union Jack adorns the cenotaph at Whitehall, London, while the Arch of Victory at Ballarat, Australia, displays the symbol of the Australian Commonwealth's military forces, the rising sun. Germany's Iron Cross sits atop the First World War Memorial at Niedaltdorf, beneath the words "*den gefallenen Helden*" (the fallen heroes).[45] Such monuments to chivalry and the nation-state confirm the existence of a heroic past in anticipation of similar sacrifices to be made in the future.

But as Volker Depkat has shown, scholars of war memory have mistakenly assumed that war memorials all remain within the paradigm of the nation-state.[46] Some Great War commemorations left out national symbols in favor of a simple list of the warriors who lost their lives, or contain sculptures bearing no words: These tributes appeared more transnational than national. Although she is called "Mother Canada" and serves the purpose of recognizing her compatriots' sacrifices, the sorrowful female figure standing over the Vimy Ridge memorial in France neither wears nor holds any symbol to convey her nationality.[47] The *Picardie Maudissant La Guerre* memorial in Péronne, France, depicts an aproned mother with a dead soldier lying across her lap, reminiscent of a *pietà*. She looks sternly in front of her with an outstretched fist, cursing the war (or the enemy of her nation?). Here, too, there is no indication of nationality except the inscription "*A Nos Morts*" (to our dead).[48] Virtually all French Great War monuments eschewed any hint of glory or celebration of war. Still other remembrances blended national symbols in transnational settings. At the cemetery in Ypres, Belgium, headstones marking German graves are in the shape of the Iron Cross.[49] However, the Bavarian War Widows Association warned members that they may be restricted from displaying nationalistic symbols on the graves of their husbands, because rules and regulations regarding German soldiers' resting places in foreign lands would come from the sovereign heads that governed the ground in which they were buried.[50] The Gold Star Mothers and Widows paid homage to the wartime alliance between France and the United States on their visits to American cemeteries, each of which included numerous symbols of both nations' military might, in addition to a transnational "Angel of Victory" in flight.[51]

Transnational artists rendered sentiments like Elisabeth Macke's into images that depicted the war's devastation on widows. An Expressionist artist like August Macke, Käthe Kollwitz used a technique known as woodcut to create the seven images constituting the series she called simply "*Krieg*" (war) in 1921 and 1922. Two of those seven pictures represent war widows. Bereft of any symbol of nationalism, Kollwitz's art symbolized the grief families from all combatant nations expressed.

Writers, too, called the concept of nationalism into question. Randolph Bourne's 1916 essay "Trans-national America" in some ways forecasted William Faulkner's and Ernest Hemingway's placeless characters, and the pensive, less patriotic mien of some First World War monuments and sculptures. Bourne's *Atlantic Monthly* piece rejected the "100% Americanism" campaigns that attempted to force the United States' multiethnic groups to adopt what were thought to represent American ways as failures. The much-vaunted "melting pot," too, marked an invented tradition in the service of U.S. preparation for and intervention in the World War.[52] But Jewish newcomers vacillated between providing wartime relief to their co-religionists suffering in the Jewish Diaspora, and loudly trumpeting their allegiance to the United States once it entered the war; they did so even when their adopted homeland fought against a nation, Austria-Hungary, to which American Jews had sent thousands of dollars in aid. Jewish immigrants represented the "second wave" of immigration into the United States from southern and eastern European countries, the torn loyalties of immigrants during the First World War, the desire on the part of immigrants to come to the aid of ravaged populations in their homelands, and the shifting nature of national identity.

Käthe Kollwitz, "Die Witwe I," 1922. One of the two images of war widows in Kollwitz's *Krieg* series. ©2010 Artists Rights Society (ARS), New York / VG Bild- Kunst, Bonn.

In the nineteenth century, most American Jews had called Germany, Spain, and Portugal home, and the U.S. Jewish community retained much of the flavor of those countries. Between 1900 and 1924, however, 1.75 million Jews immigrated to America's shores primarily from eastern Europe. To new-comers, the United States represented the hopes and aspirations for believers who hoped that the New World would release them from the oppression and poverty they had experienced elsewhere. eastern European Jews especially were motivated by financial success, according to Jonathan D. Sarna. But sub-scribing to the U.S. values ascendant during the early twentieth century, such as hard work and financial gain, came at a price of losing their traditions and identity. The war years demonstrated the tensions between the old and the new. The American Jewish community marshaled its resources to aid the vic-tims of the European war as soon as the conflict began. After U.S. interven-tion, many Jews perceived a reciprocal relationship between the U.S. government and their community, because the nation offered religious freedom in exchange for Jews' loyalty proven during wartime.[53] All told, Jewish Americans raised around $63 million in relief funds during the First World War.[54]

The Central Relief Committee for the Relief of Jews Suffering through the War explained the special needs of its co-religionists. The distress of Jewish people "was and is, we still regret to have to assert, greater than that of all those who have suffered through the war. They suffer as Jews, from all the horrors of war, besides suffering through prejudice, bigotry, and ignorant fanaticism." A prayer recited at an October 16, 1916, committee meeting praised foreign Jewish soldiers fighting "for the souls that have sheltered them," confirming the transnational nature of Jews' modern existence. After U.S. intervention, the Union of Orthodox Jewish Congregations of America held a patriotic rally asking for donations to the Third Liberty Loan. Leaders celebrated the fact that the union had given 124 of its children to the service of the United States, proving that it was truly 100 percent American. American Jews invented a certificate to bestow upon their soldiers, consisting of images of a bald eagle, the statue of liberty, and the Star of David, symbolically fusing their loyalty to their homeland with their religious identity.[55] Like other immigrant groups—most notably German Americans—U.S. entrance in the First World War provoked sometimes awkward, sometimes contradictory allegiances.[56] Transnational and international identities among Jews and so-called "hyphenated Americans" did not necessarily, or fully, replace the allegiance they felt toward the United States.

Conflict underlay the unified national identity that governments strove for both during and immediately following the war. The United States' multicultural past ensured that its government would need to go to great lengths to maintain that unity. Recent comparative histories indicate that European countries fractured along religious, class, and cultural lines as well.[57] Between 1914 and 1918, mobilization of all economic and social sectors of at-war societies created competition between compatriots for the left-over resources that were not devoted to the war effort (and all economies surrendered at least some peacetime goods in favor of war materiel production; food rationing occurred in France, Britain, Germany, Italy, and Austria-Hungary, while the U.S. government opted—in vain—to rely on "the spirit of self-sacrifice" instead). The economic blockade initiated by the British to deliberately starve German civilians spawned struggles between rich and poor and urban and rural dwellers over meager food supplies. The fragile unity among disparate populations that governments managed to knit together to prosecute the war became unraveled by the very same conflict.[58]

The Great War marked an increase in already established international and transnational trends in relations within European nations and between Europe and North America. During the war, nations supporting businesses wishing to skirt the economic blockade of Germany traded secrets with one another through already established diplomatic ties in a process Heather Jones has called a "transnational learning process."[59] Nineteenth-century imperialism resulted in heightened trade and exchange between nations; France, Britain, and Germany drafted soldiers from their African colonies to help them fight the war. After the armistice, the U.S. occupation of the Rhineland resulted in 767 additional German American families by January 1921, but given the large numbers of Germans crossing the Atlantic to make the United States their new home prior to the Great War, unions between American "doughboys" and German *Fräuleins* merely continued a long-established relationship between the two nations. Around 700 British soldiers formed international marriages with German women by 1925; these unions, too, resulted from troops stationed in the Rhineland. Historian Eugen Weber attributed the explosion in France's foreign-born population to the Great War. Of the 231 Gold Star pilgrims walking the gangplank up to the steamer bound for France in 1930, 56 were of foreign birth, with the majority of those hailing from Germany.[60]

Families with members residing on both sides of the warring Allied and Central Powers forces negotiated carefully along the fault lines between the international- and transnationalization of their national identities during and after the war. War widows and mothers drove much of that navigation. Philomene Maas, U.S. soldier Alfred Maas's widow, hailing from Heidelberg, Pennsylvania, asked the Quartermaster General if she could extend her Gold Star pilgrimage and travel to Trier, Germany—about thirty miles south of the former U.S. occupation zone—to visit her relatives.[61] At the American cemetery in Suresnes, France, six Gold Star mothers were chosen to lay wreaths on unidentified soldiers' graves. One of them, Cecilie Schmidt, had traveled to France with her relatives from Munich, Germany. Between the U.S. and German sides of this family, two sons had fought on opposing sides of the war; only the American man had forfeited his life.[62]

Plying the waters of international marriages could be complicated, particularly during wartime. German civilians sometimes assumed that American-born women wedded to German men had intimate knowledge of the U.S. military. As the U.S. reformer Jane Addams toured European cities with her traveling companion Alice Hamilton in 1915, their Berlin host (probably American-born Neena Hamilton Pringsheim) related a story to them about a German widow who had received in the mail a piece of a shell that had reportedly killed her husband. The widow confronted Pringsheim with the shrapnel, demanding to know if it was a U.S.-made bullet.[63] Elisabeth Rotten, Swiss-born reformer working in Germany, helped German women who had lost their citizenship when they married non-German citizens, and she aided French and Belgian families deported from German-occupied territories throughout the war. Essentially, Rotten and her organization, Information and Assistance Bureau for Germans Abroad and for Foreigners in Germany, helped families everywhere who were displaced by the war.[64] Beyond the ties binding international families together, the Gold Star Mothers and Widows' itinerary in Paris reinforced relations between U.S. and French allies, as the pilgrims visited the American Church of Paris, the Lafayette Escadrille Memorial (a monument to U.S. aviators), the Place of the United States, and statues of "founding fathers" Benjamin Franklin and George Washington, in addition to memorials related to the Allied war effort.[65] All of these incidents brought to the forefront, and occasionally dramatized, cross-border relationships between people multiplied by the World War.

What do the choices made by war widows such as Philomene Maas and Harriet Pierson reveal about their sense of their own national, international, or transnational, identities? When war widows perceived themselves as their dead soldier-husbands' living proxies, they too embodied the invented tradition of the sacrifice of self for the good of the whole nation. But the conventional gender roles to which Great War–era men and women supposedly longed to return interrupted that formula. Whether victorious or defeated, the war—and the government that fought it—had taken the widow's life partner and her and her children's presumed breadwinner. The widow could be restricted from (and was certainly not entitled to) assuming her husband's paying position because she was female; thus, the "living proxy" paradigm went only so far. The allowances paid to soldiers' wives and pensions doled out to their widows, systems that were extant in most warring nations, assumed this time-honored, gendered provider–dependent formula.

In addition, whether a war widow accepted her role as her husband's stand-in during venerable commemoration ceremonies, as opposed to feeling like a betrayed loser, may have depended on her view of the war itself. If she interpreted the cause as worthy and the war itself as good for the nation, perhaps her loss could be overridden. Widows who performed their role publicly by laying wreaths at their husbands' battlefield cemeteries in France communicated to the government that sponsored the journeys their great pride in the patriotic ceremonies that accompanied their pilgrimages. Newspapers reporting on the events reinforced their feelings when they described mourners as teary-eyed at first, then pride-filled when they recalled their men's battlefield heroism.[66]

War widows' sentiments about the conflict and its cause, however, may have depended on how they perceived their government's treatment of them. The British government compared what it owed to disabled veterans with what was due to its war widows. In the former case, the state acknowledged that it owed the ex-soldier the means to regain the highest industrial capacity that his disability would allow him. In the case of the war widow, the government emphasized that it did not owe her "an earning capacity," but rather it offered to assist her in adding "to her income where her domestic needs make a remunerative occupation desirable in her own interest or in that of her children," tying women closely to their maternal roles. Of the sixteen occupations deemed acceptable for widows, five could be considered domestic work. Another six were typically considered "women's work" by the Ministry of Pensions. The Ministry also listed training that widows should not undertake because such occupations were to be left open for disabled veterans. Because Britain defined war widows as only those "awarded" with a pension, its training program for them amounted to an acknowledgment that the compensation it provided was inadequate, an admission matched by that made in the U.S. Congress.[67] Despite the government's responsibility for widows' losses, however, many undoubtedly felt grateful for its willingness to prepare them for any kind of job.

War widows who failed to interpret the war and its cause as worthwhile felt defeated and humiliated by their poverty and the scrutiny they endured by government pension committees. One German war widow's encounter with the conspicuous consumption of the wealthy while in the company of her hungry, war-orphaned children prompted her perception that the rich viewed themselves as being above having to pay for Germany's loss in the war. This was matched halfway around the world when Rebecca Hinds expressed similar disillusionment with the war and its effects, but unlike the German widow she lived in a "victorious" nation. Forgoing remunerative work, Hinds, a Tasmanian survivor, tended to her war-injured husband for years before he finally succumbed to his wounds. When the Australian War Memorial organization asked her to fill out a form verifying her spouse's identity to ensure that his name appeared on a commemorative "roll of honour," she did the group's bidding, but without enthusiasm. "I am not in favour of all this kind of thing, as we wives and mothers do not need them to remind us of those we have lost," she explained quietly. Hinds's dire financial situation resulted from her having to tend to her sick husband's needs. "I think it would be fitting to put the money to better use for those that are living," she argued. The notion of sacrifice did not convince her. "[The soldiers] gave their lives 'tis true and I often wonder what for?"[68]

As a result of female disfranchisement, racism, and poverty, many war widows may have felt little connection to their nation before the war; their estrangement undoubtedly did not diminish upon their husbands' deaths. German writers and artists blamed women for the war, for their nation's defeat in it, and for the economic chaos that developed in its wake; this did little to smooth the already turbulent waters of impoverished widows' relationship to the societies in which they lived. In addition to somehow causing the war, females were believed to have gained from it without having to endure any pain themselves, unlike their male counterparts.[69] Widows such as Rebecca Hinds, hailing from a presumed victorious nation, may have believed that they had more in common with other victims living in defeated nations than with their own compatriots. Nationalism, and national identity, too, went only so far.

The Dutch pacifist Aletta Jacobs confirmed survivors' transnational commonalities at the International Congress of Women convening at The Hague in 1915. All women, regardless of nationality, mourned for mothers who lost their sons, for young widows, and for children who had lost fathers, she proclaimed. An essentialist feminist typical of her day, Jacobs believed that women evaluated the war differently from men.[70] Women astutely compared damage caused by the conflict with its cost and judged the enterprise to be counterproductive and ineffective. On the other hand, men thought in terms of winning and losing for the nation's businesses and for its political power. But, Jacobs predicted, there could be no winners in such an overall negative undertaking. In addition, the interests of humanity must trump the desires of a single nation, she argued. Delegates to the Hague conference could serve their countries, acknowledged Jacobs, but they must heed their higher responsibility to interests of humanity. For Jacobs, there could be no such thing as a war widow's truly serving as her dead husband's living proxy, because, in her mind, women differed fundamentally from men.[71]

But soldiers in the field shared similar feelings of awe and horror over the sheer numbers of war dead and of those who survived and mourned them, rather than ruminating on whether their "side" was winning or losing as Jacobs would have it. Captain Lawrence Gameson, a physician in the British Royal Army Medical Corps, succored the sick and tended to the dead during and after battle. When he stumbled upon a badly decomposed body of an

Englishman, Gameson quickly buried the body after retrieving two letters from the soldier's breast pocket: one from his wife and the other from his mother. The wife's missive included a greeting from the dead soldier's young daughter. Struggling to fall sleep later that night, Gameson wondered "what in God's name must the grand total be of ours and the enemy's—if this one man had three generations of women to mourn him."[72]

German photographer Ernst Friedrich published a bestselling book called *War Against War!* six years after the fighting stopped. The book's strategy hinged on the attachment the viewer feels to the humanistic aspects of the warrior as a transnational, rather than national, subject.[73] Friedrich laid bare the destructiveness of modern warfare on the body and psyche of the soldier. His purpose was to communicate the hypocrisy of national military rhetoric in hopes of preventing future conflicts. This mirrored the approach taken by other pacifists of humanizing the enemy and weakening the hatred assumed to be fueling the war.[74] By unveiling the war's human wreckage, pacifist artists countered the images published by patriotic artists. The patriots dramatized impersonal forces to thrill viewers with high-tech weapons and detach them from the soldiers deploying them. Friedrich's volume included no pictures of the home front or of females. Instead, the photographer addressed women in his narrative when he implored "mothers of all lands [to] unite" to take militaristic toys out of their sons' hands.[75] Threatened by the book's popularity, the government ordered Berlin police to confiscate copies of it in store front windows at bayonet point.[76]

Helene Hurwitz-Stranz's anthology of war widows' memories communicated a similar sense of the vastness of humanity ruined by the war, but also a hopeful vision of solidarity among its victims, regardless of nationality. One widow predicted that

> when the Geneva Convention protects the rights of wounded soldiers, then it will be possible to protect the war victims' economic situation in all nations. I see in the acceptance of this protection an effective guarantee of the peace. If the war victims' movement can make a moral claim to help bring the world to a victory, then the many tears of the war widow and orphans will not have flowed in vain.[77]

This anonymous mourner referred to the provisions of the Third Geneva Convention, adopted in 1929 and enforced in 1931, relating to the treatment of prisoners of war. The bereaved saw a potential for a worldwide war victims' organization that did not materialize until nearly one hundred years later.[78] Karl Reutti, a German social scientist, echoed the widow's sentiment, perceiving the "four-year World War not as an historical event in the life of a single nation, but rather a development in the natural history of humankind." The war served to forewarn humanity of the dangers of hypernationalism, declared Reutti, under which all humanity had suffered. War survivors from both sides of the conflict could form a new international movement for world peace.[79] Another aggrieved wife opined that nearly all of the mourners in her city felt a deep commitment to never seeing another war rob them of their men and their father's children. Only in peace, she wrote, could families and people thrive. "Each war widow and mother, who with blood in the hearts of their children during this difficult year in which so many promises were broken," she pledged, "will work toward the goal of peace." Another of Hurwitz-Stranz's contributors confirmed that orphaned children loathed the war that had robbed them of their fathers, and predicted that they would not forget that they and their mothers were owed the "thanks of the Fatherland," a phrase typically employed in reference to Germany's disabled veterans.[80] While the same could not be said for Germany, in France pacifism overtook nationalism as a response to the war, according to historian Eugen Weber.[81]

In addition to transnational concerns for humanity, national identities were eroded by awareness of the universal nature of wartime and postwar experiences. Despite national distinctions and differences in status (whether victorious or defeated), people living in Europe and North America witnessed many of the same circumstances. Bereavement in the face of the deaths of millions of soldiers and civilians guaranteed that, as Jay Winter put it, the "cultural history of the Great War was a common history."[82] Mona Siegel could find no ideological consensus in her survey of French war monuments; instead, she saw only agreement on the horrific scale of loss and an understanding of the shared sacrifice that the war required.[83] Other commonalities included poorly communicated death and injury reports, an aspect of the war experienced by nearly all of the war widows discussed in this volume: Macke, Boldt, Marsh, and the countless U.S. war widows who communicated with the Quartermaster General's Office about their dead husbands' bodies.[84] An exception is Harriet Pierson, who received accurate information about her husband's death quickly after it occurred.[85]

All of the major warring nations sponsored commemoration events and erected statuary, including monuments unveiled in France and Belgium by other nations and remembrances containing the remains of soldiers representing the presumed "enemy" nation. All countries were forced to deal with bodies that had been cut down in a foreign land.[86] Warring powers all used the notion of sacrifice to procure troops and domestic compliance.[87] France, Germany, Italy, Britain, and the United States each offered pensions or compensation paid to war widows.[88] Mourning wives wore "widows' weeds" all across Europe and North America, while Britain, Canada, Australia, and the United States invented badges to venerate war widows' and war mothers' statuses. With the exception of women like Elisabeth Macke, in all the major participating nations wives found that their financial status deteriorated when their soldier-husbands died.[89] All belligerent powers either sent or received wartime and/or postwar relief from other nations, including those nations that, for the United States, were soon to be designated "enemy." As Volker Depkat has noted, rather than driving nations apart, international conflicts actually brought disparate nations closer together. Wars intertwine nations' memories of war together, and armed conflict is a key element in defining national identity.[90]

International women's publications, stemming primarily from the multinational female suffrage movement, continued their production throughout the war. In addition, German women's magazines opened their pages to news and analysis of foreign women, particularly those in combatant and enemy nations. To counterbalance such internationalism or transnationalism that might reek of disloyalty to the nation-state, however, editors also offered nationalistic pieces. Journals such as *Die Frau* and *Die Frauenbewegung* featured articles on women's work in "highly cultured" nations; a report on female labor in France included statistics on women workers in Sweden, Denmark, and the United States as well. *Die Frauenbewegung* also offered articles on the status of women's rights during the war in other countries.[91] In contrast, Else Lüders's essay, titled "*Das Doppelgesicht des Krieges*" (The Janus-faced Nature of the War), explored women's responses to armed conflict, both pacifistic and nationalistic and patriotic. But even Lüders's nationalistic rumination alluded to transnational female commonalities. While some mothers regarded war from an antiwar standpoint and argued for peace at any price, most shared stronger feelings about their Fatherland, proclaimed the author. Unlike Elisabeth Macke, who emphasized women's common experiences across and above national boundaries, Lüders claimed that women were not women first, but Germans. Lüders maintained that German women were proud of the war-related deaths that had occurred, mirroring statements made by women in the United States, Germany's presumed enemy. Unfortunately, lamented the women's rights activist, some pacifist women dwelled only on the misery of the war, failing to be enlightened by its strength, glory, and righteousness: These were the two sides of war. She concluded that women in all belligerent nations were united in their eager acceptance of the guns of August.[92] But this raised the possibility that while women from disparate nations clung to their homelands, the sentiment actually bound them together across national borders.

In the same vein, economist Heinrich Lübbering's article in a magazine called *Frauenwirtschaft* (Women's Economy) warned readers against a dangerous trend he observed to be enveloping his country: the wearing of foreign fashions by German women. But even his nationalistic diatribe diverted readers' attention toward the opponent. Despite their flag-waving support for their nation, women were still shamefully and frivolously copying the morals and the appearances of the enemy, even as their own men spilled their blood for the sake of German culture, according to Lübbering. After berating his countrywomen for copying foreign styles, the economist then insisted that they pay attention to how things operated in France. Lübbering acknowledged that the war had opened German businessmen's eyes to the link between politicians and tailors in France, where fashion, he acknowledged, remained that nation's economic crown jewel. Germany should learn from its adversary and follow "suit." He cautioned his readers not to blame female consumers for this unwholesome trend, but the women's movement, he demanded, should be charged with reversing it. "Leave Paris! Leave London!" the economist implored his readers; "*Deutschland über alles* (Germany above all)—also in fashion!"[93] German women's magazines offered readers international news, but editors carefully skirted wartime censors by flaunting their allegiance to the nation-state.

Humanitarian organizations constitute another way in which the Great War fostered transnational identities, although some refused to aid victims in former enemy nation-states, and political considerations occasionally hampered relief efforts. Aid arrived in Central Europe largely from the United States and generally in the form of food and clothing. War widows facilitated the transnationalization process as they were almost exclusively poised as the recipients of humanitarian aid.

Relief organizations first formed to extend aid to war-torn populations in the mid–nineteenth century. Swiss industrialist Henry Dunant saw a need for private aid groups in 1859, and the International Committee of the Red Cross formed in 1863. The *Vaterländischer Frauenverein* (Patriotic Women's League) helped found the German Red Cross in 1866. Clara Barton established the American Red Cross in 1881.[94] Relief to the victims of the Great War, including those suffering from the economic blockade against Germany, provoked tensions between transnational concerns and loyalty to one's nation. Heather Jones has argued that international aid groups such as the International Committee of the Red Cross managed to maintain impartiality fairly well as they labored to dispense aid and ward off war-induced medical and nutritional crises during and after the Great War. Nation-based humanitarian organizations were not as successful and indeed, according to Jones, were co-opted by and aided the belligerency of the nation-states they represented.[95]

Some members of these groups did not believe that the enemy shared the same humanitarian impulses that they detected among their own compatriots. Vera Brittain cited an example of a British Voluntary Aid Detachment (VAD) nurse treating her German patients with disdain. Tammy Proctor raised the likelihood that relief organizations actually aided the war in her work. This "constructivist nationalism," as Jones called it, demonstrated the principle behind Benedict Anderson's "imagined community." VAD workers succored injured soldiers, but only if they thought the wounded were British.[96] Matthew Stibbe noted that at the end of the war, internationalist-minded relief workers had little to celebrate as there were no multi-state agreements made to promote universal human rights and rein in nationalistic interpretations of the conduct of the war.[97]

Looking at malnourishment in Germany attributable to the food blockade, and the humanitarian missions that hunger spawned after the war, one can come only to the gloomy conclusion that nations went to great lengths to starve the enemy in order to win the war, only to turn around as the presumed victors and rescue the very people whom they had deliberately reduced to desperation. After intense political wrangling between French and British diplomats, and Herbert Hoover representing the United States, shiploads of food finally reached starving Germans four months after the armistice, on March 25, 1919.[98] Calls to aid needy German widows and orphans moved some Americans to open their wallets and purses and give freely. Others shut their bank accounts tight against charitable relief, convinced that stories of German misery amounted to more "Hun trickery."[99] This unanticipated negative impact of wartime propaganda caused German Foreign Minister Wilhelm Solf to redouble his assurances that accounts of sunken eyeballs amid drawn faces wandering the streets of Berlin were really true.[100] American Red Cross secretary W. W. Husband, working in Berlin after the armistice, assured U.S. *chargé d'affaires* Ulysses Grant-Smith that "if our people still fear that the whole scheme of things here [hunger] is only another German camouflage and that they may renew the war after a rest, for God's sake do what you can to dispel the illusion."[101] Doubts among the general public about German leaders' veracity moved humanitarian-minded people to create crusades to solicit donations and ensure the former enemy's survival.

The campaign to save Germany's inhabitants repeated the time-worn notion of an innocent home front versus guilty government and military. Requests for charitable giving nearly always referred to widows and orphans rather than to the German people generally. Such a strategy only made sense, because Germans (male Germans, that is) were still considered the enemy by the United States.[102] (Because the United States did not sign the Treaty of Versailles, an official state of war continued between the two countries until the August 1921 Treaty of Berlin.) Relief programs claimed that they were poised to feed women and their children, but not men; hunger was not only political, as C. Paul Vincent has written, but gendered as well.[103] The postwar continuation of the paradigm of home front versus the battlefront persuaded civilians to provide needed relief, because they believed they were aiding blameless women and children, and not culpable German officials, who before the war and before female suffrage were male. Gender and transnationalism worked effectively hand-in-hand, because women (and their children) were historically less connected to the nation-state.

But in the long run, separating the home front from the trenches in terms of blame for wartime policies perpetuated an understanding of nations and their wars that served only to ingrain conventional ideas about the empowered versus the powerless. Contempt for those remaining *daheim* (at home) had enabled the German government to treat its citizens with callous disregard as the Berlin war elite sacrificed agricultural labor, fertilizers, draft animals, and its transportation system, all to the war effort. Having confiscated farmers' draft horses and their fodder for use by the military, the government encouraged them to use potatoes (human food) to sustain their dwindling livestock instead. Then it robbed them of their pigs and cattle as well. While the British blockade stymied food supplies into Germany (aided by neutrals' compliance with trade agreements beginning in 1915), thus forcing the enemy to depend entirely on indigenous food supplies, the German government's zeal to win the war by sacrificing its agriculture reduced its civilian population to desperate starvation. Furthermore, as Elizabeth Domansky has argued, German leaders did not even value their soldiers.[104] The Italian government, too, displayed little care for its fighting men when it refused to feed its own incarcerated soldiers, fearing that to do so would encourage surrender.[105] Such policies nurtured the resentment, the disillusionment, and the dissociation with tradition mentioned at the beginning of this chapter that troubled the soldiers of the warring nations and their survivors when the guns of August were finally silenced.

After the war, German President Friedrich Ebert proclaimed that his nation's warriors had not, in fact, been defeated in battle.[106] This encouraged the interpretation that the home front was to blame for the armistice when in fact Germany's demise had resulted (in part) from government policies designed to win the war by starving the people. At least those providing relief began to appreciate the fact that the German home front had suffered equally with soldiers in battle. But relief propaganda depicting women and children as victims contributed to the ways in which the war perpetuated female helplessness, instead of promoting women's agency.[107] Distancing the home front from battlefront ignored Germany's returning soldiers and dismissed its male population that had not been drafted or joined the military, all of whom were equally vulnerable to hunger pangs. Finally, it did little to encourage an honest critique of the relationship between a nation's wartime policies and the needs of its citizens. After the Weimar Republic collapsed and the Nazis took power in 1933, they attempted (partly successfully) to restore the centrality of marriage and traditional roles for women.[108] During the next bloody worldwide conflict they conscripted nearly every civilian into some aspect of wartime service to the nation-state except mothers with two or more children under the age of fifteen. Unlike the Great War, during World War II only in the final year of the conflict and in the aftermath did Germans suffer from food deprivation, because the state procured provisions from the pillaged eastern territories. With the exception of the excused mothers, women working in concert with the Nazi state were responsible for the relative stability of the German home front, according to Karen Hagemann, and (because in this conflict the two were inseparable) the battlefront as well. Nazi propaganda perpetuated a number of myths about women that enabled them to maintain the façade of separated home and battlefronts, however.[109]

During the Great War, citizens and government officials alike exhibited humanitarian impulses throughout the war and postwar years, but those sentiments were frequently couched in nationalistic terms, either genuinely felt or out of fear of retaliation. Writer and publicity agent William H. McMasters stated his sentiments bluntly, however. He issued a precautionary explanation to U.S. Secretary of State Robert Lansing about his work promoting the Citizens Committee for Food Shipments, because, as the Bostonian put it, he was aware "of the ridiculous espionage upon all American citizens who identify themselves with any movement, even charitable, in which the interests of Germans are involved."[110] Because at least some citizens prior to U.S.

intervention believed that their government was anti-German, and was consequently spying on them, gauging exactly where Americans may have sat on the continuum between nationalism, internationalism, and transnationalism is difficult work. Governmental officials representing the United States reflected the views of the presidential administration for which they worked, but people such as U.S. Ambassador to Germany James W. Gerard and founder of the American Relief Administration Herbert Hoover expressed heartfelt concern for starving Europeans. (Hoover did not extend sympathies to Germans until just following the armistice, however; indeed, he blamed them for the strained European conditions up to that point.) Despite their humanitarian impulses, they also explained the actions they took to alleviate the food crisis as a desire to promote American-style democracy in Europe and to stave off Bolshevism.[111] Organized labor troubled Matthias Erzberger, German envoy to the Armistice Commission, who warned of the possibility of a transnational revolution. Alluding to the perceived harshness of the armistice, Erzberger asserted to members of the commission in January 1919 that "a broken people may satisfy the lust of a victor, but I tell you today with all urgency: I warn you. Your own people are not immune from world revolution, whose most effective pacemakers are repression, robbery, misery, and starvation."[112] American Red Cross secretary W. W. Husband repeated Erzberger's caution, but, he added, if a Soviet-style government prevailed in Berlin, all aid to Germany should be canceled.[113] The care shown to starving Germans from political officials came with rather rigid ideological strings attached.

The politics driving postwar relief followed directly from Allied and neutral nations' wartime practices. The British were able to strangle German commerce with their economic blockade. Through their sea power and as a result of dexterous diplomacy, they succeeded in preventing neutral nations from supplying Germany with needed food and other products. By the end of 1916, the Allies had gained control of German trade. American entry into the war proved disastrous for all the Central Powers. On June 22, 1917, President Wilson appointed an Exports Council tasked with stopping any U.S. products from reaching the enemy. Next, he signed an embargo diverting any shipment of corn, fodder, gasoline, steel, fertilizers, and ammunitions from U.S. ports without special permission. The British blockade had evolved into an Allied and U.S. weapon of epic proportion.[114]

The November 1918 armistice continued the blockade, although it assured the enemy that the Allies and the United States would "contemplate the provisioning of Germany during the Armistice as shall be found necessary."[115]

Postwar political wrangling among the victors ensured that those needing provisions would not be supplied until March 1919. The Allies had demanded possession of the German merchant marine, while Berlin insisted that it be given the ability to pay for food in exchange for its fleet. It offered 100 million gold marks as partial payment. The French balked, claiming that the gold Germany said it would spend on food belonged instead to them. In response, the Germans refused to surrender their ships. The impasse was broken by the testimony of General Herbert Plumer, commander of the British Army of Occupation. The general's men were begging to go home because they could no longer stand the sight of bloated German children pawing over discarded food at British barracks. Faced with pressure from the United States, the British, and the Italians, French Prime Minister Georges Clemenceau finally relented and allowed Germany to use its gold to pay for food. According to C. Paul Vincent, until Plumer's eyewitness testimony Allied and U.S. politicians had sacrificed the welfare of starving people by viewing the German people as something other than human.[116]

U.S. social reformer and pragmatist Jane Addams understood the pitfalls of instituting policy solely on the basis of abstractions. During her June 1919 tour of Central Europe sponsored by the American Friends Service Committee (the Quakers) and Hoover's renamed organization, the European Children's Fund, Addams and Alice Hamilton observed conditions, filed a report, and distributed $30,000 worth of food and 25 tons of clothing.[117] Later, in her seminal 1922 book *Peace and Bread in Time of War*, Addams lashed out at the limitations imposed by viewing the world through the distorted lens of nationalism. She viewed concerns over national honor and "other abstractions dear to the heart of the diplomat" as having impaired previous attempts at solving public health problems, and she had hoped that a concrete, international response by the League of Nations would alleviate the food crisis in postwar Europe. Had the international body bridged the gap between the deprivation suffered by people and the official, detached methods used to solve international dilemmas like food shortages and massive starvation, she argued, the entity would have earned respect. But because the League remained strangled by old-fashioned diplomacy and was "indifferent to the widespread misery and starvation of the world," it squelched hopes for a new international politics of care.[118] Had the body responded to the postwar food crisis in Europe, according to Addams, "it would have been recognized as indispensable."[119] Addams's brand of transnational thinking during the war remained exceptional. Correspondence between State Department officials and humanitarian groups reveals that while relief interfered with wartime policies during the conflict, after the war ended sympathies regarding aid for needy Germans among the U.S. State Department and private citizens were (mostly) in alignment.

Judging by State Department records, the task of supplying relief remained primarily the business of men. Heather Jones asserted that the war created a "reciprocal gendered economy" in which men relinquished their civilian jobs in favor of defending their women and children in battle. When the guns ceased, women provided care for the defenders when they came marching home, often physically and psychologically battered.[120] There is ample evidence to support this interpretation. Females from all belligerent countries entered into service with the Red Cross, the Young Men's Christian Association, and other aid organizations in vast numbers. As Alice Hamilton toured European cities during the war, she wrote that she experienced a moment of *déjà vu* as she watched women in Berlin organizing relief efforts. In London, Paris, and Brussels, Hamilton explained, females had gone about their business of patching the world up as men continued to tear it apart on battlefields.[121] In the United States, too, women such as Julia Wickham Porcher helped the war-damaged by sending their discarded clothing to grateful French war widows.[122]

But men did not simply hand over their dominant roles in public life to women as easily as these examples suggest. Correspondence to the State Department from Americans desiring to feed hungry Germans came primarily from male heads of spontaneously organized groups such as the California Thanksgiving Offering for Germanic Widows and Orphans, the *Deutschamerikanische Hilfe* (German American Relief), the Committee for the Relief of Destitute Women and Children in Germany and Austria, and the German and Austrian Relief Society (in the case of the German and Austrian Relief Society, an exception, the president was Mrs. A. F. Stoeger).[123] Already established groups also wrote to the State Department, including the Red Cross and the International Good Templar, along with various churches and synagogues; these too were directed by men. In addition, several individual male correspondents declared their desire to send relief to Germany on their own.

Publications informing readers about conditions in Germany were circulated by churchmen and male physicians throughout the United States. Drs. Robert M. Green, George G. Smith, and Walter L. Burrage, for example, appealed to subscribers of the *The Boston Medical and Surgical Journal* to contribute to the American Relief Committee because, as of July 1916, the numbers of needy widows and orphans were constantly multiplying.[124] Charles S. Macfarland, secretary of the Church of Christ in America, urged believers to help the American Relief Committee's work in Berlin and its local fund-raising body, the American Auxiliary Committee. The church member asked pastors to make Memorial Day that year a special War Relief Day in their congregations, noting the benefits that such work would have for Sunday-school children. Striking a transnational chord, Macfarland argued that it made no difference whether Prussia or Russia overran Poland, because thousands of innocent people would be driven from their homes and deprived of livelihoods regardless of which army claimed victory.[125] Perhaps the discrepancy between this evidence and Jones's contention is that when circumstances called for corresponding with the U.S. government, those involved believed that the missives should be from a man. In addition, the formidable forces of the Men and Religion Forward Movement, founded in 1912, may have displaced female leaders of church-affiliated relief organizations.[126]

While these examples all show men in charge of relief efforts, *recipients* of U.S. aid were uniformly assumed to be females and children. In that respect U.S. humanitarian aid to Germany demonstrated a different kind of reciprocal gendered economy created by the war, in which men purposely set out to destroy the enemy's home front (presumed to be female-dominated), women suffered the brunt of war's wreckage, and males in turn offered them relief. More cynically, relief also represented the victors' desire to dominate the postwar world politically as part of their just deserts.

Between 1915 and 1917, officials at the American Embassy in Berlin formed the American Relief Committee in Berlin for Widows and Orphans of the War (ARC), which opened a kitchen that served meals to those in need. In this case the organization followed Jones's idea of a gendered reciprocal economy, because Ambassador James W. Gerard's wife, Mary Daly Gerard, headed the organization and German Princess Stephanie von Hohenlohe at least lent her name to the project (however, men conducted all ARC correspondence with the State Department). The food service claimed to be non-partisan "and made no distinctions as to nationality," according to its advocates.[127] But by July 1916 supplies in the city were running low and the charity was in danger of closing. In response, Ludwig Grosse, secretary of the ARC, sent out a plea to "prominent New York ladies and gentlemen" to become members of an Auxiliary Committee so that contributions could be sent to Berlin to keep the ARC functioning. Acknowledging that the sinking of the *Lusitania* by German U-boats in May 1915 had curtailed donations, Grosse nevertheless proclaimed that fundraising had been a success.[128] "America," assured the ARC, "is willing to give of her plenty wherever humanity demands" and would not allow herself to appear to neglect human need. In its correspondence and its publications, the ARC proved itself to be a humanitarian organization with American exceptionalist underpinnings, touting its ability to promote friendly relations between the United States and Germany. Just three months prior to the U.S. declaration of war against Germany, Ambassador Gerard (who was regarded as being pro-German in the United States and leaning pro-British by German officials) proclaimed that relations between the United States and Germany had never been so close.[129] After the war, the ability of relief work to perform politically was reinforced by Ulysses Grant-Smith, U.S. *chargé d'affaires* in Copenhagen. He, too, proclaimed that "the people are clearly relying on the 'American spirit' to save Germany from famine, and also save it politically, and if this happens, the future German Government will surely be modeled along American lines."[130]

Washington did not always approve of Ambassador Gerard's relief endeavors. By November 1916, the ARC's activities had come under the scrutiny of Frank L. Polk, legal counsel to the State Department. Polk demanded that Gerard send him more information about money raised for the Berlin organization and its transmission through the State Department and disbursal through consular officers in Germany. In Polk's opinion, such transactions implied a breach of the British blockade of Germany, making the U.S. government a direct participant in an effort to nullify the British strategy for bringing economic pressure to bear on its enemy.[131] When the State Department received requests from U.S. citizens to join the relief effort in Berlin, the officials denied that they had any knowledge of such aid programs.[132] The Ambassador's largesse, and presumably that of his wife, became hamstrung by the political constraints of war.

Coinciding with concerns for Berlin's needy widows and orphans were State Department worries about how to feed its own employees, followed by other American nationals living in the blockaded country. Both cases reveal the workings of Benedict Anderson's "imagined community" as countrymen expressed a desire to help only "their own." U.S. officials corresponded with diplomats in other nations to learn how they were dealing with the food crisis in a process Jones calls the "transferring of norms between belligerents."[133] Argentina, for example, managed to send meat to its compatriots in Germany through unofficial means.[134] These efforts were curtailed by suspicions of what exactly U.S. citizens were doing in Germany in the first place. Joseph C. Grew, an aide to Ambassador Gerard, used the term "bona fide Americans" to supply food only to them, and Assistant Secretary of State William Phillips warned Consular Bureau Chief Herbert C. Hengstler that, in Gerard's opinion, "there are many Americans in Germany who are not entitled to this food, and he [Gerard] referred especially to Americans who have returned to Germany to live and who are to all intents and purposes Germans in spirit, as well as those Americans who have bitterly attacked and continue to attack this country."[135] Gerard's munificence extended only to his countrymen whom he regarded as loyal. W. W. Husband of the American Red Cross seconded this attitude when he railed against U.S. women married to Germans who had to his mind lost the "American spirit."[136] The imagined community of compatriots operated on a rather selective basis.

After U.S. intervention, the humanitarian spirit among some American citizens did not always coincide with State Department views of the adversary. As late as March 19, 1917, less than a month before the declaration of war, officials received requests for advice on sending aid to Germany. One inquiry came from F. N. Stevens of Manassas, Virginia, who asked if the State Department knew of any restrictions on helping needy women and children in Germany. The writer stated, "I suppose it is just as well to say that we are not of German descent nor do we sympathize with the German cause except as to the suffering women and children not only those of Germany but all the others."[137] The kinds of suspicions that had spawned William H. McMasters's cynicism in 1915 intensified with U.S. intervention and remained even after the war ended. In responding to citizens' requests to send help, the U.S. State Department employed a tit-for-tat strategy similar to one that the Berlin government had used when it retaliated against the British blockade by sinking British submarines in order to hamper the commerce of its foe.[138] The chairman of the War Loan Organization of Philadelphia, an organization that had raised thousands of dollars for the U.S. war effort, asked Secretary of State Robert Lansing to suspend the requisitioning of German milk cows for France (as per the armistice agreement) calling such a move "child murder on a large scale," because starving German mothers were unable to provide breast milk to their infants and needed cow's milk instead. As an alternative, Chairman J. B. Mayer suggested that the U.S. government instruct treaty negotiators in Paris to allow Germany to pay for and retain its milk cows. Mayer assured Lansing that he and his organization were "100% American" in their support for their country, but "we appeal to you . . . because Americans do not wage war against women and children." William Phillips, replying on behalf of Lansing, responded acerbically. The German milk cows represented only a restoration, because Germany had taken France's cows in the first place and without regard to suffering children, in districts that it had occupied during the war. In any case, wrote Phillips, because all restrictions on trade were open, Germany was at liberty to purchase its own milk cows.

Mayer did not retreat, however. "I was not aware," he penned, adopting Phillips's same biting tone, "that such irreconcilable spirit is still prevalent at our National Headquarters." He went on to explain that he had written initially because, in the words of President Wilson, the United States had not quarreled with the German people.[139] The London *Daily Herald*, too, rejected the politics of revenge when it reported that, contrary to the popular British belief that German civilians would never come to the aid of British military prisoners held in Germany, in fact such an organization dedicated to that very cause had already been formed.[140]

Private citizens critical of aid to Germany also made their sentiments known to the State Department. J. J. Hammel informed on an organization called the American Relief for the German People (ARGP) when he wrote to the Assistant Secretary of State. The ARGP, which claimed to have the State Department's support, had written to Hammel with its appeal for aid to Germany in the German language, a tongue with which Hammel was apparently familiar, as he translated it for the Assistant Secretary. "Just think of the German mothers who sacrificed their grown sons upon the altar of the fatherland," wrote the ARGP, according to Hammel's translation, "and who are now with tearful eyes looking upon their minor children, who being underfed because of the *devilish hunger blockade*, will finally be victims of the *merciless wrath* of the allies." Hammel found the language objectionable. In response, Lansing wrote to the parent organization of the ARGP, the Welfare Committee for Prisoners of War (WCPW), stating that, because the United States was still at war with Germany, the U.S. State Department could not permit itself to be connected with a statement containing "unwarranted and defamatory remarks concerning the governments associated with the United States in the prosecution of the war." Carl Boschwitz, representing the WCPW, immediately sent a note of apology to the State Department, claiming that it knew nothing of the ARGP's circulars.

Dr. Hermann Gerhard, ARGP director, proved less contrite. While he apologized for the wording, he defended his organization by noting that, even though the United States was still at war with Germany, he understood that large American "packing houses and other industries have resumed business relations with Germany." In this statement, Gerhard pointed to the privileged position of big business in American society. Companies were free to conduct *commerce*, but nonprofit charities were subject to censorship when they tried to send *aid*. Adopting a defensive tone, Gerhard continued, "we trust that we are not in conflict with any laws or policies of the Government in engaging in the work of charity to relieve human suffering and starving children, even though they be the children of those people with whom we have been engaged in conflict."[141]

Charles Osner, chairman of the Committee for the Relief of Destitute Women and Children in Germany and Austria, espoused a transnational approach to solicit funds to send to Germany in November 1919. This was a brave move given the reactionary politics in the United States in 1919, including the blackballing of international activists like Jane Addams by the infamous Lusk Committee of the New York legislature and the deportation of presumed radicals such as Emma Goldman during the 1919–20 Red Scare. But in at least one instance Osner's transnational strategy backfired badly. Based in Seattle, the relief worker issued an appeal to "all charitably inclined people, irrespective of nationality and creed." He acknowledged that all of Europe depended on U.S. support as a result of "four years of terrible warfare." Osner identified Germans and Austrians as the Europeans who were in the worst shape. Although he did not single out the blockade as Gerhard had done, he noted that starvation in Germany was due to the population's having to depend on its own resources. He included a German Red Cross circular to support his point on the direness of the German situation.

Another Seattleite, Edgar N. Gott, caustically rejected Osner's bid. Gott resented the presumption that he might, because of his German-sounding last name, have been inclined to aid the former foe. He began his response to the aid activist by relieving himself of any "Hun taint," claiming that his ancestors had sailed from England in the 1600s. Using the same tit-for-tat measuring stick used by Phillips, Gott argued that if Germans and Austrians were suffering the most out of all Europeans, it was because of the atrocities committed by the Germans on the civilians of France, Belgium, England, Serbia, Montenegro, and Italy. Doubting the veracity of accounts of starvation in Germany in any case, Gott believed that people living in the nations destroyed by the Central Powers should be offered aid first. He then expressed distrust that money donated to Germany would reach those in need. Finally, Gott objected to the use of the German language on some of the enclosures that Osner had sent along with his solicitation, deeming it a language that "this Country can well do without."

Osner gave back as good as he got. Playing on the translation of Gott's name (the English translation of the German word *Gott* is God), he suggested that his correspondent cultivate the godly virtues of love and charity. His response then turned political. Claiming that no war had ever been fought without the kinds of atrocities that Gott had mentioned in his letter, he listed several perpetrated by the U.S. government (including General William Tecumseh Sherman's "march to the sea" during the U.S. Civil War) with a few conducted by the Allies (including the hunger blockade of Germany and Austria) thrown in for good measure. Gott, after receiving Osner's letter, sent the entire packet of correspondence between the two men to the State Department, asking the Secretary of State whether he had indeed endorsed Osner's project, as the activist had claimed. Breckinridge Long, Third Assistant Secretary, mailed Gott a response that the Boeing Company manager must have found unsatisfactory. In some ways, Long's reply simply duplicated a form letter that the State Department sent to most of the inquiries it received regarding aid to Germany. He informed Gott that trade and communication with German and Austria had been resumed and that there were in place no impediments to the disbursal of funds for relief in either country. He did add, however, that "it must be understood that the organizers and promoters of such [aid] shall refrain from making any statement derogatory to this government or to the governments associated with it in the war."[142]

Like the protesting Edgar N. Gott, the American Legion stood opposed to the sending of any form of aid to Germany. Blind to the greater interests of humanity that lay above the narrow-minded nationalism to which Osner, Aletta Jacobs and Jane Addams had alluded, Legion headquarters sent Charles Evans Hughes (Secretary of State during the Warren G. Harding administration) a letter decrying the sending of dairy cows from the United States to Germany to feed infants whose mothers were too malnourished to breastfeed. The movement to ship the bovines was perpetrated by German "sympathizers" living in the state of South Dakota, according to Legion assistant national director Alvin Owsley. Owsley warned Hughes ominously that people from local Legion organizations who were protesting the shipments were armed.[143] Hughes replied with the same measured response that he had sent to others complaining of the alleged activities of German relief organizations: Trade between the United States and Germany was legal, and such protests were beyond the purview of the State Department. When Germany failed to pay war reparations as mandated by the Treaty of Versailles in 1922, the French invaded the Ruhr early the following year; this action resulted in a flurry of relief efforts from the United States.

Women and children, often regarded as "innocents" by relief workers, were presumed to be uninvolved in the war because of the ways in which the home front diverged from battlefront. U.S. aid workers almost exclusively aimed their benevolence at them. While few would deny food to someone they met who was hungry, the practice of targeting women and children, and especially widows and orphans, served to keep widows in their place as females needing male protection set apart from the public realm, a practice that had begun during the war with Family Allowance (but did not really continue with widows' pensions, because amounts granted were rarely enough to sustain a widow and her children). Divided fronts also served to highlight the gendered, contradictory nature of the nation's imagined community. On the one hand, the war making elite kept home and battlefronts isolated from each other in order to perpetuate the myth of separate spheres for men and women, enabling war makers to justify the war as necessary for the protection of helpless females. On the other hand, the nature of mechanized warfare conducted among industrialized nations required women's active involvement in the fighting.

Great War relief reinforced another time-honored trope of armed conflict: To the victor go the spoils. The spoils, like relief, were also gendered. The winning nations gained control over some portion of the losing nations' resources. Industrialization and imperialism had ensured that prewar Germany relied on imported food and other necessities required for economic growth from neighboring countries. As a weapon of war, the economic blockade brought Germans to their knees and then enabled the victors to manage resources and sustain the supposed innocent women and children in the home front that the blockade had been designed to subdue. Defeated Germans equated their nation-state with the helpless "state" of being female, as Josef Wackerle's painting indicated.

Nation-states are defined by the geographic borders that separate them from their neighbors. They invent common histories—temporal borders—that include presumed racial and ethnic commonalities, languages, and religious and political ideologies that distinguish them from those living across the border as well. Industrialization and imperialism accelerated when citizens (aided by their governments) traversed those self-imposed boundaries and exploited the human and natural resources that lay beyond the nation's boundaries. The Great War resulted in part from both of those developments, while at the same time the conflict brought people of different nationalities closer together. While distinctions are easy to find, the World War also demonstrated the commonalities of different nations' and widows' experiences of armed conflict above and across national boundaries. For some, those unifying aspects fostered a rejection of war and of the intense nationalism that led to it. For some transnationals, such as the German reformer Helene Stöcker (profiled in the next chapter), eschewing the confines of nationalism and gender roles went hand-in-hand.

"The Other Trench"

Remarriage, Pro-natalism, and
the Rebirthing of the Nation

The medieval town of Magdeburg, situated on the Elbe River in north central Germany, has a history that is wedded at important junctures to the institution of marriage. It was consecrated in a.d. 805 by the Roman Emperor Charlemagne, and in 929 the German King Henry I bequeathed the city to Edward the Elder's daughter Edith as a *Morgengabe*—a gift to the bride by the groom's family on the morning after the wedding feast. The word "Magdeburg" meant "pure maid" in Old High German, and presumably the English-born bride had lived up to that expectation.[1] Edith, who had married Henry I's son Otto I, loved the town of Magdeburg and spent much of her life there. Upon her death her descendants buried her in the crypt of Magdeburg's Benedictine Abbey of Saint Maurice.

In 1524 Martin Luther brought the Protestant Reformation to Magdeburg, where he had begun his education years earlier. The city's printers adopted his ideas with gusto, hastening its influence by distributing several religious tracts.[2] In 1525, the theologian, priest, and author of *The Estate of Marriage* renounced his vow of chastity and at the age of forty-two married Katharina von Bora, a twenty-six-year-old former nun who, under the spell of the Reformation, had fled her Cistercian convent at Nimbschen, Germany. A Magdeburg colleague of Luther's, Nikolaus von Amsdorf, made the Luther–von Bora match. The plucky Katharina proved her housekeeping skills as a consummate gardener and cattle breeder. The duo established the former Augustinian monastery in Erfurt as their residence, and six children soon followed. The union between the former monk and the one-time nun was not only a productive one but also a happy one. When Katharina became a widow in 1546, she discovered that her husband had taken the unusual step of naming her as his sole heir.[3]

By the time of the First World War, Magdeburg faced challenges endemic to countless municipalities across Germany and in all the warring European nations. The war consumed millions of lives and drained local and national resources. In the aftermath, scores of army units began making their way back to their homelands as per the November 1918 armistice agreements. Many returning soldiers were physically, mentally, and emotionally damaged from the bloodiest conflict the world had ever witnessed, a fight they had believed would last only a few months. Veterans sought restitution in the form of health care, compensation, and, for those physically able, at least the promise of employment from the governments that had sent them into battle. At the same time, war survivors began their hopeful, if embittered, trek toward a decent standard of living for themselves and for their children. Many of these were war widows. They, too, sought justice in the form of compensation for lost breadwinners and for the paying positions that industry, urged on by governments, had taken from them.[4]

In Magdeburg, officials turned to marriage as a solution to its war-induced woes by encouraging nuptials between members of the two groups of survivors sitting on the lowest rung of economic well-being. Another local matchmaker, menswear store owner Benno Basch, facilitated the dating service by entreating the local welfare office to arrange meetings between ex-soldiers and war widows. Matchmaking must have seemed, serendipitously, a solution to more than one problem. The injured required physical care from an attendant; the widow needed additional income, particularly if she had children to feed from her first marriage; and the nation needed survivors to remarry so that they could produce more youths and help their society rebuild and regenerate after a devastating, life-consuming war. In one instance, a Magdeburg housewife had been married to a bakery owner prior to the guns of August; she reportedly could not operate her husband's business by herself after his death. The shop brought in only 2.5 to 2.75 marks per day, she complained, a scant income that proved to be enough to pay rent on the store and the widow's apartment, but nothing else. While the aggrieved had been advised to take bookkeeping lessons, she refused to be separated from her children to do so. She soon found a new husband—one who understood the bakery business—through the marriage broker. The couple exchanged vows within six months after their first meeting. The bakery thrived, and, according to a social worker, the matchmaking had "created family happiness." One hundred twenty couples took nuptial vows through the Magdeburg program.[5] Marriage bureaus appeared in other German towns as well. Legal unions between dutiful housekeeping and childrearing wives dependent on sturdy, capable bread-earning husbands complemented Germany's desire to return to the normalcy of well-ordered families that in turn reflected a highly disciplined society after the war. Sociologist Hans Harmsen told the Magde-burg story in his 1926 critique of the influence of the German government's welfare laws on war widows. The demographer and eugenicist warned his readers that if females were not suitably married and fecund, their nation faced the ominous prospect of sterility.[6]

A survey conducted among Germany's IV Army Corps demonstrated that 97 percent of the wives married to soldiers of that unit who had been killed in 1914 were under the age of forty and therefore stood as potential conduits to the replenishment of the population from its wartime decline. Whether war widows viewed themselves primarily as wives or as women partially determined the choices they made after their husbands' deaths: If women, then they felt free to remarry; if wives, they may have felt pressured to remain loyal to their fallen soldier-husbands. If they took vows a second time, they may have felt liberated from the burden of the sacrifice they had made when their husbands enlisted and from their "duty to the fallen sol-dier." If they remarried, mourners positioned themselves as potential moth-ers for a first or second time, depending on whether they had had children by their soldier-husbands. The vast majority of the 1914 war widows from the IV Army Corps already had offspring.[7] Elisabeth Macke and Johanna Boldt followed the general IV Army Corps pattern, although neither of their husbands had belonged to that particular unit. Macke and Boldt each had birthed two children before their men were killed. Both were among the 30 to 40 percent of widows who eventually remarried, but only Macke had chil-dren with her second husband. Tracing war widows' fertility remains a dif-ficult task, because upon remarriage most war widows changed their names and lost their pensions and their direct connection to the nation-state (unless they voted or held public office). Macke is exceptional, because she penned her memoirs and retained her first husband's name in her last name, becom-ing Elisabeth Erdmann-Macke when she wed Lothar Erdmann in 1916.

In addition to these considerations loomed the often more pressing ques-tion of economics. According to Karl Nau's findings in his 1930 study of Darmstadt war survivors, the bereaved who remarried often fared at least as well as they had during their first marriages.[8] Bearing additional children, of course, obligated families to feed more mouths. But war widows, like all women in European societies after the Great War, understood the decision to become pregnant as not merely an individual choice or even an option for the couple but as a matter deeply affecting the society in which they lived, particularly if they read or heard pro-natalist propaganda. Politicians, intel-lectuals, teachers, and religious leaders of all political persuasions in France,

Germany, Great Britain, and Italy constructed alarmist pro-natal campaigns to publicize the falling birth rates within their countries and to offer solutions.[9] Great Britain lagged behind both France and Germany in pro-natalist propaganda production, and Germany fell in behind France, particularly during the war.[10] European natalist groups included the National Alliance for the Increase of the French Population, the Superior Council on the Birthrate (also French), the German *Reichsbund der Kinderreichen Deutschlands zum Schutze der Familie* (League for a Child-rich Germany for the Protection of the Family), and the English National Birth Rate Commission.[11] Much of the pro-natalist literature included dire warnings about what a low population would mean for a nation threatened by invasion from its neighbors. Large-family activists, in other words, worked hand-in-hand with the remilitarization of the nation-state in the wake of the Great War. In addition, transnational eugenicists in Europe and the United States cooperated to create and sustain national policies based on the presumed inferiority of certain perceived racial groups and designed to encourage births among "racially valuable families."[12] Birth rates in England, France, Germany, and the United States had been falling well before the war, but during the conflict statistics indicated precipitous plummets in the numbers of babies being born within each warring nation.[13]

But in their memoirs and in other writings, war widows themselves seldom addressed the low birth rate problem; nor did pro-natalist campaigns single out bereaved wives as potential allies in their literature. On the contrary, French legislators viewed encouraging war widows to remarry as actually detrimental to the nation's fertility, because they believed that in choosing younger women as wives Frenchmen would be more likely to sire large families.[14] Karl Reutti confirmed this notion when he compared birth rates among widows and women in general in Germany and found that widows were far less likely to have children.[15]

In addition, to urge war widows to remarry and to validate new relationships by bearing children would have been to implore them to be women first rather than war widows, to disregard their wartime sacrifices and move on into the next phase of their lives. In other words, beseeching them to take another husband would have been akin to suggesting that widows and their compatriots forget about the war, a path that few were willing to follow. Despite relatively vigorous peace movements in both France and Germany (Germany's effectively shut down by the mid-1920s, while France's, more robust because of its greater destruction and losses, flourished throughout the interwar years),[16] official war remembrance in the interwar period continued unabated in the form of Armistice Day ceremonies, unknown-soldier rituals, and pilgrimages to France.

While not ignoring male soldiers' fighting spirit, women's rights leader Gertrud Bäumer, an ardent German nationalist, implored her readers to remember women's overlooked contributions to the war, which she argued were equal to men's.[17] In addition, aggrieved wives subscribing to a periodical called *Die Kriegerwitwe* (The Warrior's Widow) read articles with titles such as "On the Commemoration of Munich's Fallen" and poems glorifying "Our Distant Heroes' Graves"; bereaved women of the Gold Star variety in the United States embarked on journeys to their husbands' graves in remembrance of their sacrifices, lobbying the U.S. Congress intensely for that privilege; Australian women begged to be granted a role in Anzac Day commemorative rituals; all these mourners wanted their participation in the war—and therefore the war itself—to be recalled time and time again.[18] Only a lonely French school teacher, Gaston Clémendot, advocated forgetting about the war and furthermore eliminating history from the curriculum altogether to enable schoolchildren to bypass learning about the conflict at all; but his notion was ultimately rejected by the French national teachers' union.[19]

Moreover, rather than dismissing the war, militarized states signaled that they needed to be perpetually positioned to fight future battles.[20] While the world witnessed the signing of the 1922 Five-Power naval treaty, limiting the number and size of major warships of the United States, Japan, Britain, Italy, and France, by the end of the decade France had fortified its defenses against Germany with its Maginot Line, and the goal of the 1928 Kellogg-Briand Pact—to renounce the use of war as a political tool—proved elusive as signatories such as the United States refused to surrender their right to self-defense. Meanwhile, hawkish officials in Germany used the vengeful Treaty of Versailles as a rationale to remilitarize. By 1926 the chief of the Office of Ministerial Affairs, General Kurt von Schleicher, prepared to rebuild his nation's armed forces. German nurses who had participated in the Great War supported this movement.[21] The remilitarization and brutalization of German society was more pronounced than in the other war powers and helps explain women's inability to assert their constitutionally mandated equal citizenship, even though their votes were courted by right-wing political parties.[22] Along with politicians and national militaries, war widows' participation in countless commemorative ceremonies helped the world remember, not forget, the Great War.[23] But to remain active war memoirists, war widows had to stay widowed. To some, courtship and remarriage implied self-indulgence and frivolity, the supposed feminine characteristics—typified by the American lifestyle, according to some—that they blamed for Germany's defeat.[24]

In addition to revering their dead soldier-husbands' memory, war widows took their economic situation into account when faced with an option to remarry. Those with children remarked repeatedly on their devotion to their offspring as an extension of their loyalty to their dead soldier-husbands, but most were too busy finding work and enlisting child care so that they could work, or taking in finishing work in the textile industry to stretch their pensions, or planning their little ones' futures to consider their own futures, which they often saw as the equivalent of their children's.[25] Many commented that in caring for their offspring they reaffirmed women's traditional role as child caregiver, and this role had social and national implications. When children achieved *Selbstständigkeit*, or economic independence, it marked them as respectable, hardworking adult citizens and widowed mothers as successful parents. Widows like Johanna Boldt achieved *Selbstständigkeit* for themselves as well, and they were encouraged in this by social workers and by feminist writers.[26] Remarriage and birthing more young would not likely help them reach this benchmark. While some widows recorded feeling obligated to honor their fallen husbands' memories and the homeland to which the men had sacrificed their lives, they did not view their duty to the nation as including having *more* children—not, at least, according to their autobiographies (and not reflected in birth rates, which, except for a 1920 rise, remained at prewar levels). In some cases, widows rejected coming to pronatalists' aid because they felt that to do so would only provide the nation with additional sheep vulnerable to the next slaughter.[27]

Widows' remarriage, their choice of whether to enlarge their families or not, and national pro-natalist campaigns took place in the context of the demobilization and regeneration of nations that after 1918 were supposedly once again at peace. For European crusaders encouraging the filling of empty cribs, whether one's nation stood on the winning or losing side of the war made little difference.[28] Instead, the same fears of weakness in men and sterility in women flourished across Britain, France, and Germany. In addition, while U.S. promoters of large families did not perpetuate propaganda to the same extent as did their European counterparts, some joined racialist campaigns designed to encourage white middle-class women to offer their nations counterweights to nonwhite populations seen as being overly fecund and likely to drive white people into the uncomfortable position of minority status. In all nations with pro-natalist programs, campaigners compared national fertility to military strength, an aspect of nationhood that, despite four long years of a bloody war that had produced almost nothing but mountains of corpses, remained a sought-after goal in the aftermath of the Great War.[29] Weimar culture adopted not only the tools necessary to create an efficient workplace—called "Fordism" after the American car manufacturer Henry Ford—but also the rationalization and reliance on "experts" emphasized in nearly all aspects of everyday life.[30] Arguments to the contrary— that having children should remain in control of individuals rather than the state, and that more babies translated into more soldiers and therefore more bloodshed in the future—were voiced primarily by feminists, transnational pacifists, and schoolteachers involved in the French peace movement. But the fiery desire for national strength, seen not only as requiring female fecundity but, more important, as reflecting the nation's manly virility, could not be doused in the postwar years.

War widows contemplating remarriage foresaw a variety of scenarios, but none of them looked very good. Magdeburg welfare workers, along with well-meaning relatives such as Johanna Boldt's brother-in-law, assumed that wives could not conduct their husbands' businesses in their absences or upon their deaths. That women could not or should not live independently of men formed part of the rationale behind all of the legislation passed by warring nations to pay allowances to soldiers' wives and pensions to their widows. At the same time, however, widows trying to court potential breadwinning husbands publicly faced accusations of disloyalty and immorality. Magdeburg marriage brokers skirted this unseemly circumstance by introducing potential mates to each other within the confines of the local welfare office. Other widows were not as lucky. In the state of Victoria, Australia, for example, police investigated widows who were the object of numerous accusations of immorality. One widow was found to have "questionable morals" because she had been seen at the movies with a man.[31] The Bavarian War Widows Association protested the fact that authorities scrutinized war widows' private affairs in determining their pensions prior to a new 1920 National Pension Law.[32] In Italy, popular and Catholic culture frowned upon second marriages for widows, making courtship a frightening prospect under any circumstances. A widow who remarried before ten months had elapsed after her first husband's death was considered disloyal and immodest; the law punished her by confiscating her dowry and her inheritance from her first husband. Even though they were pitied for their reduced circumstances, war widows' independence from a male protector and their untethered sexuality represented, in the view of some, social instability and marked them as a danger to society.[33] Mourners gazing into a crystal ball at their futures viewed a slippery slope: Either they risked their neighbors' condemnation and possible legal penalties for seeking out new marriage partners, or they remained forever "in the shadow of the war," perpetually wearing widows' weeds.[34] If leaning toward remarriage, they stood to gain what society viewed as male protection and, they hoped, a standard of living equal to that which they had enjoyed during their first marriages. On the other hand, in choosing the altar most lost the ability to manage their economic lives on their own (except in France, where widows' pensions were retained upon remarriage). Barring a willingness to bear a child out of wedlock, remaining widowed spelled out a barren future, a state of affairs that raised eyebrows in postwar societies in the throes of pro-natal campaigns. Having illegitimate children remained largely a stigmatized endeavor, although by 1915 German military authorities, under the sway of pro-natalists, extended servicemen's allowances to include their illegitimate children.[35] Given these unpleasant scenarios, some war widows, such as Harriet Pierson, opted to remain war widows for the rest of their lives. While "mourning" may not be an appropriate word to describe her everyday life in her remaining years, Pierson's desire to be buried in her nation's most highly honored military cemetery indicates that the Great War did indeed cast a long shadow upon her existence.[36]

Widows with children considered potential conflicts caused by the introduction of a second husband to her children from her first marriage. Given the honor—or in the German phrase, the "thanks of the Fatherland"—that widows believed were due them from their government for having sacrificed their husbands to the war effort, their children by their warrior-husbands may have represented something more than living symbols of an earlier union. One of Hurwitz-Stranz's widows pondered the impact of a stepfather on her *Familienleben*, or family life, in her essay.[37] Another memoirist had nothing positive to say about her subsequent nuptial; unlike the Magdeburg widow's remarriage, her union did not create family happiness. She did not explain her estrangement from her second husband but confided that her children remained her only comfort and support. That she lost her pension upon exchanging new vows probably did not help. Another autobiographer discouraged war widows from seeking remarriage, also decrying the impact of the stepfather on her offspring, but noting in addition that widows who had reached *Selbstständigkeit* would feel claustrophobic when tethered once again to a husband. Another memoirist stated that she found more solace in the company of other war widows who had experienced the same losses rather than in the company of a man. The Bavarian War Widows Association, too, disparaged second nuptials.[38]

All in all, the prospect of a new relationship simply held too many nega-
tives for some women. Sex reformer Grete Meisel-Hess, however, had a different perspective on the issue. War widows, argued Meisel-Hess, desired
another wedding because they expected to marry a better man the second
time around. In addition, they sought remarriage because they were frightened of the prospect of living without the protection of a husband.[39] Remarried war widows could place unforeseen burdens on their second husbands
as well. Elisabeth Macke married Lothar Erdmann two years after August
Macke's battlefront death, offering her beloved children a new parent. Lothar
Erdmann's diary revealed him to be a caring father, but because of her continued spiritual connection to her first husband, his marriage to Elisabeth
was ultimately an unhappy one.[40]

Still others, including never-married women, perceived a keen competition
for a reduced number of available grooms. According to Katharine Anthony's
1915 survey of European women's lives, prospective brides lacked marriage-
able men to wed because of colonization, immigration, industrial accidents,
and war. Already in 1914 Britain claimed an excess of more than 1,300,000
females, supposedly the largest imbalance in Europe. Germany's 1925 census
counted an estimated surplus of 2 million women. Expectations of failure may
have kept a certain number of mourners from seeking a second union. [41]

Despite widows' somber outlook, however, remarriage struck at least
some in postwar societies as much-needed regeneration and therefore as a
cause for celebration. Americans trumpeted what they saw as their wartime
ally's good fortune in the area of renewed nuptials, even as they advertised
Britain's "lost generation." The April 1926 edition of the Portsmouth, New
Hampshire, *Herald* reported that 100,000 English war widows had remarried, a "decent" showing eight years after the end of the war in a nation where
men were "at a premium," because it had been recorded that 248,367 dead
soldiers had left pension-eligible widows.[42] In a rosy review of new British
nuptials, the London *Daily Mail* predicted that at the current rate of 2,000
weddings a month in 1920, *all* English war widows would be remarried by
1928, surely an inspired goal.[43] However, only about 40 percent of German,
British, and French war widows had proceeded to the altar by 1924, and in
no nation did all war widows remarry. Indeed, 40 percent remained the pinnacle figure.[44] Because pro-natalist crusaders touted legal unions as the best
context for bringing more children into the world, their preaching, too, constituted ringing endorsements of the institution of marriage.

In addition to the more emotional issues of loyalty to their first husbands,
priorities given to their war orphaned children, and the moral implications

of both, legal and economic considerations entered into war widows' calculations as they contemplated renewed vows. In this arena widows' chances for autonomy and a decent living depended on where they lived. German widows surrendered control of their property to their second husbands upon remarriage, unless their betrothed had signed a pre-nuptial contract outlining spousal property rights. Female wage workers, on the other hand, retained their earnings upon taking vows.[45] Remarrying German widows forfeited their pensions, although they received a gratuity in the amount of three times their most recent annual payment. While the bonus may have been welcomed, the widow—unless employed for wages—lost the independence of controlling an income apart from a man. Sociologist Hans Harmsen blamed the practice of withdrawing widows' pensions from those who remarried for the increasing numbers of the bereaved who chose cohabitation rather than the altar.[46] Bavarian widows and their organization analyzed Germany's 1920 pension law and its relation to mourners' remarrying. For those remarrying prior to the new law, the *Versorgungsamt* (Pension Office) appraised the war widow's economic situation upon her new marriage: The group asserted that wealthy widows received the full amount (1,000 marks) whereas the neediest were less likely to obtain their due. They also accused authorities of awarding lower sums to wives of soldier-husbands who had not died "gloriously" in combat.[47]

British mourners, too, lost their pensions upon remarriage, unless their first husbands had been officers. Like their German counterparts, they received "wedding gifts" from the Ministry of Pensions. The London *Daily Mail* touted the government's endowment to the newlywed couple as a year's worth of a widow's pension and a year's allowance for any children she may have had. This the betrothed couple accepted as a "nest-egg" that would "start a new home and [open up] a second chapter of married life." In Australia, aggrieved wives could keep their pensions for two years after remarriage until a 1931 law abolished the provision. French women resuming married life kept their pensions outright until a 1925 law penalized them, resulting in a decreased amount for remarried war widows.[48] Even though new unions were celebrated in societies strained by wartime losses, war widows recording their experiences and ruminations did not relish the prospect of second nuptials.

Around 16 million people lost their lives as a result of the Great War, a figure that translated into an alarming downturn in the number of each nation's citizens, amounting to a 3.8 percent loss in the German population and a 4.3 percent decline for France. All of Europe that lay west of Russia lost 7 percent of its population to the First World War.[49] Deaths from the war afforded survivors, especially women and immigrants, an opportunity to redefine what constituted citizenship in the postwar years (the injuries sustained by 21 million people in the conflict caused other, immeasurable changes as well[50]). Before the Great War, marriage and children were considered private family matters that nevertheless constituted what was perceived as women's primary contribution to their nations. After the war, private versus public divisions were no longer as clear. On the one hand, all of the memoirists writing in Helene Hurwitz-Stranz's anthology consented to anonymity. It is unclear if this agreement was made at the behest of the editor, the publisher, or the widows themselves, but in any case, their obscured identity reinforces the gulf between public and private that continued to veil women's lives after the war. On the other hand, pro-natal campaigns brought women's reproductivity increasingly into the public and political arena.[51]

If the war's sorrows, coupled with challenging postwar economies, led widows and women to opt not to marry or to have many or any children, then their nations had to adjust to lower numbers of citizens, varying, of course, on death rates, immigration levels, and other factors. Women had already proven themselves ready and capable of filling voids at schools, factories, farms, and civil service positions during the conflict, and they surrendered those jobs with varying degrees of reluctance upon demobilization.[52] The return to peacetime economies—including welfare measures designed to support war survivors and pro-natal campaigns—encouraged women to regard peacetime as a return to traditional gender roles and dependence upon a man. The Weimar Constitution and the government it represented upheld the sanctity of family life but promised to protect the rights of illegitimate children and took final responsibility for rearing children. "Child-rich" families were encouraged, and abortion was outlawed except when medically necessary; contraceptives could not be advertised or displayed, but they were legally manufactured and distributed by megalithic German pharmaceutical companies, which sold 80 to 90 million condoms annually.[53] Those women reporting on their individual circumstances remarked on their resistance to the re-inscription of normal gender roles, except as that restoration meant a return to low prewar birth rates that had accompanied industrialization before the guns of August. Women gained a political voice in Britain, the United States, and Germany through the ballot, proving themselves not only as "republican mothers" but as political citizens as well.[54]

Concerns over falling birth rates due to industrialization and the advent of modern life had risen in most European and North American countries long before the World War. The link between war, the nation-state, and the national birth rate emerged in the nineteenth century during the Franco-Prussian War, when demographers noted the military implications of discrepancies in combatant countries' birth rates.[55] Specifically, the German birth rate fell during that conflict from 38.1 in 1870 to 33.8 in 1871 but did not rise after the war ended. The rate plunged again from 30.7 in 1910 to 26.8 per thousand by 1914; in 1917 it dropped to a low point of 14.4, and then jumped up to 26.7 in 1920. Subsequently, it declined steadily through the mid-1920s.[56] German men and women continued to marry at prewar levels, meaning that their nation's low birth rates were due primarily to marital infertility (although the divorce rate climbed between 1920 and 1924). The English, too, continued to seek nuptials: Only the French seemed to have soured on the institution.[57] Germany withstood the lowest postwar net reproduction rate of any European country except its former ally, Austria.[58] The French birth rate stood at 25.5 in 1870; it dropped to 22.6 in 1871, followed by a decline to an average of 19 per thousand between 1910 and 1914. It rose again to an average of 20.1 between 1920 and 1924, after which it declined steadily through the remainder of the decade.[59] Historian Mary Louise Roberts demonstrated that there was no "crisis" of infertility; the birth rate in France was not alarmingly low, and in fact a healthy postwar bounce had occurred.[60] German sex reformer Helene Stöcker cautioned that a declining birth rate does not necessarily indicate a drop in population, because factors such as immigration and better health care, translating into fewer deaths, also affected a nation's population.[61]

In the United States, the birth rate per thousand inhabitants was 38 in 1890; by 1915 it had dropped to 32, remaining level for the next couple of years. In 1918 it headed downward steadily until reaching a low of about 20 in 1938.[62] In comparison to those of Germany and France, the United States' population did not respond as drastically to the war, and its birth rate did not plummet as dramatically as was the case in those two nations. France's birth rate in the late nineteenth century had not been as high as Germany's. Both France and Germany experienced a jump in birth rate immediately following the war, but the rises constituted neither a boom nor a trend, because neither nation sustained that postwar burst in births for more than a year or two.

During the war, conjugal relations were impeded by soldiers' departing for faraway battlefields and uncertain leave-times. Industrial warfare could not abide with the old ways of camp-following wives who cooked, cleaned, mended, and made love with their warrior-husbands in army tents: There

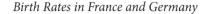

Birth Rates in France and Germany

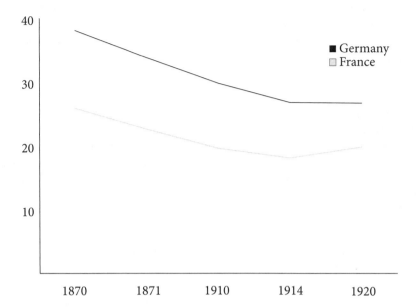

Births per 1,000 inhabitants. The 1870, 1910, and 1914 figures for birth rates in France and Germany are from Walter T. K. Nugent, *Crossings: The Great Atlantic Migrations, 1870–1914* (Bloomington: Indiana University Press, 1995), 20; 1871 figures for Germany and France are from Louis I. Dublin, "War and the Birth Rate—A Brief Historical Summary," *American Journal of Public Health* 35 (April 1945): 316; 1920 German figure is from Richard Bessel, *Germany After the First World War* (Oxford: Oxford University Press, 1993), 229. The 1920 figure for France represents the average French birth rate between 1920 and 1924; data from Elinor A. Accampo, "The Gendered Nature of Contraception in France: Neo-Malthusianism, 1900–1920," *Journal of Interdisciplinary History* 34, no. 2 (Autumn 2003): 236. Compiled by Erika Kuhlman.

was no room for tag-alongs in narrow Great War trenches. Combat units traditionally made up for absent sexual partners by inviting prostitution. German military authorities began collaborating with the medical profession and pro-natalists to establish treatment clinics for soldiers, because venereal disease—spread by prostitution—if left to fester caused sterility.[63] But fighting men did not give up sex, nor were they encouraged to. One pro-natal French postcard circulating among *poilus*, for example, depicted a couple embracing atop an armored tank.[64] Other images showed soldiers' leaves as opportunities not only to lift the sagging birth rate but also to create more fighters for depleted trenches. Fathering more children, in other words, became part of the man's military mission.[65] Efforts by the military and others to restrict when, where, how, and with whom soldiers could have sex represented the ever-increasing state control of its citizens' sexuality.[66]

While local governments typically regulated female sexual deviants and prostitutes, during the Great War male sexuality came under increased government scrutiny. At the beginning of the war, men's sexual lives and reproductive capacities were treated as separate entities, but the two became linked as Germany grew more concerned with natality; venereal disease in men had to be treated to ensure their future fertility and the nation's *Wehrkraft*, or military power. According to Elisabeth Domansky, the German state exerted its authority to a much greater degree than did France or Britain.[67] The largest German women's organization, the *Bund Deutscher Frauenvereine* (Federation of German Women's Associations, or BDF) with its 250,000 members, confirmed state intrusion in maternal affairs when it promoted its Woman's Year of Service, a campaign designed to encourage maternity among women as their service to the nation equivalent to conscription.[68]

As Atina Grossmann has pointed out, Germany led the world in sex research and sex reform activism. German scientists facilitated discussions of birth control and other sexual matters at international sex reform conferences. Magnus Hirschfeld, for example, founded the Berlin Institute for Sexual Research in 1919, and other sexologists from around the world (including Havelock Ellis and Alexandra Kollontai) joined Hirschfeld in the 1928 World League for Sex Reform, which called for tolerance toward sexual deviancy and the legalization of birth control and abortion. Margaret Sanger resisted the meeting because of the organization's ties to homosexuality, abortion, and communism, remaining devoted to her pet issue of contraception. But Sanger's ties to Germany and its sex reform movement were steadfast; she, along with the Rockefeller Foundation, funded German efforts to study and dispense birth control in Germany.[69] One Berlin newspaper heralded Sanger's presence in the capital city, noting that Americans' reputation as being puritanical had been relieved not only by "the dancing girl" (presumably Josephine Baker) "but also by the woman, Margaret Sanger."[70] But opinions on contraception were divided in Germany's bourgeois women's movement. BDF President Gertrud Bäumer perceived motherhood as women's national duty, but fellow member Marie Stritt called the bill to outlaw birth control and eradicate venereal disease a "degradation of and an assault on women."[71]

For women in heterosexual relationships, government regulation came in the form of surveillance not only of prostitution but of birth control and abortion restrictions as well. The state took advantage of rigorous centralized control over people's lives during war to pass legislation pertaining to female sexuality. Such provisions were either negative, meaning punishment for displaying and advertising contraception, or positive, consisting of material inducements and tax relief for large families, a salary structure that would enable civil servants to have children earlier, and better housing and maternity protection. Gertrud Bäumer lent her formidable name and pen to the positive proposals.[72] By 1915 military authorities had sharpened the existing legal restrictions on birth control by banning the display and advertising of contraceptives and abortifacients (condoms were exempt because of their ability to prevent the spread of venereal disease), distributing information about them, and selling them door-to-door. Measures forcing prostitutes to undergo medical exams, preventing public access to birth control, and prohibiting abortion except to save the mother's life had passed legislative bodies but never became law because of the November Revolution, which ended Germany's monarchical government and replaced it with a parliamentary state called the Weimar Republic.[73]

It seems unlikely that the legislation would have had much effect in any case. Couples did not typically use birth control devices except for condoms, which were exempt. A Berlin sex researcher interviewed 300 men being treated for VD in a military hospital in 1916. More than 60 percent named withdrawal as their most frequently used form of contraception.[74] Despite support from Protestants, Catholics, and liberal and conservative politicians, the pro-natalist movement still could not compete with the advocates of birth control, especially in the economic crises of the late 1920s and early 1930s.[75] In 1926 the government reduced the severity of penalties to women and to abortion providers and legalized abortions for women for whom pregnancy posed a danger to the woman's health (not simply to save life).[76] Meanwhile, in France, the Chamber of Deputies in 1920 passed by a vote of 521 to 55 a bill that imposed stiff penalties for advertising or selling any articles related to birth control or abortion. The same legislation passed the Senate a few days later. It was the most oppressive anti–birth control and abortion measure in Europe.[77]

During the war, the German government made sexual intimacy part of the war effort by ensuring soldiers' health and their marital procreation. After the November Revolution, authorities were reluctant to relinquish control over sexual matters traditionally considered private. The Prussian Ministry for Social Welfare, for example, established marriage and procreation counseling centers throughout the province, although these were poorly utilized.[78] Concerns deemed important to "family health" were now considered issues of national priority. Medical experts, public health officials and private and state welfare agencies showed a unanimous hostility toward small families, indicating an overall consensus regarding pro-natalism in Germany.[79]

In a rational, scientifically oriented society, the first step toward control of female sexuality was knowledge. Why, wondered political, welfare, and religious leaders, were women unwilling to birth more babies after the guns were silenced and the nation had supposedly returned to normalcy? Unfortunately, "rational" pro-natalists paid scant attention to the potential mothers themselves. Gertrud Bäumer complained of this oversight when a conference held in Berlin in October 1915 called the Maintenance and Growth of Population excluded women's opinions; French feminist Nelly Roussell expressed similar alienation from pro-natalist discourse in her country for the same reason.[80] At least one birth supporter in Germany, Friedrich Naumann, did take women's feelings into account as he pledged to revitalize women's presumed maternal instincts.[81]

Most pro-natal propagandists operated on the assumption that a vague phenomenon called "modernity" had precipitated the fall in birth rates and could be blamed for the continuing low numbers of babies being born. Bäumer harangued against the "naked materialism" and the desire to raise one's "self-esteem" that pervaded modern life.[82] Warning that Germany would disappear unless it filled empty cribs, educator and Württemberg politician Mathilde Planck blamed greed and self-indulgence for women's unwillingness to birth more babies.[83] Others pointed fingers at industrialization, an acute housing shortage, and other urban phenomena including women's rights organizations (despite the fact that female activists also knit their brows at Germany's low birth rates) and education for females. German demographer Max Reuscher presaged that cultivating an intellectual life would leave women physically and morally drained and uninterested in family life.[84] Such comments reveal the contradiction between wartime measures and pro-natalist arguments. Neither allowances nor pensions were ever adequate for a woman to support a family without taking at least part-time work, nor were they meant to. But pro-natalists deplored and belittled wage work for women. According to eugenicist Alfred Grotjahn, female paid labor was "irrelevant to national production but fatal for population growth." Industrial output itself was compromised by female workers, according to French pro-natalist Louis Duval-Arnould, who likened them to effete immigrant laborers.[85] Yet pro-natalist writers—most of whom came from the professional classes—viewed the bourgeois woman as decadent, while the working-class female sacrificed herself; bourgeois housewives sought their own self-interest, rather than that of the nation.[86] (However, demographers noted that after the World War, German working-class families also grew smaller, narrowing perceived differences between the classes.[87]) On the other hand, some baby enthusiasts blamed men for the appalling decline in the birth rate. The anonymous author of one pro-natalist tract asserted that it was men's waiting too long to marry that had produced the empty crib syndrome.[88]

Part of women's disinclination to have more children was fear of childbirth, a reluctance that few public health workers were willing to admit; pronatalists, too, were loath to draw attention to the statistics. In 1915 U.S. feminist Katharine Anthony noted wryly that "there is no evidence that the death rate of women from child-birth has caused the governing classes many sleepless nights though the infant mortality rate has begun to do so." Anthony provided statistics from Prussia showing that between 1891 and 1900, 11 percent of the deaths of all women between the ages of twenty-five and forty years occurred in child-birth. Between the Franco-Prussian War and August 1914, Germany lost 400,000 mothers' lives, or ten times what it lost in soldiers' lives during the war with France.[89]

Minna Cauer pointed out that 18 German mothers lost their lives in childbirth daily, while in a year the maternal mortality figure stood at 6,570.[90] Across the Atlantic, A. B. Wolfe's review of Margaret Sanger's 1917 book *The Case for Birth Control* included Sanger's report that the number of deaths among women aged 15 to 44 in childbirth reached 9,876 in 1913, second only to the number resulting from tuberculosis, which stood at 26,265.[91] While BDF member Rosa Kempf touted childbearing as women's greatest sacrifice to the Fatherland, she also believed that the risks inherent in childbearing did not receive enough press (and were ignored in pro-natalist propaganda) relative to the dangers men faced in war.[92]

At the time of the First World War, the use of antisepsis to prevent maternal infection during childbirth was a relatively new phenomenon. In the late nineteenth century the trend in maternal mortality in European countries was uniformly high but variable; for example, in 1850 the rate of maternal deaths per 10,000 births was 51.5; in 1875, it reached a high of 70, then plummeted to around 38 in 1877. These wide annual variations in the number of maternal deaths were almost certainly due to the alterations in the virulence and prevalence of streptococcus. By 1910 the wide differentials had been lost. Medical experts in various countries responded differently to the introduction of antisepsis, either accepting the new germ theory upon which the use of antisepsis was based or discounting it, creating the disparity in maternal death rates in different countries. But a clear trend emerged by 1900, resulting in a downward slope of maternal death rates until the mid-1930s. However, there was a curious upward spike in maternal deaths after 1910. Why did maternal mortality suddenly increase, when medical experts and demographers expected improvement?[93]

Physician and medical historian Irvine Loudon noted that a rise in the number of abortions performed produced the sudden spike in maternal deaths.[94] While it is difficult to determine the commonality of the procedure, Cornelie Usborne argued that abortion probably constituted the most important factor in the long-term decline in the German birth rate.[95] Abortion and other forms of birth control were both anathema to pro-natalists, at least those who did not have eugenicist leanings. The prevalence of both suggests that there existed among women a strong desire to control their own reproductivity, a factor that may explain women's choices in the postwar years.

One report indicated that the low birth rate in Germany had less to do with gender ideology or maternal instinct than with empty stomachs. The Kaiser Wilhelm Institute for Labor Physiology in Berlin had filed a report on the impact of the economic blockade on citizens' health shortly after the signing of the armistice. "Doubtlessly the reduction of the birth rate has some relation to this phenomenon [the cessation of menstrual cycles among women for more than a year]," according to the Institute report.[96] The purposes of the blockade had been exactly that, proclaimed the English periodical *Weekly Dispatch*. Two months prior to the armistice, the journal had gleefully reported that thousands of "unborn Germans are destined for a life of physical inferiority." The head of official U.S. relief efforts in Europe, Herbert Hoover, sent a cadre of physicians and others to Berlin in 1918 to confirm that the inhabitants were suffering as badly as Germany's President Friedrich Ebert had claimed. The group reported that not only was the birth rate sinking, but child mortality had jumped by 30 percent. Pro-natalists' pleadings failed to move a hungry and malnourished German population to bear more children.[97]

As for a cure for the low birth rate, eugenicist and leading public health official Otto Krohne argued that what was needed to counter the selfishness of modern life was the selfless nationalism brought about by war. Only this, he declared, would erase his countrymen and -women's moral failure to fill empty bassinets.[98] Very few pro-natalists viewed the war as one of the causes of the low birth rate. In the immediate aftermath of the conflict, people expressed plenty of anxiety about the high death toll, but that angst did not translate into a desire for peace, at least not among those concerned by falling birth rates. While recalling the horrors evoked by the war's grim statistics—3 million Frenchmen dead or severely wounded, out of 8 million mobilized—the French senator Léon Jénouvrier suggested that the Gallic people must be persuaded that the nation's population was not depleted from the war, but rather from babies not being born.[99]

But not everyone could be convinced. Havelock Ellis's 1917 book *Essays in War Time* argued that the alarmist talk of "race suicide" on the part of pronatalists and eugenicists missed the genuine obliteration of humanity that was occurring on Great War battlefields.[100] The German women's magazine *Die Frauenbewegung* (The Women's Movement) reported on a 1917 study conducted in Copenhagen in which the causes of Europe's low population were enumerated. Heading the list were losses due to battle; next were heavy losses in prisons of war, followed by civilian losses due to war; fourth were deaths due to refugee problems; last on the list were low birth rates.[101]

The militarists soldiered on, however. One anonymous German author lingered in competitive mode a decade after the war had ended. He or she gleefully reported that Germany's birth rate in 1928 was bigger than France's. The French, the writer chided, knew this but masked their inner weaknesses with protective belts of steel and cement and weaponry, an allusion to plans for the Maginot Line.[102] Historian Karen Hagemann called this attitude the "friend/enemy dichotomy," whereby citizens of at-war nations cannot let go of wartime antagonisms. Bitter feelings, she recorded, lasted well into the postwar years.[103]

Other Germans took a more sober view of their neighbor's natality. An official at the Prussian Ministry of the Interior noted that while France took 70 years to lower its birth rate by 8 per 1,000 births, Germany's plummeted in only 12 years.[104] Gertrud Bäumer scanned such statistics warily. When one peeks into the nursery, the women's rights leader admitted, one sees the army corps, particularly when contemplating Germany's bulging neighbor to the east, Russia. Conservative Germans saw in Russia not only a military but an ideological threat: The proletariat revolution could spread if western European defenses were low, a circumstance that went hand-in-hand with low birth rates. Germans obsessed that Russia's enormous population could overflow into the less-populated regions of Europe; in view of that possibility, a Catholic pro-natalist wondered how any government could tolerate the presence of contraceptives at all.[105] "We bring only one more to life each year," lamented the never-married, childless Bäumer, "while they [the Russians] bring two or three."[106]

BDF co-founder Helene Lange (also unwed and without offspring) ratcheted Bäumer's urgency up a notch by warning that Germany stood to lose its international reputation as cultural leader if it could not jump-start a rise in births. "From the woman's standpoint," proclaimed Lange, "the population question is not simply a matter of military power . . . but rather linking [larger families] to our hopes for a 'bigger Germany' in a cultural sense." Writing in November 1915, Lange admitted that, given that the war was dragging on longer than anticipated, it was tempting to equate more babies with a stronger military.[107] On the other side of the Rhine River, French writers also drew comparisons between themselves and their arch-rivals. Germany, pronatalists cried, had produced five soldiers for every two birthed in France. Not a little fear-mongering occurred among Gallic birth enthusiasts, who distributed postcards displaying the dreaded "two against five" theme.[108] For both nations, low birth rates translated into military weakness; conversely, high birth rates signaled national vitality.[109] One French postcard depicted a soldier on leave, coming home to his wife and his farm during sowing season; the result, shown in an inset, is a baby *poilu* complete with rifle and a *képi*, the French military cap. Fathering children, an extension of a man's military duty, united home front with battlefront. Given the high numbers of widows and mothers dressed in mourning on European streets, such postcards, while meant to be humorous, must have seemed ironic at best, morbid at worst.[110]

Manly virility, an aspect of masculine youth thought to have grown flabby during peacetime, played a key role in the reasons given by U.S. congressmen for voting in favor of American intervention in the war in 1917.[111] In addition, boys had to be instilled with hatred toward the enemy if they were to become successful soldiers. The U.S. reformer Jane Addams argued that antagonism between different nationalities was a learned behavior.[112] Before the war, French schools instructed boys to grow up to be militaristic citizens and to hate Germans, according to historian Mona Siegel; the two went hand-in-hand.[113] In battle, French soldiers were encouraged to make a "good thrust" with their bayonets and with their manhood; the result would be a double victory, the first on the battlefield and the second in the nursery. The proliferation of pro-natalist propaganda represented increasing male sexual anxieties after the war, wrote historian Mary Louise Roberts.[114] The emphasis on manly virtue did not escape feminist pro-natalists such as Helene Lange, who argued it was high time that men took responsibility for the sinking German birth rate. She thought that educating boys about marital sex offered the best avenue toward assuring that men did their part in fillings empty bassinets.

Lange's efforts to equalize gender relations aside, most women still accepted primary responsibility for the birthing and caring of children after the war. In this respect, the conclusion of hostilities meant a return to "gender normalcy," because with the demobilization of male soldiers, "normal" family life could begin again . . . at least for those whose loved ones did return. In addition to gender normalcy, nation-states also acted to ensure racial normalcy in the aftermath of the war.[115]

In 1920, Germany passed the *Reichsversorgungsgesetz* (RVG) law that revamped its previous system, unifying and simplifying the nation's pension structure. Several of the law's provisions related to war widows, including the stipulation that upon remarriage widows surrendered their war pensions but would receive a gratuity. In addition, the law stated that widows who wed foreign or stateless men would forfeit their "wedding gift" as well.[116] The RVG helped the government insinuate its way into the reproductive lives of its female citizens by encouraging them to choose compatriots as mates and as fathers of their children and penalizing them if they failed to do so. The French government, too, took steps to determine who would sire the children born within French borders. Male foreign laborers relocating to France were welcomed as replacements for husbands lost in the Great War, but only if "racially appropriate": These included Italian, Spanish, and Polish men. African and Asian workers, though already in France, were discouraged.[117]

Between 1870 and 1939 physicians, scientists, churchmen, politicians, and others noted with alarm the decline in birth rates specifically in western Europe. Genetic theories developed and spread that analyzed this decrease; interpretations of the hereditary character of social behavior coincided with the rise of genetic theories. "These ideas helped transform discussion of population growth into arguments about the perceived decline of the inherent qualities of elites, nations, or races," explained historian J. M. Winter. Winter noted wryly that if Hitler did anything positive, it was to discredit these ideas; after World War II no one evoked public fear through eugenics. Pro-natalist arguments were made on class and race bases; some individuals were worried only about decline in their own nations, while others were concerned about the "yellow peril" and its African equivalent above and across national boundaries.[118]

The Great War hastened racial "mixing." The French, German, and British armies had all benefited from 600,000 or so "nonwhite" colonial soldiers fighting in Europe during the conflict. A French college professor mused that his country's military had had to turn to its colonies for defense because the deplorable population decline had resulted in France's becoming enfeebled. A British Member of Parliament explained France's use of African troops as the failure of its "white manhood."[119] Ironically—given their own nation's use of African troops—German men and women, including politicians, intellectuals, and religious leaders, objected to the stationing of French colonial troops in the French zone of the occupied Rhineland after the war, generating fears about colonials allegedly attacking white women. Their crusade became known as the Rhineland horror campaign.[120]

Meanwhile, as France and Germany took steps to return to racial "normalcy" after the war, the U.S. Congress passed restrictive immigration laws in the 1920s aimed at excluding Asian immigrants, and the government deported Mexican immigrants in the early 1930s.[121] But immigration restrictions were not enough for Abraham Lincoln biographer and *Delineator* editor Honoré Willsie. "If America had closed her doors to immigration in 1830 and the birthrate of that period had continued for seventy years," mused Willsie, "instead of the seventy-six millions of people that we boasted of in 1900, we should have had one hundred millions [*sic*]. This one hundred million would have been a homogeneous people of strongly Anglo-Saxon type and ideal. The chaos that has resulted from the constant introduction of new types would have been avoided." Bemoaning falling birth rates in New England whence had come "the American spirit," Willsie concluded that because women play a key role in establishing national birth rates, they should consider having more babies.[122]

In Germany, racial hygienists and social hygienists had a common interest in reproduction; but not all medical experts and social scientists agreed on the admissibility of "Aryan" racial categories or the value of abortion and sterilization for presumed non-Aryans. Members of the Munich Racial Hygiene Society and the Pan-German League demanded new territories to export "racially compromised" Germans. But the Ministry of Justice deemed induced abortion and sterilization on racial grounds illegal. The German government was obsessed in this period with quantity, not quality, so eugenics did not play a large role.[123] However, Paul Weindling perceived a shift away from moral to racial arguments after 1918 because the revolution and postwar chaos challenged national survival. In 1919 the Prussian Statistical Office predicted that the German nation faced extermination; medical officials condemned the peace terms as an attempt to obliterate the German "race." Consequently, positive eugenics and racial biology were heralded as avenues to national salvation. At each phase of the Weimar Republic the eugenics lobby strengthened its hand, beginning with the Rhineland horror campaign.[124]

The response to pro-natal propaganda among feminists sounded relatively weak, although gauging genuine sentiment during war is a difficult prospect given censorship. As soldiers marched and battles raged, women's rights advocates in Germany and France, desiring to be included among the ranks of the patriotic, urged mothers and potential mothers to provide their nation's military with more children.[125] In 1916 and 1917, Gertrud Bäumer's *Die Frau* and Minna Cauer's magazine *Die Frauenbewegung* each printed one essay critical of Germany's pro-birth campaigns, written by Gesine Nordbeck and Rosa Schwann-Schneider, respectively. But in both cases, the periodicals followed up the critiques with pro-natal pieces (penned by Bäumer in *Die Frau* and Mathilde Planck in *Die Frauenbewegung*).[126] To put it another way, pro-natalists got the last word in both publications. At times, the suppression of differing opinions was blatant. In France, a postcard circulating on battle-fields depicted a newborn hatching from an egg and, eyeing the battle scene before it, grouses, "if this is life I prefer to go back inside." Military authorities requested that the card be re-drawn with a different caption.[127] Even after the war, French pacifist critics of pro-natalist literature faced censors. In 1932, Jeanne Humbert quoted from Victor Margueritte's 1931 book *The Human Homeland* in her antiwar speech; police arrested her under the charge of dispersing anti-natalist propaganda. The passage from Margueritte's book that the government found objectionable was this: "first have no children as long as countries have the right to kill them."[128] In the late 1930s, Madeleine Pelletier's arguments that contraception and abortion would improve women's quality of life led to her arrest; she died in a mental clinic in 1939.[129]

Female pacifists' responses to the pro-natal movement ranged from reinforcing the presumed link between maternity and pacifism—which did not specifically address raising national birth rates—to renouncing pro-natalism by calling for potential mothers to launch "birth strikes." The pacifism espoused by Lida Gustava Heymann and Anita Augspurg, members of the German section of the Women's International League for Peace and Freedom (WILPF), emphasized women's innate nonviolence, which operated as an extension of their maternal instincts, versus men's presumed natural inclinations to aggression.[130] In this formula, politicized women could help reduce the likelihood of war by voting against it. In opposing the WILPF, the BDF argued that women's natural desire to protect their children led them to support the war. The WILPF's essentialist notions were central to organized pacifism before, during, and after the war, even among members of the mixed-gender pacifist organization *Bund Neues Vaterland* (Federation for a New Fatherland), founded in November 1914. This organization and other mainstream pacifists counted on the Social Democratic Party (SPD) and one of its leaders, Clara Bohm-Schuch, to instill a "will to maternity" among women. While not discussing national birth rates, pacifists like Bohm-

Schuch encouraged motherhood as a buffer that would act as a counter to (presumably male) violent aggression.[131]

Rosa Schwann-Schneider, critic of the pro-birth movement, posited that women's wartime experiences drove the flagging birth rate. Schwann-Schneider could find no other reason for Germany's empty cribs than the simple fact that women were unwilling to bring children into a brutal world. Potential mothers reported not wanting to be pregnant. "Something is broken [in the world]," proclaimed Schwann-Schneider, "and will not be whole again." A gender essentialist (one who assumes that feminine and masculine traits are inborn rather than learned), she asserted that men could not understand women's reluctance because they had not given birth. Schwann-Schneider then made a statement akin to announcing that the emperor had no clothes: Women were not to blame for the low birth rate. Instead, the war—and by extension those who had instigated it and fought it—was the real culprit.[132] A soldier's wife in Strassdorf, Germany, confirmed Schwann-Schneider's contention when she wrote to her husband, a prisoner of war, in August 1917: "I am so sick and tired of human life that I want to cut my own and my children's throat. . . . You have to be the most stupid person on God's earth when you have children." The rest of her letter paints a dismal picture of parenthood during war.[133] Research conducted later confirmed the view that people blamed the war for social ills. By 1935, when Adolf Hitler reinstated conscription, the outlawed Social Democratic Party sent informants out to observe and interview people about their attitudes toward the possibility of another war. In Saxony, the SPD informant reported that war widows, when asked about another war, suggested pointedly that the government meet its obligations to Great War victims first before it made any moves to begin a new one.[134] In addition, survivors recording their lives in Helene Hurwitz-Stranz's anthology outlined their reasons for not bringing children into a world where war still threatened.

The conundrum of essentialist feminism and pacifism made it difficult for purveyors of this way of thinking to make much headway in the interwar years. If women argued that only they held the key to a peaceful world, then once suffragists achieved the vote, they had to demonstrate that indeed the female political voice wanted peace. But as Elizabeth Harvey and others have shown, and as Gertrud Bäumer demonstrated repeatedly, women did not vote uniformly on any issues, women certainly did not consistently argue against war, and in fact they tended to support right-wing, conservative parties during and after the Weimar Republic.[135] Even the mighty BDF, divided and facing financial difficulties, was "demoralized and in disarray" by 1932 as a result of women's disinterest in feminist issues.[136] Hurwitz-Stranz's contributors often presented their peaceful natures as being an aspect of their roles as mothers; but by claiming that their children had a right to live in a peaceful world, they were making arguments that became tied less to gender and more to human rights.

Helene Stöcker also offered a way out of the essentialist-feminist-pacifist bind. Stöcker thought that both sexes had an interest in rejecting war, and, departing from most German feminists of her day, she did not regard women as "natural" pacifists; rather, she argued that women had a right to bear and educate their children in a world free of war.[137] Founded by Stöcker and others in 1904, the *Bund für Mutterschutz* (League for the Protection of Motherhood, or BfM) called for the reform of sexual ethics and the transformation of the relationship between women and men. The group called for legislation to support single mothers and their children. The BfM demanded legal equality for illegitimate children and the right of women to sue for divorce. Finally, the group encouraged reform-minded men to join the organization and work in partnership with the women, while most German women's organizations worked separately from men.[138] The BfM, with Stöcker at its helm, represented the epitome of the modernist culture that pro-natalists blamed for the nation's low birth rate.

The outbreak of World War I was a decisive moment in Stöcker's life. Whereas she had been a staunch believer in the progressive nature of human development, the war rent this notion asunder. The call for women's patriotic support of their nations fell on Stöcker's deaf ears. For Stöcker, the rallying cry of *Vaterlandsliebe* (love of homeland) was abhorrent because in its exclusion of non-Germans, it contradicted her all-embracing respect for humanity. Gesine Nordbeck, a Swiss citizen, agreed. She offered an alternative perspective to Gertrud Bäumer's view of women's patriotic duty to the state as mothers in the pages of Bäumer's own venerable publication *Die Frau*. Nordbeck deemed wartime as a time in which *zwei Gesetzen* (two ways of thinking) animated public discourse. The first held that the state did what God and Christianity would have people do. The other she deemed *echt* (real) Christianity, which directed humans to love their neighbors as they did themselves. Nordbeck reminded her readers that Germany didn't have to be big or powerful to earn its inhabitants' love: Rather, people loved their Fatherland, asserted Nordbeck, because their ancestors had lived there and because they bore their children there. "Having read the letters written by wounded soldiers in field hospitals who write to their mothers stating that they hope they don't have to go back to the front," penned Nordbeck, "we now have to ask ourselves, in regards to the birth rate question, whether it isn't better not to have any children than to send them out into this grim scene."[139]

Stöcker encouraged women to join a birth strike, not only to deny the state sheep for the next slaughter but also because mothers could not raise healthy children during a war.[140] Her slogan for the BfM during the conflict became "the protection of motherhood through the protection of humanity," combining her two foremost causes: mothers and their rights, and pacifism.[141] Agreeing with fellow feminists Katharine Anthony and Rosa Kempf that the dangers of childbirth went unnoticed, Stöcker declared that women who bore "life at the risk of their own, wanted to do so for the sake of life, not of death."[142] Stöcker's advocacy of birth control in its most extreme form of the birth strike offered women the ability to shape the future of their nations after the war. If citizenship mandated men's armed service to the state, then women could at least shrink the size of the military by refusing to birth more children. In addition, women could breach the link between citizenship and military service. This move would enable females to share equally in citizenship with their male counterparts. Stöcker's rhetoric mobilized war widows to challenge nationalistic paradigms by refusing to join the pro-natal movement.

When attacked as unpatriotic, Stöcker responded that, because childhood and infant mortality still threatened women and their children (especially so during wartime, considering the effects of total war in the form of the hunger blockade), birthing babies under such conditions squandered national wealth and amounted to the abuse of motherhood. Stöcker used the term "rebirth" at end of war to summon the need for a moral and intellectual regeneration, not the crib-filling meaning of rebirthing as advocated by pro-natalists. German militarism, she reminded readers, formed the underlying force behind the violation of Belgian neutrality and ultimately the vengeful Treaty of Versailles. What was needed in Germany, she argued (in agreement with Nordbeck), were policies that reflected the notion that people should treat others as they would like to be treated.[143]

The debate over whether the phenomenon of nationalism had turned premodern people into modern citizens, united, obedient, loyal to the "national fraternity" and liberated from the slavery of traditional social hierarchies (as in feudalism), or whether nationalism constituted a conservative reaction *to* modernity and social change has only recently included women's social, political, and economic conditions. Women have played an important role in nationalism, given the ideology's adherence to the notion of ethnic purity. If

"German blood" formed a required component of the German citizen, then the nation-state needed to control the female body, from which flows the blood. "Controlling women," concluded Patrizia Albanese, "becomes a way of protecting or reviving the nation" after war.[144] During the Weimar period, Germany offered women liberation from traditional roles, including access to the ballot, open doors to education, and relaxed abortion restrictions. But Adolf Hitler reversed the last of those forward steps. Fascism, ascendant in Germany and Italy in the interwar years, symbolized a revolt against modernity. In France, women did not receive the vote until after the Second World War, and emancipation for them after the First World War, according to Eugen Weber, "moved with positively glacial speed."[145] When women are drawn into the equation, it becomes difficult to see how nationalism could be interpreted as a liberating force, even while acknowledging that some political and social gains were made.

And what happened to the modern, twentieth-century New Woman who had arrived before the Great War began?[146] While modernity and its meanings continued to be debated in the aftermath of the war, the history of war widows indicates that women were increasingly defining for themselves what it meant to be a modern female citizen. Except for the 40 percent of war widows who remarried, being a female citizen required enough *Selbstständigkeit* to be able to make one's own livelihood and choose whether and when to birth children. Johanna Boldt provided for her two children and appeared to have chosen remarriage when it suited her. While widows were willing to sacrifice their own desires and needs for the sake of their offspring, those leaving behind a written record declared an unwillingness to do the state's bidding. Rosa Schwann-Schneider, who borrowed the idea from Helene Stöcker, reminded *Die Frauenbewegung* readers in the spring of 1917 that "in our times, the state is there for the individual, not the other way around!"[147] Indeed, "just as conscription can only be forced on a self-governing nation by raising the spectre of fear of conquest," wrote a reviewer of Adelyne More's book *Uncontrolled Breeding*, "so the slavery of perpetual maternities can only be forced on awakened womanhood by the specious appeal of self-immolation for the good of the State." The author of *Uncontrolled Breeding* saw only one ray of hope: "At present it is possible for powerful interests to play one nation against another, so that none will take the first step [toward disarmament]. If after the war the same mad fertility race is to continue, no settlement, no form of international organization will avail to prevent a recurrence of the catastrophe [of the Great War]." It would be up to transnational feminists to prevent it.[148]

Epilogue

The Second World War ignited just twenty years after the signing of the peace treaty that ended the First World War. In the later conflict political ideologies, such as fascism and communism, were at stake. Many more nations aimed much more toxic weapons against one another. The horrors of trench warfare identified so closely with the earlier war had transformed into an air war that peppered battle lines, pummeled villages and towns, and punctured European landmarks in city centers. In the later conflict the fighter pilot was too common to be considered "romantic." The *Vaterland* was reduced to rubble in places, unlike the First World War that had left the German landscape largely undisturbed. Because of newly developed technologies, propaganda spread more quickly. While genocide—a word coined during the Second World War—shamed humankind in both conflicts, the Holocaust obliterated many more millions of people than did the 1915 Armenian genocide. The atomic bomb that ended World War II spawned a new breed of international antagonism known as the Cold War. Destruction and death overall occurred on a much more vast scale.

Almost 300,000 U.S. military personnel lost their lives in the later conflict, and 83,500 war widows survived them. Little had changed for Second World War widows when compared with their Great War foremothers. In the 1940s more women heeded Uncle Sam's call and helped produce the weapons that killed other women's husbands. In Germany, the Nazi regime required six months of service to the state from single women, regarded as the female equivalent of young men's compulsory military service (feminist Minna Cauer finally got her wish—she had championed female service during the earlier conflict).[1] In both wars, female employment in war-related industry was, by and large, intended to be only for the duration.[2] Like their Great War predecessors, widows received compensation from the U.S. and German governments for their losses, but once again that benefit was contingent upon the woman's remaining a widow. The stigma attached to a widow's choosing a second husband had allegedly disappeared, and yet war widows continued to worry what others thought of their plans. The specter of the frivolous, self-indulgent female derided during the Great War reappeared in the 1940s.[3]

Feelings of grief and despair over losing one's life partner had not changed much, either. Mrs. Abe C. Webb's sorrow over her husband's death during the war nearly drove her to take her own life. In July 1946, the Canton, North Carolina, war widow penned a letter to her husband's army chaplain, Ben L. Rose, a fellow North Carolinian by then living in New York City. Mrs. Webb confessed to Rose that she had lost her Christian faith since facing the death of her husband. She began her letter by asking Rose if he remembered Webb, a member of Troop E 113th Cavalry who had been killed in a vehicle accident on May 8, 1945. She reminded the chaplain that Webb had attended his services frequently during his army stint. Mrs. Webb confessed to Rose that while her husband had been away she had prayed and had had faith that he would return to her and their two small children. She assured Rose that she had not doubted Webb's homecoming and had kept God's commandments, and now she could not understand why her husband's life had not been spared. "I blame God," she cried, "for taking part of me away."

Reverend Rose responded to the war widow's inner turmoil by enumerating the instances in the Bible where God tested believers. To comfort her, he assured her that her husband's faith had been with him on the day that he died. No follow-up letter from Mrs. Webb appears in Rose's papers, which he donated to the North Carolina State Archives in 1999. About Mrs. Webb's missive, the Presbyterian minister appended a typewritten notation dated September 1, 1999, explaining that the enclosed letter had been written by a grieving wife whose husband had been killed in the service. "The sad part of it," admitted Rose, "is that Abe Webb was killed . . . the very day the Germans surrendered." Webb and some of his buddies had been poking around among some abandoned machinery on an air field that the U.S. Army had taken, according to the chaplain. Webb had been toying with a forklift when it turned over on him and crushed him to death. "He lived through nine months of combat," lamented Rose, "and was killed on the day hostilities ended by a sad turn of events." Mrs. Webb's letter to Rose does not indicate whether she knew of the exact circumstances of her husband's death. If the First World War set any precedents, she may well have not been fully informed. Would knowing the precise details have helped or hurt this widow's ability to cope with her soldier-husband's death? Would the anger that she had directed at God have instead been aimed at the military or at the senseless destruction of the war itself?[4]

Mrs. Webb's sad state is reminiscent of Nancy Payne Marsh's 1918–19 letters to the U.S. military following her husband's death. In Marsh's case, the exact circumstances surrounding her mate's illness and death were finally accurately reported to her by another army chaplain. Prior to that February 1919 letter, Marsh had received two contradictory accounts of her husband's final days. Although Marsh did not appear to be consoled by her Gold Star pilgrimage to her husband's grave in France, many Great War widows were at least appreciative of their government's form of restitution for their losses. No Gold Star voyages were offered to Second World War widows, however, even though many more American soldiers lost their lives on foreign soil. The government again created a series of U.S. military cemeteries overseas and a set of rules regulating the erection of headstones and monuments to honor them that it hoped would inspire national unity. The body of another Unknown Soldier arrived stateside for the ritual hero's burial at Arlington National Cemetery, while popular-magazine articles recommended that the fallen be laid to rest on battlefields where they had helped achieve an American victory. But ultimately it was up to widows, children, parents, and siblings—in that order—to determine where their soldiers' bodies would finally rest. Once again, a majority chose to bring the remains of their loved ones back home.[5]

Lilian Rixey's 1946 *Life* magazine article about U.S. war widow Bernadine Secord Doyle reported that more than two-thirds of Second World War widows were under the age of thirty, and 21,000 mourning wives had already birthed children by the time they learned of their husbands' deaths. Doyle, at age twenty-four, fit both those categories as she cared for two young boys. She confided to *Life* readers that after a year and a half since her loss, she felt herself ready to live and love again. Rixey confirmed that after their spouses had been dead a year or more, most widows desired another mate. The reporter interpreted this time period as indicative of the widows' loyalty to their soldier-husbands. "Not since the post–Civil War period have widows been praised for devoting their lives to their husbands' memories," proclaimed Rixey, neglecting to mention the lobbying efforts of the Gold Star mothers and widows, or perhaps not realizing that widows did participate, although not as vocally as mothers had. But then Rixey went on to suggest that Civil War widows' loyalty had been only superficial. Reminiscent of the American Legion Post president who doubted Emma Downer's devotion to her dead soldier-husband, Rixey explained that during the Civil War "gossips usually whispered that a widows' decorous loyalty was determined only by the extent to which she had nothing better to do."

When Shelton Doyle Jr. responded to his draft notice, his bride followed him from army camp to army camp until his unit shipped overseas. Doyle was killed at Aachen, Germany, in 1944 just before the Battle of the Bulge. The second lieutenant had carried with him a $10,000 government life insurance policy. Combined with his Social Security (a program not yet in place during the First World War) and her war pension, Doyle's widow and the two children managed on an income of $141 a month ($1,750 in present-day dollars), reported Rixey. Bernadine's father invited his daughter and grandchildren to move into his house, where her expenses amounted to $75 a month. Her father-in-law cautioned her that he would stand by her in any financial emergency so long as she remained a widow, and her mother-in-law confided to her that she hoped that Bernadine would not remarry. Rixey noted that if the widow were to wed again her income would be cut to $38 a month because she would lose both her widow's pension and her husband's Social Security check.

Assuring readers that "today no one would deny a war widow her right to remarry," Rixey nevertheless enumerated the problems widows faced when thinking about taking second vows. Widows tied down with children were challenged even to meet men, she opined, let alone date them. The widow must take into consideration her in-laws, who may be frightened of losing contact with their grandchildren. "Would her first husband's parents ever really forgive the war widow who puts that stranger in the place of their dead soldier son?" pondered the writer. Rixey presumed that war widows were not in position to support themselves or their children when she proclaimed that a prospective husband would have to be prepared to provide for a ready-made family. The *Life* magazine article included several interviews with people who knew Bernadine and her family. One respondent identified herself as a war widow who had remarried; she advised Doyle that if she did decide to wear a gold ring again, she should defer in all decisions to her new husband, including the disciplining of her two boys.[6]

Meanwhile, across the Atlantic, 1.2 million German victims of the Second World War left widows to mourn their deaths in Berlin's western zones of occupation and in the newly created Federal Republic of Germany. Added to these were vast numbers of divorced, never-married, and other widowed women, creating what historian Elizabeth D. Heinemann has called an army of "women standing alone" in postwar Germany. An initial postwar census conducted in occupied West Germany revealed an imbalance of 7 million women over their male counterparts.[7] Because Allied bombing campaigns had been so destructive, and because younger men were often absent, able-bodied women in Berlin became *Trümmerfrauen*, or "rubble women," clearing away debris with buckets and rebuilding structures with mortar. Somewhat reminiscent of Heather Jones's "gendered reciprocal economy" created in the First World War, in this case surviving women re-made what military men had destroyed. Second World War women, though, were much more intimately involved in the destructive part of that formula than they had been during the earlier conflict.[8]

The new government created by the Federal Republic of Germany replaced the Allied-administered government in 1949. Mourning wives in West Germany suffered from the same problems plaguing their Great War predecessors: They needed to know where their next meal would come from (in this conflict it was the postwar years that were the leanest for Germans), how to secure their pensions (which were modest), and how to find employment (very difficult in circumstances that included continued discrimination against wage-earning women). Lawmakers in West Germany formed distinct categories of war widows,; these in turn affected the amount of pension they received. For example, they deemed "lightly widowed women" to be young, to have been married only a few years before the husband died, to be able-bodied, and to be childless. These widows received the smallest pensions. Second marriages for West German women in most cases meant losing their widows' pension, and many Second World War widows chose "*Onkelehe*" (cohabitation) instead to retain their benefits. "You can get by without a husband," quipped one Second World War widow. "I mean, you don't have to go out and buy a cow just because you want a little milk."[9] But the moral stigma attached to this arrangement had not disappeared, either. German war widows labored under the added burden of their association with a conflict that everyone wanted to forget as quickly as possible.[10] In East Germany, where the German Democratic Republic was formed in 1949, war widows and their pensions were effectively eliminated by laws that banned sex discrimination, forcing war widows—with or without children—to find other sources of income.[11]

Like their Great War predecessors, German war widows in the Second World War donned some kind of visual indicator of their widowhood, although not the deep mourning dress and accessories that Johanna Boldt wore. War orphan Hubertus Thiel told the story of his father's disappearance during the waning days of the Third Reich in April 1945, and of his mother's widowhood. Thiel's father, Hans-Jürgen, had worked as a forester and game warden before the war and had responded to his draft call in 1939. On April 25, 1945, during a lull in combat he visited an aunt living in Berlin, who begged him to stay, renounce the war, and take off his uniform because there could be no more point to the fighting. The *Waffen*-SS soldier replied that he could not because his men needed him. He left Berlin, and his family never heard from him again. Hubertus Thiel, then a Bavarian *Volksschule* student, remembered that his mother, Ilse Thiel, wore a black armband to commemorate her husband's death on every *Totensonntag*, Germany's day of remembrance. Frau Thiel taught school until 1958, when she asked the German government to declare her missing soldier-husband dead so that she could receive a widow's pension. She never remarried and died, alone, in her house in Würzburg, Bavaria in 1990.[12]

Despite the many similarities between First and Second World War widows, there were some departures from tradition in the lives of widows victimized by the later conflict. By the 1950s and 1960s, many women in Europe and North America began to renounce the ways in which their identities were based solely on their marital status. Headstones marking the graves of females were less often marked with the words "wife of" or "mother of."[13] Germany's many "stand alone women" undoubtedly had much to do with these changes. Geertje van Os drew lines connecting the welfare state, a result of the Great War, and women's greater sense of self-reliance, because widows' pensions had helped them to become less economically dependent on men. In addition, van Os demonstrated that the later conflict marked the disappearance of mourning clothes among Dutch widows. She attributed this transformation to the fact that by the time of the Second World War, people had become afraid of death, while concomitantly demanding more personal happiness in life. Widows wearing black posed a constant, irritating reminder of death's existence, and their mourning appearance and rituals became taboo, too.[14]

Bernadine Doyle evaded the subject of mortality altogether in her wartime household. She thought it best to hide their father's last days from his children. "I have tried to save my sons the shock of their father's death as much as I could," she confided to Lilian Rixey. "I thought it best not to tell them anything at all. In my father's home we are always careful not to mention the word 'death' in front of them." As Doyle continued, she explained that her oldest son, Jimmy, then aged four, continued to post letters to his father in the army even after Doyle knew he had died. When V-E Day came, Jimmy naturally wanted to know when Daddy was coming home. Bernadine explained to him that the Germans had hurt him and that he had gone to heaven.[15]

By the time of the war in Vietnam, Americans' negative reaction to mortality had grown acute. Twenty thousand U.S. wives lost their husbands in that conflict. A *Time* magazine journalist noted that in the United States, survivors were confronted by well-meaning friends and relatives who failed to comfort them because the subject of death embarrassed them. Professional therapists were called upon to help the bereaved and guide them through an identifiable "grief cycle." The U.S. military harnessed the power of experience as it set up "rap sessions" among women who had been widowed for some time and those who had only recently learned of their mates' passing. The women's liberation movement and sexual revolution of the late 1960s had instigated a change among these younger-generation war widows; an additional purpose of the sessions was to help mourners make the shift from widow to single woman again, and to rebuild "their social and sexual lives. At first, most are unable to consider remarrying," explained the *Time* reporter, "but they eventually come to see themselves as available single women, although with special memories and, often, children." One psychiatrist involved in the process cautioned that American society had not yet progressed sufficiently to accept widows' swift change from mourner to alluring female: The sexual revolution had apparently gone only so far. "People want widows to marry," he suggested, "but not to date," an astute observation about war widows that could have been made during the Great War almost two generations earlier.[16]

Organizing had aided widows in both the First and Second World Wars in nearly all the belligerent countries as they sought compensation for the loss of their breadwinning husbands. Janis Lomas compared British war widows' experiences with those of Australia, where the government published the names of dead soldiers' wives. Mourners there formed an organization, the War Widows' Guild of Australia, in 1945 and it became a lobbying powerhouse for social justice and welfare: Members asked for more money from their government and they got it. In England anonymity prevented war widows from organizing.[17]

In the twenty-first century, war widows are finding one another with much more ease, and their organizations are becoming more transnational. The nature of warfare has changed, as well. The ubiquitous "woman behind the man" paradigm seen in U.S. and German World War propaganda posters, wherein women take over men's jobs on the domestic front while their warriors fight on the battlefront, has now largely vanished. The U.S. military has become more open to placing women in combat roles in the twenty-first century. The feminized home front has given way to stay-at-home dads kissing their uniformed wives as they march off to war (although women still made up only 14 percent of the U.S. active military in 2008).[18] Combat-ready wives will have the inevitable consequence of creating more war widowers. At the same time (and perhaps not merely coincidental to the growing feminization of the military), national militaries frequently engage in humanitarian missions. In addition, international alliances such as the North Atlantic Treaty Organization have often replaced single-nation combatants. Transnational religious organizations have targeted Western nations, and these have fought back against a stateless enemy.[19] But while some aspects of combat have changed, other wartime traditions remain intact. The nation-state continues to prescribe how survivors should interpret warriors' deaths, for example. During the 2003 war in Iraq, the U.S. president comforted military families by using language that hearkened back to the Great War: "The families of the fallen," declared George W. Bush, "can rest assured that your loved ones died for a noble cause."[20]

War widows in the twenty-first century are receiving international recognition. In 2010, diverse organizations lobbied the United Nations, a body formed at the end of the Second World War, for recognition of International Widows Day in order to publicize the plight of widows victimized by armed conflicts, including the wars in Iraq and Afghanistan.[21] Those battles led to a transnational organization called CIVIC, or Campaign for Innocent Victims of Conflict, formed to benefit the greater number of civilians hurt in conflicts. One of Helene Hurwitz-Stranz's memoirists had imagined such a group forming after the Great War. Activist and humanitarian Marla Ruzicka visited hospitals and refugee centers after the United States began its bombing campaign in Afghanistan in October 2003. Troubled by the lack of accountability for explosions hitting civilian targets, she founded CIVIC in late 2003. Ruzicka died in 2005 from a roadside bombing in Iraq. CIVIC's headquarters are in Washington, D.C., where the organization advocates that warring powers, regardless of national affiliation, make restitution to civilians harmed by the armed conflicts they provoke.[22]

The U.S. military action in Afghanistan inspired another transnational social justice and welfare movement, this one headquartered in the San Francisco Bay Area. Melanie Gadener, a student at the University of California Berkeley, used the corporate business models she developed for career self-reliance to serve Afghan widows in need. In March 2004, Gadener met Heba Tarzi when Tarzi came to the United States as a participant in the Afghan Women Leadership Exchange Program. Wanting to extend the servicing of widows in Afghanistan, Afghani widow Shalah Arsala, Tarzi, and Gadener designed a pilot program called Grants for Self-Reliance. Their first beneficiaries consisted of a group of five indigent

Afghani war widows and their children. The short-term grants funded by the organization helped pay for widows' basic education, vocational training, child care, transportation expenses, and supplies for the widows to begin home-based businesses. In addition, the organization established the Widows Research and Support Center in Kabul, Afghanistan, in May 2006.

War memorials now appear on the Internet, where widows from former enemy nations can share their experiences with one another. A Web site called the "Widows of War Living Memorial" appeared in 2000 to coincide with the twenty-fifth anniversary of the end of U.S. involvement in Vietnam. The Web site resulted from Barbara Sonneborn's documentary *Regret to Inform* (1998), a film featuring U.S. war widows' attempts to reconcile both their own sorrowful experiences of widowhood with those of Vietnamese war widows as well as the damage their soldier-husbands may have caused that made war widows out of Vietnamese wives. Sonneborn traveled to Vietnam and toured with a Vietnamese war widow the place where her husband died. First World War widows such as Elisabeth Macke could only *imagine* that wives residing in enemy nations felt and experienced the same sorrows and deprivations, but they rarely met their counterparts face-to-face. The interactive Web site constitutes "a place where widows of all wars can record and share their stories with people throughout the world." Cyber-memorials encourage transnational perspectives of wars because participants from both the presumed victorious and defeated nations can post to them. During the two World Wars, survivors were restricted by the U.S. military on where and what kinds of commemorative markers they could place at their loved ones' graves. Cyber-memorials carry no such restrictions. There are no authorities to mediate between a war widow's memories of her late soldier-husband and the official commemoration of the conflict itself, and no governmental entity to fabricate unity out of disparate experiences or responses. There are downsides to memorial Web sites, however. When "Widows of War Living Memorial" first appeared in 2000, it contained stories from Vietnamese and U.S. victims of the conflict. Now, ten years later, only two stories remain on the site, and the words of the Vietnamese widows have vanished.[23]

During the Great War, millions of widows, mothers, and other female family members seen in black attire on the streets of European towns and cities served as a visible and constant reminder of the fact that the war caused carnage on a vast scale. Had Bernadine Doyle survived that war instead of the Second World War, her attempt to shield her children from death would have been much more difficult, even more so had she lived in Europe instead of in the United States. The nation-states waging the First World War could ensure greater allegiance and willingness to fight on if leaders could obscure the loss of life as much as possible. Because it was traditionally women who displayed war's sorrows and losses through the wearing of widows' weeds, rather than celebrating war's glory, it was their rituals and customs that had to be harnessed and controlled by the combatant governments that had sent male citizens to fight. This tug-of-war between the nation-state's need to glorify war and widows' mournful responses to the deaths caused by the war constituted yet another Great War "trench."

Much was at stake as nations and their militaries insisted on "victory" as the only possible outcome of the conflict for their "side." In the defeated nation of Germany, women suffered blame for their supposed inability to buoy up the feminized home front long enough to achieve victory. Perceived as indulging in the emotions of the loss of their men, the bereaved reinforced the stereotypical sentimental woman, as opposed to the presumed rational, stalwart man; *Simplicissimus* editors underscored this difference when they placed Josef Wackerle's painting of mourning widows and Hans Bauer's article celebrating soldierly manhood on the same page in their publication. Overwrought responses to loss made women vulnerable to the assertion that it was they who had abandoned the nation's war imperative. This fabrication appeared often enough that two women's magazines, *Die Frau* and *Die Kriegerwitwe*, were forced to repudiate it in their pages. Reinforcing the myth of a domestic front isolated from battlefront lent further credence to the falsehood. If people believed Field Marshal Paul von Hindenburg's claim that the heroic German military had spared the *Vaterland* from war's horrors, then they could be persuaded that it was the home front's lack of support for the war that had caused military defeat. Since World War I, separating the domestic front from the battlefield has become much harder. The United Nations estimated that 90 percent of war's casualties at the end of the twentieth century were civilian, not military, a figure that is nearly double the estimated percentage of civilian deaths inflicted during the First World War.[24]

Both the defeated and victorious nations sought control of their citizens' responses to war. Evidence suggests that their efforts were largely successful, at least in terms of public, official war remembrance. Gold Star Mothers and Widows tried very hard during and after the conflict to erase the visible link between war and death through the Gold Star emblem that replaced black crepe. Canadian, Australian, and German governments adopted similar practices of rewarding survivors for their loved ones' deaths in battle. Supporters pointed out that to be reminded of casualties by mourners lamenting war's butchery hurt morale and sparked ruminations on whether the war was really necessary. (Twenty-first-century warring societies have worked to achieve the same goal by refusing to allow coffins containing soldiers' bodies to be photographed or tallied.[25]) Not only did Gold Star activists and others labor to obscure the prevalence of loss from the war, they sought to create out of soldiers' deaths a *cause célèbre* through the adaptation of insignia and the militarized pomp and circumstance surrounding the pilgrims' journeys to France. Most of the correspondence between widows and the Quartermaster General regarding the voyages and between mourners and the Victory Hall Association reveals appreciative survivors relishing military-style rewards for their contribution to their husbands' sacrifice and to the nation. Successful attempts to control the public response to wartime deaths made it easier for nation-states to wage the next war twenty years later. But such control was not seamless. The historical record also includes some stinging exceptions to citizens' acquiescence to militarization. In these letters widows rebuked the government and military for their suffering, and they refused to veil the pain caused by wartime deaths. Claims of victory seemed shallow in light of widows' expressions of grief and anguish. Women's hopes for the individual happiness they expected to derive from their choice of lifelong companions and partners heightened their sense of loss, in addition to their grief over the loss of their breadwinners.

The issue of modern mourning attire did not arise in the same way in Germany, although the underlying reason behind the drive to discard black crepe did appear. To remind readers of proper wartime behavior, in September 1914 *Die Frau* reproduced an excerpt from Friedrich Schleiermacher's 1813 sermon that he had delivered as Confederated German forces drove Napoleon's French army back across the Rhine. The nineteenth-century theologian had urged German women not to mourn but to be thankful and grateful that they had sacrificed their loved ones for the noble struggle. Feminist writer Else Lüders shook her finger accusingly at wives and mothers who responded with grief and anger at their losses. She found their behavior to be "thankless" in the face of the heroism displayed by Germany's valiant fighting men. Be proud of heroic deaths, she implored, instead of sorrowful.[26] After the signing of the peace treaty the war widows' periodical *Die Kriegerwitwe* published numerous articles supporting the soldier and his nation's war effort, although the organization also criticized the government's miserly pensions and its dealings with survivors who received them.[27] As a total war, the Great War involved many more citizens than previous conflicts, ensuring that traditional gender divisions would inevitably begin to blur. "Modern" war widows in the United States facilitated that erosion when they rejected black attire and adopted military-style emblems instead. After 1917 all except two of the political parties in Germany argued for greater female participation in public life. But women participated in and were recruited primarily by right-wing conservative parties such as the *Deutschnationale Volkspartei* (German National People's Party), in which time-honored duties for females remained the order of the day. In the land of "reluctant feminists," rigidly conceived gender roles rarely released females from tradition, and women paid the price when they were scapegoated for their nation's defeat.[28]

But not all German war widows were so accepting of their fates. Elisabeth Macke's letters reflect her cynical attitude toward the German military's inability to account honestly for her husband's death. Her experiences as a war widow brought her little comfort, and led to her transnational perceptions of war widowhood. In addition, mourners penned their memoirs in Helene Hurwitz-Stranz's anthology and in the publications of survivors' organizations. Their words reveal a plurality of nationalistic sentiment, abiding connections between war widows, disillusionment with their government, and transnational attitudes toward war widowhood and directed at the war itself.

Notes

1. AN ARMY OF WIDOWS

1. Josef Wackerle, "Die Witwen," *Simplicissimus* 24, no. 3 (15 April 1919): 45 (I have translated all German into English except where noted).

2. Tamar Mayer, "Gender Ironies of Nationalism: Setting the Stage," in Tamar Mayer, ed., *Gender Ironies of Nationalism: Sexing the Nation* (London: Routledge, 2000), 1–2. My title comes from Geertje van Os, "Widows Hidden from View," in Jan Bremmer and Lourens van den Bosch, eds., *Between Poverty and the Pyre: Moments in the History of Widowhood* (London: Routledge, 1995), 235.

3. Erika Kuhlman, *Reconstructing Patriarchy after the Great War: Women, Gender, and Postwar Reconciliation between Nations* (New York: Palgrave Macmillan, 2008), 148.

4. Vivian Bruce Conger, *The Widows' Might: Widowhood and Gender in Early British America* (New York: New York University Press, 2009); S. J. Kleinberg, *Widows and Orphans First: The Family Economy and Social Welfare Policy, 1880–1939* (Urbana: University of Illinois Press, 2006); Thomas A. J. McGinn, *Widows and Patriarchy, Ancient and Modern* (London: Duckworth, 2008); Cindy L. Carlson and Angela Jane Weisl, *Constructions of Widowhood and Virginity in the Middle Ages* (New York: St. Martin's Press, 1999); Louise Mirrer, *Upon My Husband's Death: Widows in the Literature and Histories of Medieval Europe* (Ann Arbor: University of Michigan Press, 1992); Allison M. Levy, *Widowhood and Visual Culture in Early Modern Europe* (Burlington, VT: Ashgate, 2003); Michel Parisse, *Veuves et veuvage dans le Haut Moyen Age* (Paris: Picard, 1993); Nicole Pellegrin and Colette H. Winn, *Veufs, Veuves et Veuvage dans la France d'ancien régime: Actes du Colloque de Poitiers, 11–12 Juin 1998* (Paris: Honoré Champion Éditeur, 2003); Ursula Machtemes-Titgemeyer, *Leben zwischen Trauer und Pathos: Bildungsbürgerliche Witwen im 19. Jahrhundert* (Osnabrück: Rasch Verlag, 2001); Irmgard C. Taylor, *Das Bild der Witwe in der deutschen Literatur* (Darmstadt: Gesellschaft Hessischer Literaturfreunde, 1980); sociologist Helena Znaniecki Lopata has done important work on widowhood in the United States; see Lopata, *Widowhood in an American City* (Cambridge, MA: Schenkman Publishing Company, 1973).

5. Marjo Buitelaar, "Widows' Worlds: Representations and Realities," in Bremmer and van den Bosch, 6.

6. Sandra Cavallo and Lyndan Warner, "Introduction," in Cavallo and Warner, eds., *Widowhood in Medieval and Early Modern Europe* (London and New York: Longman, 1999), 3.

7. Jean H. Quataert, *Reluctant Feminists in German Social Democracy, 1885–1917* (Princeton, NJ: Princeton University Press, 1979), 24.

8. J. M. Winter, "Communities in Mourning," in Frans Coetzee and Marilyn Shevin-Coetzee, eds., *Authority, Identity, and the Social History of the Great War* (Providence, RI: Berghahn Books, 1995), 344; no one at the time knew how many each belligerent country had lost, and even afterward only approximate numbers could be given, according to Robert Weldon Whalen, *Bitter Wounds: German Victims of the Great War* (Ithaca, NY: Cornell University Press, 1984), 38.

9. Leonard V. Smith, Stéphane Audoin-Rouzeau, and Annette Becker, *France and the Great War, 1914–1918* (Cambridge: Cambridge University Press, 2003), 70; Francesca Lagorio, "Italian Widows of the First World War," in Coetzee and Shevin-Coetzee, eds., 177; Joy Damousi, *The Labour of Loss: Mourning, Memory, and Wartime Bereavement in Australia* (Cambridge: Cambridge University Press, 1999), 71; for the United States figure, see chapter 3.

10. Jay Winter, *Sites of Memory, Sites of Mourning: The Great War in European Cultural History* (Cambridge: Cambridge University Press, 1995), 46; Karin Hausen, "Die Sorge der Nation für ihre 'Kriegsopfer': Ein Bereich der Geschlechterpolitik während der Weimarer Republik," in Jürgen Kocka, ed., *Von der Arbeiterbewegung zum modernen Sozialstaat* (Munich: Saur Verlag, 1994), 725.

11. Sigmund Freud, "Our Attitude Towards Death," *The Standard Edition of the Complete Psychological Works*, XIV, trans. James Strachey (London: Hogarth Press, 1957), 291.

12. Drew Gilpin Faust, *This Republic of Suffering: Death and the American Civil War* (New York: Knopf, 2008), 148–62; David Cannadine, "War and Death, Grief and Mourning in Modern Britain," in Joachim Whaley, ed., *Mirrors of Mortality: Studies in the Social History of Death* (New York: St. Martin's Press, 1981), 188–218.

13. Lynn Abrams, "Companionship and Conflict: The Negotiation of Marriage Relations in the Nineteenth Century," in Elizabeth Harvey and Lynn Abrams, eds., *Gender Relations in German History* (Durham, NC: Duke University Press, 1996), 103–5.

14. Sydney Grundy, *The New Woman: An Original Comedy* (London: Chiswick Press, 1894).

15. Beth L. Bailey, *From Front Porch to Back Seat: Courtship in Twentieth-Century America* (Baltimore: Johns Hopkins University Press, 1988), 13–19; for working-class U.S. women, see Kathy Peiss, *Cheap Amusements: Working Women and Leisure in Turn-of-the-Century New York* (Philadelphia: Temple University Press, 1986), 49.

16. Elaine Tyler May, *Great Expectations: Marriage and Divorce in Post-Victorian America* (Chicago: University of Chicago Press, 1980), chapter 4.

17. Helene Hurwitz-Stranz, ed., *Kriegerwitwen gestalten ihr Schicksal: Lebenskämpfe deutscher Kriegerwitwen nach eigenen Darstellungen* (Berlin: Heymann, 1931), 22, 26, 40, 78, 81, 85.

18. Alexander Watson, *Enduring the Great War: Combat, Morale, and Collapse in the German and British Armies, 1914–1918* (Cambridge: Cambridge University Press, 2008), 82; Aribert Reimann, *Der grosse Krieg der Sprachen: Untersuchungen zur historischen Semantik in Deutschland und England zur Zeit des Ersten Weltkriegs* (Essen: Klartext Verlag, 2000), 129.

19. Damousi, 1.

20. Irmgard Steinisch, "Different Path to War: A Comparative Study of Militarism and Imperialism in the United States and Imperial Germany, 1871–1914," in Roger Chickering and Stig Förster, eds., *Anticipating Total War: The German and American Experiences, 1871–1914* (New York: Cambridge University Press, 1999), 31–32; Kathryn Kish Sklar, Anja Schüler, and Susan Strasser, eds., *Social Justice Feminists in the United States and Germany: A Dialogue in Documents, 1885–1933* (Ithaca, NY: Cornell University Press, 1998), 2.

21. Jeff Lipkes, *Rehearsals: The German Army in Belgium, August 1914* (Leuven, Belgium: Leuven University Press, 2007), 766, note 94.

22. Fussell's *Great War and Modern Memory* is the most influential of these, but see also Henry E. May, *End of American Innocence: A Study of the First Years of Our Own Time* (New York: Knopf, 1959); Modris Eksteins, *Rites of Spring: The Great War and the Birth of the Modern Age* (London: Black Swan, 1990); Douglas Peter Mackaman and Michael Mays, eds., *World War I and the Cultures of Modernity* (Jackson: University Press of Mississippi, 2000) includes James P. Daughton's article "Sketches of the *Poilu's* World: Trench Cartoons of the Great War," 35–67, but this deals with women as *poilus* imagined them; Janet Watson's essay "The Paradox of Working Heroines" in Mackaman and May's volume, 81–103, treats women extensively.

23. Ellen Carol Dubois, "Harriot Stanton Blatch and the Transformation of Class Relations among Women Suffragists," in Noralee Frankel and Nancy S. Dye, eds., *Gender, Class, Race and Reform in the Progressive Era* (Lexington: University Press of Kentucky, 1992), 163; as Kimberly Jensen notes in her book, the war's legacy for female equality in the United States was ambiguous at best, *Mobilizing Minerva: American Women in the First World War* (Urbana: Univeristy of Illinois Press, 2008), viii; Richard J. Evans quotes Field Marshal Paul Hindenburg's letter to BDF president Gertrud Bäumer after her public repudiation of the armistice, Treaty of Versailles, and League of Nations as saying, "we German men bow down our heads before the German women in reverence," in *The Feminist Movement in Germany, 1984–1933* (London: SAGE Publications, 1976), 211; Birthe Kundrus, "Gender Wars: The First World War and the Construction of Gender Relations in the Weimar Republic," in Karen Hagemann and Stefanie Schüler-Springorum, eds., *Home/Front: The Military, War and Gender in Twentieth-Century Germany* (New York: Berg, 2002), 163.

24. Mary Nolan, *Visions of Modernity: American Business and the Modernization of Germany* (New York: Oxford University Press, 1994), 108–9, 120–27; Nancy Nenno, "Femininity, the Primitive, and Modern Urban Space: Josephine Baker in Berlin," in Katharina von Ankum, ed., *Women in the Metropolis: Gender and Modernity in Weimar Culture* (Berkeley: University of California Press, 1997), 146, notes that Berliners throughout the Weimar Republic expressed a love for all things American; in the same volume, Sabine Hake, "In the Mirror of Fashion," 193.

25. Correspondence collected and edited in Sklar, Schüler, and Strasser, 1 and entire.

26. Buitelaar, 9, 11; Brian Levack, *The Witch-hunt in Early Modern Europe* (New York: Longman, 1987), 131–32.

27. Elaine Pagels, *Adam, Eve, and the Serpent* (New York: Vintage Books, 1989), 16–18; see also I Corinthians 7:8.

28. Steven N. Austad, "Why Women Live Longer than Men: Sex Differences in Longevity," *Gender Medicine* Volume 3, no. 2 (June 2006): 79.

29. Katherine Ashenburg, *The Mourner's Dance: What We Do When People Die* (New York: North Point Press, 2002), 94.

30. Lou Taylor, *Mourning Dress: A Costume and Social History* (London: George Allen and Unwin, 1983), 133–36.

31. Samuel Belkin, "Levirate and Agnate Marriage in Rabbinic and Cognate Literature," *The Jewish Quarterly Review* 60, no. 4 (April 1970): 275.

32. Barbara Evans Clements, "Introduction," in Barbara Evans Clements, Barbara Alpern Engel, and Christine Worobec, eds., *Russia's Women: Accommodation, Resistance, Transformation* (Berkeley: University of California Press, 1991), 5; van Os, 234.

33. See Kimberly Jensen's discussion of "Citizenship and the Masculine Martial Ideal" in the United States, 14–20; Susanne Rouette, "Mothers and Citizens: Gender and Social Policy in Germany after the First World War," *Central European History* 30 (1997): 65–66, comments on this phenomenon in Germany; quoted in Frank Lorenz Müller's review of Sven Oliver Müller, *Die Nation als Waffe und Vorstellung: Nationalismus in Deutschland und Grossbritannien im Ersten Weltkrieg* in *The English Historical Review* CXXI, no. 492 (2006): 874.

34. Dorothy A. Mays, *Women in Early America: Struggle, Survival, and Freedom in a New World* (Santa Barbara, CA: ABC-CLIO, 2004), 51.

35. Harriet Hyman Alonso, *Peace as a Woman's Issue: A History of the U.S. Women's Movement for World Peace and Human Rights* (Syracuse, NY: Syracuse University Press, 1993), 10–12.

36. See chapter 5 of this volume.

37. James G. Frazer, *The Golden Bough: A Study in Magic and Religion* (New York: Macmillan, 1958), 29.

38. Homer, *The Odyssey*, trans. Rodney Merrill (Ann Arbor: University of Michigan Press, 2002), 99.

39. Damousi, 1.

40. Vera Brittain, *Verses of a V.A.D.* (London: E. MacDonald, Ltd., 1918), and *Testament of Youth: An Autobiographical Study of the Years 1900–1925* (New York: Macmillan, 1933).

41. For German statistics on soldiers' occupations, see Whalen, 41; Gerald E. Shenk, *Work or Fight! Race, Gender and the Draft in World War I* (New York: Palgrave Macmillan, 2005), 153; Jeanette Keith, *Rich Man's War, Poor Man's Fight: Race, Class, and Power in the Rural South during the First World War* (Chapel Hill: University of North Carolina Press, 2004), 2, 116–17.

42. Whalen, 23–25; David M. Kennedy, *Over Here: The First World War and American Society* (1980; reprint New York: Oxford University Press, 2004), 213, 217.

43. Barbara Dodd Hillerman, "Chrysalis of Gloom: Nineteenth-Century American Mourning Costume," in Martha V. Pike and Janice Gray Armstrong, eds., *A Time to Mourn: Expressions of Grief in Nineteenth-Century America* (Stony Brook, NY: Museums at Stony Brook, 1980), 101–4.

44. Stéphane Audoin-Rouzeau and Annette Becker describe soldiers' elaborate commemorations of their comrades in *14–18: Understanding the Great War* (New York: Hill and Wang, 2002), 204–5.

45. For example, after the U.S. Civil War, homes established for widows were called "Soldiers' Widows' Home" in Wisconsin, Illinois, and Kansas, whereas the records pertaining to the Gold Star Mothers and Widows pilgrimages usually use the term "war widow" (see chapter 3); Anna Schnädelbach, *Kriegerwitwen: Lebensbewältigung zwischen Arbeit und Familie in Westdeutschland nach 1945* (Frankfurt: Campus Verlag, 2009), 7, note 1, places the term in the context of World War II, but the literature suggests that both *Kriegerwitwe* and *Kriegswitwe* were commonly used during the Great War.

46. "Disillusionment" is the term most widely used to describe postwar attitudes in the United States; see Kennedy, 221–30; for general discussions of postwar disillusionment see Eric J. Leed, "Class and Disillusionment in World War I," *Journal of Modern History* 50, no. 4 (December 1978): 680–99; in addition, Marc Ferro contends that the only "victor" in the Great War was the United States, see Paul Fussell, *The Great War and Modern Memory* (New York: Oxford University Press, 1975), 317, and British poet Edmund Blunden's comment that the only victor in the Great War was war itself, see Blunden, *The Mind's Eye: Essays* (1934; reprint Freeport, NY: Books for Libraries Press, 1967), 38.

47. Elizabeth A. Marsland, *The Nation's Cause: French, English, and German Poetry of the First World War* (London: Routledge, 1991), 34.

48. Chickering and Förster, 3.

49. Karl Jünger, *Deutschlands Frauen und Deutschlands Krieg; Ein Rat-, Tat- u. Trostbuch* (Stuttgart: Lutz, 1916), 9; Ingrid Sharp, "Blaming the Women: Women's 'Responsibility' for the First World War," in Sharp and Alison S. Fell, eds., *The Women's Movement in Wartime: International Perspectives, 1914–19* (Basingstoke: Palgrave Macmillan, 2007), 69–70.

50. Leonhard Frank, *Der Mensch ist Gut* (Zurich: Max Rascher, 1918), 26 (translation Robert Weldon Whalen).

51. Lagorio, 177–78.

52. Eine Hauptmannswitwe, "Was leistet das Reich für die Kriegsbeschädigten und Kriegerhinterbliebenen?" *Neue Lebensfahrt: Mitteilungen für Kriegerhinterbliebene, Beilage zum Reichsbund*, Volume 3, no. 21 (November 1, 1920), n.p. This book's title comes from this essay. The architect Witold Rybczynski defines comfort as a feeling of well-being: For a fascinating discussion of the history of the notion of comfort, see Rybczynski, *Home: A Short History of an Idea* (New York: Penguin, 1986), 224–32.

53. Faust, 243.

54. Lagorio, 185; Michael Lanthier, "Women Alone: Widows in Third Republic France, 1870–1940" (Ph.D. diss., Simon Fraser University, 2004), 149–54: Janis Lomas, "'So I Married Again': Letters from British Widows of the First and Second World Wars," *History Workshop Journal* 38, no. 1 (1994): 218.

55. Franziska Seraphim, *War Memory and Social Politics in Japan, 1945–2005* (Cambridge, MA: Harvard University Asia Center, 2006), 74.

56. Hans Bauer, "Standrecht," *Simplicissimus* 24, no. 3 (April 15, 1919): 45.

57. Michael Lanthier, "War Widows and the Expansion of the French Welfare State," *Proceedings of the Western Society for French History* 31 (2003): 255.

58. Elisabeth Domansky, "Militarization and Reproduction in World War I Germany," in Geoff Eley, ed., *Society, Culture, and the State in Germany, 1870–1930* (Ann Arbor: University of Michigan Press, 1996), 427–63.

59. Jennifer Anne Davy, "Pacifist Thought and Gender Ideology in the Political Biographies of Women Peace Activists in Germany, 1899–1970," *Journal of Women's History* 13.3 (2001): 35; Susan Zeiger, *In Uncle Sam's Service: Women Workers with the American Expeditionary Force, 1917–1919* (Philadelphia: University of Pennsylvania Press, 2004), 11–25.

60. Domansky, 440, discusses the impact of working in munitions factories on women workers' health.

61. Paul Berry and Mark Bostridge, *Vera Brittain: A Life* (London: Chatto & Windus, 1995), 429–31.

62. Bäumer's German original quoted in Ute Gerhard, "National oder International: Die internationalen Beziehungen der deutschen bürgerlichen Frauenbewegung," *Feminist-ische Studien* 3 (1994): 42.

63. Constance Potter, "World War I Gold Star Mothers Pilgrimages, Part I," *Prologue,* 31, no. 2 (Summer 1999): 140–45; ibid., "World War I Gold Star Mothers Pilgrimages Part II," *Prologue,* 31, no. 3 (Fall 1999): 210–15.

64. Norman Rich, *The Age of Nationalism and Reform, 1850–1890* (New York: Norton, 1970); Benedict Anderson, *Imagined Communities: Reflections on the Origins and Spread of Nationalism* (London: Verson, 1990).

65. Frank Lorenz Müller, review of Sven Oliver Müller, *Die Nation als Waffe und Vor-stellung: Nationalismus in Deutschland und Grossbritannien im Ersten Weltkrieg* (Göttingen: Vandenhoeck & Ruprecht, 2004) in *The English Historical Review* CXXI, no. 492 (2006): 874–76.

66. Jay M. Winter's work is voluminous, but three of his most important books are Winter and Richard Wall, eds., *The Upheaval of War: Family, Work and Welfare in Europe, 1914–1918* (Cambridge: Cambridge University Press, 1988); Jay M. Winter, *Sites of Memory, Sites of Mourning: The Great War in European Cultural History* (Cambridge: Cambridge University Press, 1995), and Jay M. Winter, *Remembering War: The Great War Between Memory and History in the Twentieth Century* (New Haven, CT: Yale University Press, 2006); comparative works include Susan Grayzel, *Women's Identi-ties at War: Gender, Motherhood, and Politics in Britain and France During the First World War* (Chapel Hill: University of North Carolina Press, 1999); Stéphane Audoin-Rouzeau and Annette Becker, *14–18: Understanding the Great War,* trans. Catherine Temerson (New York: Hill and Wang, 2002); Tammy Proctor, *Civilians in a World at War: 1914–1918* (New York: New York University Press, 2009); Alan Kramer, *Dynamic of Destruction: Culture and Killing in the First World War* (New York: Oxford University Press, 2009); and Laura Lee Downs, *Manufacturing Inequality: Gender Divisions in the French and British Metalworking Industries, 1914–1939* (Ithaca, NY: Cornell University Press, 1995).

67. George Mosse, *Fallen Soldiers: Reshaping the Memory of the World War* (New York: Oxford University Press, 1990); G. Kurt Piehler, *Remembering War the American Way* (Washington: Smithsonian Institution Press, 1995), 92–125.

68. Fussell, *The Great War and Modern Memory;* Cannadine, 187–242.

69. Cannadine, 212–13.

2. *TROSTLOSE STUNDEN:* GERMAN WAR WIDOWS

1. Anica Helmar, "Einsame Frauen," *Frauen-Rundschau* 7, no. 7 (April 1, 1906): 183; I have translated all of the German into English unless otherwise noted.

2. Helmar, 183–88. Frau Hillemann's other reason for moving to the city, a secret she kept from her pastor, is to improve her daughter's prospects at finding a husband; see chapter 5; Olwen Hufton, "Women without Men: Widows and Spinsters in Britain and France in the Eighteenth Century," in Jan Bremmer and Lourens van den Bosch, eds., *Between Poverty and the Pyre: Moments in the History of Widowhood* (New York: Rout-ledge, 1995), 131–32, discusses the high incidence of widows living with adult daughters, and the likelihood that this would lead to the daughters' spinsterhood; other sources on

nineteenth-century widowhood include Marie Tyrol, "Totensonntag," *Frauen-Rundschau* 10, no. 23 (December 1, 1909): 602; Marie Schmidt-von Ekensteen, "Der geheimnisvolle King," *Swabische Frauenzeitung: Organ für die Interessen der Frauenwelt und der Familie* 3, no. 5 (January 29, 1899): 2–3; L. Schmidt, "Die Frau als Witwe," *Die Frauenbewegung* 3, no. 17 (September 1, 1897): 1–2; Henriette Fuerth, "Die Ehefrage," *Die Frau* 1, no. 11 (August 1894): 710; Mathilde Lammers, "Allein durchs Leben. - Betrachtungen und Ratschlage," *Die Frau* 1, no. 2 (November 1893): 103–8; Dr. J. Silbermann, "Frauenerwerb und Frauenbewegung" *Die Frauenbewegung* 3, no. 6 (15 March 1897): 57–59.

3. Jean H. Quataert, *Reluctant Feminists in German Social Democracy, 1885–1917* (Princeton, NJ: Princeton University Press, 1979), 4, 8, 27.

4. Ibid., 22–23.

5. On *Züchtigungsrecht*, see Anonymous, "Der Stand der Frauenfrage in den Culturstaaten," *Frauen-Werke* 2, no. 6 (June 1895): 43; Dr. Paul Schüler, "Die Frau im Recht – Der Lezte Wille," *Die Frau* 2, no. 8 (May 1895): 453–57.

6. Quataert, 9–10.

7. See Francesca Lagorio's interpretation of war widows in "Italian Widows of the First World War," in Frans Coetzee and Marilyn Shevin-Coetzee, eds., *Authority, Identity, and the Social History of the Great War* (Providence, RI: Berghahn Books, 1995), 178.

8. Ute Daniel, *The War from within: German Working-Class Women in the First World War*, trans. Margaret Ries (Oxford: Berg, 1997), 19; see also Fritz Fischer, *Germany's Aims in the First World War* (New York: Norton, 1967), 19.

9. Jay Winter deems Germans' enthusiastic response to August 1914 mythological, because it is largely based on staged Berlin newsreels and Philipp Witkopf's publication of student-soldiers' letters, Winter, *Remembering War: The Great War Between Memory and History in the Twentieth Century* (New Haven, CT: Yale University Press, 2006), 105; Bernd Ulrich and Benjamin Ziemann, eds., *German Soldiers in the Great War: Letters and Eyewitness Accounts*, trans. Christine Brocks (South Yorkshire: Pen & Sword Books, 2010), 22; Helene Hurwitz-Stranz, ed., *Kriegerwitwen gestalten ihr Schicksal: Lebenskämpfe deutscher Kriegerwitwen nach eigenen Darstellungen* (Berlin: Heymann, 1931), 22.

10. George Mosse, *Fallen Soldiers: Reshaping the Memory of the World Wars* (New York: Oxford University Press, 1990), 144.

11. Eric J. Leed, *No Man's Land: Combat and Identity in World War I* (Cambridge: Cambridge University Press, 1981), 155, 194.

12. Modris Eksteins, *Rites of Spring: The Great War and The Birth of the Modern Age* (Boston: Houghton Mifflin, 1989), 145.

13. Stig Förster, "Introduction," in Roger Chickering and Stig Förster, eds., *Great War, Total War: Combat and Mobilization on the Western Front, 1914–1918* (Washington: German Historical Institute, 2000), 2–3.

14. Karen Hagemann, "Home/Front: The Military, Violence and Gender Relations in the Age of the World Wars," in Hagemann and Stefanie Schüler-Springorum, eds., *Home/Front: The Military, War and Gender in Twentieth-Century Germany* (New York: Berg, 2002), 12; Belinda J. Davis, "Home Front: Food, Politics and Women's Everyday Life during the First World War," in ibid., 125, discusses the "internal enemy" concept.

15. Olaf Gulbransson, "Before the Decision," *Simplicissmus* 23 no. 30 (22 October 1918): 361.

16. Reinhart Koselleck and Michael Jeismann, eds., *Der Politische Totenkult Kriegerdenkmäler in der Moderne* (München: Wilhelm Fink Verlag, 1994), 105–13.

17. Quoted in Karin Hausen, "The German Nation's Obligation to the Heroes' Widows of World War I," in Margaret Randolph Higonnet, Jane Jenson, Sonya Michel, and Margaret Collins Weitz, eds., *Behind the Lines: Gender and the Two World Wars* (New Haven, CT: Yale University Press, 1987), 140.

18. Lagorio, 178, 185; for widows' remembrances of their soldiers, see Hurwitz-Stranz, ed., *Kriegerwitwen*; the *Volksbund Deutsche Kriegsgräberfürsorge* (Association for the Care of German War Graves) included women's organizations as signatory members, but they were not active in ceremonies; letter from the VDK to Herren Reichskanzler, February 17, 1922, I/710 #1, Friedhöfe, Denkmäler und Gedenkfeiern für die im Kriege Gefallenen, R 43, Reichskanzlei, 1.38 Militär, 1919-1945, Bundesarchiv (hereafter BA), Berlin.

19. Geoff Eley, "Introduction 1: Is There a History of the *Kaiserreich*?" in Geoff Eley, ed., *Society, Culture and the State in Germany, 1870–1930* (Ann Arbor: University of Michigan Press, 1996), 19.

20. Hurwitz-Stranz, ed., *Kriegerwitwen*; Karl Scholl, "Die soziale Lage der Kriegswitwen in Hamburg; eine Darstellung auf Grund der Ergebnisse von 300 Monographien" (Ph.D. diss., University of Hamburg, 1924); Whalen, *Bitter Wounds*; Hausen, "German Nation's Obligations," 140.

21. Belinda J. Davis, *Home Fires Burning: Food, Politics, and Everyday Life in World War I Berlin* (Chapel Hill: University of North Carolina Press, 2000); Volker Ullrich, *Kriegsalltag: Hamburg im Ersten Weltkrieg* (Köln: Prometh, 1982); Ute Daniel, *The War Within*; Susanne Rouette's *Sozialpolitik als Geschlechterpolitik: die Regulierung der Frauenarbeit nach dem Ersten Weltkrieg* (Frankfurt: Campus, 1996); Susanne Rouette, "Mothers and Citizens: Gender and Social Policy in Germany after the First World War," *Central European History* 30 (1997): 53–54.

22. Paul Fussell's *The Great War and Modern Memory* (New York: Oxford University Press, 1975); Eric J. Leed's *No Man's Land*, and Elizabeth Marsland's *The Nation's Cause: French, English, and German Poetry in the First World War* (New York: Routledge 1991) illuminate soldiers' poetry from the major warring powers. Others are specific to the German soldier, such as studies of soldiers' literature, including Patrick Bridgwater, *The German Poets of the First World War* (London: Croom Helm, 1985) and Martin Travers, *German Novels on the First World War and their Ideological Implications, 1918–1933* (Stuttgart: H. D. Heinz, 1982).

23. A widows' organization in Munich published poems and prose glorifying the fallen soldier; see Clara Priess, *"Gefallen auf dem Feld der Ehre"* (fallen on the field of honor), *Die Kriegerwitwe* 3 (1920): 1.

24. Whalen, 70.

25. Lagorio, 190, 179.

26. Ulrich and Ziemann, eds., *German Soldiers*, 36–39, 52–55, 165–67, reproduces several letters written by front soldiers to their wives back home.

27. Benjamin Ziemann, "Geschlechterbeziehungen in deutschen Feldpostbriefen des Ersten Weltkrieges," in Christa Hämmerle and Edith Saurer, eds., *Briefkulturen und ihr Geschlecht: Zur Geschichte der privaten Korrespondenz vom 16. Jahrhundert bis heute* (Wien, Köln: Böhlau, 2003), 261–63; see Birthe Kundrus, "Gender Wars," in Hagemann and Schüler-Springorum, eds., 160; for remarks on French differences in perception of this division (because much of the war was fought on French territory), see James P. Daugh-

ton, "Sketches of the *Poilu*'s World: Trench Cartoons from the Great War," in Douglas Peter Mackaman and Michael May, eds., *World War I and Cultures of Modernity* (Jackson: University Press of Mississippi, 2000), 61–62.

28. Johanna Boldt destroyed most of her husband's fifty-odd letters written to her as per his wishes. Julius had sent the letters he received from Johanna back home to her, fulfilling her desire, Hagener, "*Es lief so sicher an deinem Arm*": *Briefe einer Soldatenfrau, 1914* (Weinheim: Beltz, 1986), 29.

29. Edith Seligsohn, "Typische Fälle aus der Hinterbliebenenfürsorge," *Die Frau* 24, no. 3 (December 1916): 137–43; Whalen, 76, noted that soldiers' wives stopped getting Family Aid when their husbands died but wouldn't get a pension until at least three months after death.

30. Bavarian War Commemoration Endowment, "Deutsches Volk! Vergiss nicht deine Kriegshinterbliebenen," *Die Kriegerwitwe* 3 (1920): 1–2.

31. Martha Hanna, *Your Death Would Be Mine: Paul and Marie Pireaud in the Great War* (Cambridge, MA: Harvard University Press, 2008), 8–9; Jessica Meyer, *Men of War: Masculinity and the First World War in Britain* (Basingstoke: Palgrave Macmillan, 2008), 14; Jay Winter, "Foreword," in Ulrich and Ziemann, eds., *German Soldiers*, ix; for censorship of women's letters to the front, see Davis, *Home Fires*, 113; for military censorship of soldiers' letters from the front, see Bernd Ulrich, *Die Augenzeugen: Deutsche Feldpostbriefe in Kriegs- und Nachkriegszeit, 1914–1933* (Essen: Klartext Verlag, 1997), 78–79; Peter Fritzsche, *Germans into Nazis* (Cambridge, MA: Harvard University Press, 1998), 38; Catherine Rollet, "The Home and Family Life," in Jay Winter and Jean-Louis Robert, eds., *Capital Cities at War: Paris, London, Berlin, 1914–1919, Vol. 2* (Cambridge: Cambridge University Press, 2007), 331.

32. Hanna, 19.

33. Leed, 74, 207.

34. Fussell, 87.

35. Eric F. Schneider, "The British Red Cross Wounded and Missing Enquiry Bureau: A Case of Truth-Telling in the Great War," *War in History* 4 no. 3 (1997): 296–315; Helen B. McCartney, *Citizen Soldiers: The Liverpool Territorials in the First World War* (Cambridge: Cambridge University Press, 2005); Mona Siegel, "'History Is the Opposite of Forgetting': The Limits of Memory and the Lessons of History in Interwar France," *The Journal of Modern History* 74, no. 4 (December 2002): 775.

36. David Lewis, "Postscript to 'Mad Pain and Martian Pain,'" in *Philosophical Papers, Vol. 1* (Oxford: Oxford University Press, 1983), 131.

37. Thomas Nagel, "What Is It Like to Be a Bat?" *Philosophical Review* 83 (1974): 435–50.

38. Frank Jackson, "What Mary Didn't Know," in Paul K. Moser and J. D. Trout, eds., *Contemporary Materialism: A Reader* (London: Routledge, 1993), 180 (emphasis Jackson's).

39. Moritz Bromme, "Stumme Märtyrerinnen," *Die Frau* 21, no. 4 (January 1914): 229–33; Alison Jaggar, *Feminist Politics and Human Nature* (Totowa, NJ: Rowman & Littlefield, 1983), 353–89; Siegfried Sassoon, "Glory of Women," *The War Poems of Siegfried Sassoon* (London: Faber and Faber, 1983), 100; Elizabeth Marsland notes that this poem has been used as evidence that civilians were ignorant of the front, Marsland, 161.

40. Literary critics have argued that binary thinking dominated the modern age, seen in such oppositions as mind/body and theory/practice. If the left is the privileged side of those binaries, however, the contention that women fell short in their ability to under-

stand warfare overturned them. In other words, if women's minds were trying to "know" soldiering, but men's bodies were doing the soldiering, and if women could know only *in theory* what soldiering was like, while men practiced soldiering—then the male/female dichotomy could also be deemed false; Marsland, 28, discusses her own and Fussell's interpretation of the binary in *Great War and Modern Memory*; Lorraine Code, *What Can She Know?: Feminist Theory and the Construction of Knowledge* (Ithaca, NY: Cornell University Press, 1991), 222–64.

41. Elisabeth Erdmann-Macke, *Erinnerung an August Macke* (Stuttgart: W. Kohlhammer, 1962), 251; Hagener, 100.

42. Marsland, 34.

43. Schneider, 299.

44. David A. Davis has asserted that the Great War resulted in a compression of space and time. Davis, "The Modernist Death of Donald Mahon," unpublished paper, Modern Language Association conference, Philadelphia, 2006. faulknersociety.com/mla06davis. doc. July 2011.

45. Whalen, 70–75.

46. I am basing my assumption here on anecdotal evidence of these two women's social class in Hagener's biography and E. Macke, *Erinnerung*. For information on German soldiers, see Karl Nau, *Die wirtschaftliche und soziale lage von kriegshinterbliebenen: Eine studie auf grund von erhebungen über die auswirkung der versorgung von kriegshinterbliebenen in Darmstadt* (Leipzig: Lühe and Company, 1930), 10; Whalen, 70; Hausen, "German Nation's Obligation," 132.

47. Eric J. Leed, *No Man's Land*, 204–5; Hausen, "The 'Day of National Mourning' in Germany," in Gerald Sider and Gavin Smith, eds., *Between History and Histories: The Making of Silences and Commemorations* (Toronto: University of Toronto Press, 1997), 128–29; Rollet, 316. Many historians have countered the "alienation" thesis, including Helen B. McCartney, *Citizen Soldiers*, 89–90.

48. Leed, 74.

49. C. Paul Vincent, *The Politics of Hunger: The Allied Blockade of Germany, 1915–1919* (Athens: Ohio University Press, 1985), 9.

50. Michael Zeitlin, "The Passion of Margaret Powers: A Psychoanalytic Reading of *Soldiers' Pay*," *Mississippi Quarterly* 46 (1993): 353–54.

51. J. L. Carr, *A Month in the Country* (Brighton: Harvester Press, 1980); the preacher's wife Alice Keach fears intimacy and keeps her distance from the war-damaged artist Mr. Birkin.

52. Marie-Monique Huss, "Pronatalism and the Popular Ideology of the Child in Wartime France: the Evidence of the Picture Postcard," in J. M. Winter and Richard Wall, eds., *The Upheaval of War: Family, Work and Welfare in Europe, 1914–1918* (Cambridge: Cambridge University Press, 1988), 337.

53. Joy Damousi, *The Labour of Loss: Mourning, Memory and Wartime Bereavement in Australia* (Cambridge: Cambridge University Press, 1999), 36–37.

54. Hilde Hammer to Adolf Schärf, 9 April 1916, in Margit Sturm, "Lebenszeichen und Liebesbeweise aus dem Ersten Weltkrieg: Eine sozialdemokratische Kriegsehe im Spiegel der Feldpost," in Hämmerle and Saurer, eds., *Briefkulturen*, 245, 249–50; translation by Jamie Hively.

55. Huss, 339.

56. Discussion of the home/front division appears in Hanna, 17; Marsland, 65–66, 122.

57. Carolyn Janice Dean, *The Fragility of Empathy after the Holocaust* (Ithaca, NY: Cornell University Press, 2004), 83–86; Hubertus Thiel, "Hubertus Thiel," in Wolfgang W. E. Samuel, ed., *The War of our Childhood: Memories of World War II* (Jackson: University Press of Mississippi, 2002), 32, where the author recalls his father, a *Waffen*-SS soldier on leave, telling his mother, "if what I have heard about Jews is true, then God have mercy on us."

58. Robert Jay Lifton and Greg Mitchell, *Hiroshima in America: A Half Century of Denial* (New York: Avon Books, 1995), 40.

59. Meyer, 4–5, discusses new scholarship on the ways in which soldiers' identities remained entrenched in domesticity, instead of alienated from it.

60. Daniel, *War from Within*, 54–55.

61. Hermann Geib, "Einführung," in Hurwitz-Stranz, ed., *Kriegerwitwen*, 6–7.

62. Lagorio, 179. Elizabeth Domansky, "Militarization and Reproduction in World War I Germany," in Geoff Eley, ed., *Society, Culture*, 427–63.

63. E. Macke to Maria Marc, September 5, 1914, in August Macke and Franz Marc, *August Macke, Franz Marc: Briefwechsel* (Köln: M. Dumont Schauberg, 1964), 190.

64. Mosse, 4–5, indicates that Great War soldiers were ill prepared for trench warfare.

65. August to Elisabeth, September 21, 1914, in Werner Frese und Ernst-Gerhard Güse, *Briefe an Elisabeth und die Freunde* (München: Bruckmann, 1987), 334–35.

66. Hurwitz-Stranz, ed., *Kriegerwitwen*, 62, 65, 82.

67. Letter printed in "Heimatchronik.," *Die Frau* 22, no. 1 (October 1914): 55.

68. Quoted in Rollet, 339; Whalen, *Bitter Wounds*, 74; Schneider, 297, notes that the British War Office "sent only the curtest message to relatives, stating simply that their man at the front had been declared Missing in Action on a certain date."

69. Hurwitz-Stranz, ed., *Kriegerwitwen*, 31; Barbara Sonneborn, Director, *Regret to Inform* videorecording (New York: Docurama, 1998), 33:49, includes a scene in which a widow reads the last letter she received from her soldier-husband in Vietnam. She explains that the letter arrived after she already knew that her husband was dead. She describes the moment that she saw the envelope, written in her husband's hand, and says that for an exhilarating moment she thought that perhaps he was not dead. Then she noticed the date on the envelope.

70. J. M. Winter, "Communities in Mourning," 326, explains that the scale of the First World War made it difficult, and sometimes impossible, for families to know where their loved ones were at any given time.

71. Elisabeth to Maria, October 15, 1914, in Macke and Marc, *Briefwechsel*, 194; rumors beguiled two Parisian families as well, Rollet, 348–50, and a Berlin family, Rollet, 351–53.

72. E. Macke, *Erinnerung*, 250, 251.

73. Macke and Marc, *Briefwechsel*, 197.

74. Leonhard Frank, *Der Mensch ist Gut* (Zürich: M. Rascher, 1918).

75. Elisabeth to Franz, October 24, 1914, in Macke and Marc, *Briefwechsel*, 196.

76. Ibid., 199, 200.

77. Ibid., 206.

78. Ibid.

79. E. Macke, *Erinnerung*, 251.

80. Daniel, *War from Within*, 206–7, discusses working women's mistrust of the government as a result of its food rationing system during the war.

81. Schneider, 296–99, 305–9.

82. Anonymous, "Kriegerdenkmäler," *Die Kriegerwitwe* 3 (1920): 2–4; the article addresses the problem of how to honor the deaths of those buried in foreign lands; having lost the war made this problem more difficult.

83. Quote from Elisabeth's diary in E. Macke, *Begegnungen* (Bielefeld: Christof Kerber Verlag, 2009), 197.

84. Anna Meseure, *August Macke, 1887–1914* (Köln: Taschen, 1993), 92. In 1999, the Mackes' grandson erected a tombstone in memory of both his grandparents in Bonn's Old Cemetery.

85. Elisabeth to Franz, January 20, 1915, in Macke and Marc, *Briefwechsel*, 204.

86. E. Macke, *Begegnungen*, 29–30; Stefan Berger, review of Ilse Fischer's *Versöhnung von Nation und Sozialismus? Lothar Erdmann (1888–1939): Ein 'leidenschaftlicher Individualist' in der Gewerkschaftsspitze*, in *English Historical Review*, CXXIV (June 2009): 761–63; E. Macke, *Begegnungen*, 200.

87. Robert L. Nelson, "German Comrades/Slavic Whores: Gender Images in the German Soldier Newspapers of the First World War," in Hagemann and Stefanie Schüler-Springorum, eds., "Home/Front," 83, argues that the German military published 115 soldiers' newspapers in order to convince soldiers of the defensive nature of the war.

88. Martin Kitchen, *German Offensives of 1918* (Stroud, Gloucestershire: Tempus, 2001), 10.

89. Hindenburg's Order of the Day remarks on November 12, 1918, quoted in "Von Hindenburg's Lament," *The Argus* (Melbourne, Australia), July 26, 1919, 7; Rollet, 316, notes that other nations upheld the same defensive war myth about themselves. "Stab in the back" refers to the notion, popular among the right, that the German military was betrayed by civilians, especially anti-monarchist republicans.

90. Gertrud Bäumer and Helene Lange, "Rechtsfrieden?" *Die Frau* 26, no. 2 (November 1918): 37–40; Bavarian War Commemoration Endowment, "Deutsches Volk!," 2.

91. Ulrich and Ziemann, eds., *German Soldiers*.

92. Leed, 195.

93. D. Lendecke, "Grund zum Frieden," *Simplicissimus* 23, no. 21 (August 20, 1918): 251; "My God," says the woman in the drawing, "has the Entente no idea how boring it is without men?"; unsigned illustration, "Damenwahl," *Simplicissimus* 23, no. 43 (January 21, 1919): 528.

94. B. Wennerberg, "Przemyśl unser!" *Simplicissimus* 20, no. 11 (June 15, 1915): 129.

95. Leed, 188–89.

96. Robert L. Nelson, 77; Rollet, 318.

97. Dennis Showalter, "Mass Warfare and the Impact of Technology," in Roger Chickering and Stig Förster, eds., *Great War, Total War*, 83.

98. Franz Marc to Elisabeth, January 29, 1915, in Macke and Marc, *Briefwechsel*, 205.

99. Davis's point of comparison includes civilian versus military death rates, *Home Fires*, 185; Daniel, 193; Domansky, 436.

100. Rollet, 333; corroborated in Ulrich and Ziemann, eds., *German Soldiers*, 116.

101. Else Lüders, "Die Fürsorge für unsere Krieger-Witwen und -Waisen als soziales Problem," *Die Frauenbewegung* 21, no. 9 (May 1, 1915): 33; Alice Salomon, "Die Fürsorge für die Hinterbliebenen der gefallenen Krieger," *Die Frau* 22, no.7 (April 1915): 385, 393.

102. Bavarian War Commemoration Endowment, "Deutsches Volk!," 2.

103. Richard J. Evans, *Death in Hamburg: Society and Politics in the Cholera Years, 1830–1910* (New York: Oxford University Press, 1987), 11.

104. Hagener, 12.

105. Ibid., 18–19.

106. Johanna to Julius, September 24, 1914, in Hagener, 61–62.

107. Hagener, 27.

108. Ibid., 69; Rollet compares leave-time policies of the French and German armies, 329; French soldiers got no leave time until January 1915, while German authorities authorized leaves from the beginning of the war; Paul and Marie Pireaud saw each other fairly frequently in comparison, Hanna, *Your Death Would Be Mine.*

109. Julius to August Boldt, August 30, 1914, in Hagener, 53.

110. Johanna to Julius, August 31, 1914, in Hagener, 44.

111. Elisabeth to Maria, September 29, 1914, in Macke and Marc, *Briefwechsel,* 192–93.

112. Johanna to Julius, undated but early September 1914, Hagener, 40.

113. Daniel, 54; quoted in Katharine Anthony, *Feminism in Germany and Scandinavia* (New York: Henry Holt, 1915), 202; Johanna to Julius, October 2, 1914, in Hagener, 66.

114. Davis, *Home Fires,* 71–73; Ullrich, 39–44.

115. Johanna to Julius, October 2, 1914, in Hagener, 66–67, emphasis mine.

116. Quataert, 43, 210; the always-energetic Johanna planned for only ten days after giving birth, Hagener, 44.

117. Johanna to Julius, October 2, 1914, in Hagener, 66.

118. Nelson, 80.

119. Rollet, 318.

120. Hagener, 96–99; Schneider, 296–315, uncovers the ways in which the British Red Cross helped families obtain information about their soldier-relatives.

121. Photograph of Boldt in mourning in Hagener, 101; Detlev J. K. Peukert, *The Weimar Republic: The Crisis of Classical Modernity,* trans. Richard Deveson (New York: Hill and Wang, 1987), 27, discusses Workers' Councils; Hagener, 102, 106–7.

122. Hagener, 107–10; on double-earners see Gerda Szepansky, *Blitzmädel, Heldenmutter, Kriegerwitwe: Frauenleben im Zweiten Weltkrieg* (Frankfurt: Fischer Taschenbuch Verlag, 1986), 10–11.

123. Drew Gilpin Faust, *Mothers of Invention: Women of the Slaveholding South during the American Civil War* (Chapel Hill: University of North Carolina Press, 1996), 150; Quataert, 25–27.

124. Richard Bessel, *Germany after the First World War* (New York: Oxford University Press, 1993), 225–26.

125. Hurwitz-Stanz, ed., *Kriegerwitwen,* 54, 59, 88, 92, 114.

126. Ibid., 27.

127. Else Lüders, "Die Dankesschuld gegen die Mutter," *Die Frauenbewegung* 21, no. 19 (October 1, 1915): 1–2; Damousi, 42–43. The widows' journal *Die Kriegerwitwe* carefully noted that both widows and parents needed adequate pensions, Dr. Dübell, "Spendet Hilfe für unsere Hinterbliebenen!" *Die Kriegerwitwe* 5/6 (1920): 1–2.

128. Johanna to Julius, October 1, 1914, in Hagener, 63; Robert Weldon Whalen explains the significance of the "feudalization" of the bourgeoisie in Germany in *Bitter Wounds,* 25.

129. Helmar, 184.

130. Helene Simon, "Kriegswitwen und Beruf," *Die Frau* 22, no. 7 (April 1915): 417; Geib, 6–7.

131. Karin Hausen, "Die Sorge der Nation für ihre 'Kriegsopfer': Ein Bereich der Geschlechterpolitik während der Weimarer Republik," in Jürgen Kocka, ed., *Von der Arbeiterbewegung zum modernen Sozialstaat* (Munich: Saur, 1994), 719.

132. Davis, "Homefront," 127; Marsland, 157, notes that stressing the exclusivity of comradeship in battle demarcated soldiers from civilians.

133. Hurwitz-Stranz, ed., *Kriegerwitwen*, 28; see Helma Sanders-Brahms's film *Germany, Pale Mother* VHS (Chicago: Facets Multimedia, 1979), for misunderstandings over men's and women's wartime experiences during the Second World War.

134. Cornelie Usborne, "'Pregnancy Is the Woman's Active Service': Pronatalism in Germany During the First World War," in Winter and Walls, eds., *Upheaval* 389.

135. J. M. Winter, "The Fear of Population Decline, 1870–1940" in R. W. Hiorns, ed., *Demographic Patterns in Developed Societies* (London: Taylor and Francis, 1980), 184–85.

136. Minna Cauer, "Zur Dienstpflicht der Frau," *Die Frauenbewegung* 22, no. 5 (March 1, 1916): 18; Quataert, 23, mentions the Socialists; Cauer, 18.

137. Quoted in Kimberly Jensen, *Mobilizing Minerva: American Women in the First World War* (Urbana: University of Illinois Press, 2008), 98.

138. Daniel, 283.

139. Daniel noted that not many new women entered the workforce, 276–77; Josephine Levy-Rathenau, "Berufsberatung und Kriegshinterbliebene," in Tagung des Hauptausschusses der Kriegerwitwen und Waisenfürsorgung, *Frauenerbwerb und Kriegswitwe Referate entstattet auf der 2. Tagung des Hauptasschusses der Kriegerwitwen und Waisenfürsorge am 27. November 1915 im Reichstagsgebäude in Berlin* (Berlin: Carl Heymann, 1916), 1.

140. Davis, *Home Fires*, 1–5.

141. Bessel, 226; Hurwitz-Stranz, ed., *Kriegerwitwen*, 37–38.

142. Hurwitz-Stranz, ed., *Kriegerwitwen*, 27.

143. Anthony, 196.

144. Salomon, "Die Fürsorge," 391.

145. Bessel, 141, 227; Cauer, 18.

146. Herta Daeubler-Gmelin, *Frauenarbeitslosigkeit oder Reserve zurück an den Herd!* (Reinbek bei Hamburg: Rowohlt, 1977), 29.

147. Deutscher Verein für Armenpflege und Wohltätigkeit, *Soziale Fürsorge für Kriegerwitwen und Kriegerwaisen* (Munich and Leipzig: Duncker und Humboldt, 1915), 51–52.

148. Leed, 83; Franz Marc's obituary of August Macke declared "in war we're all the same," Macke and Marc, *Briefwechsel*, 197; at the Russian POW camps where Julius was sent, officer POWs dined on elaborate meals while rank-and-file soldiers dined from communal soup pots and slept in close quarters, spreading the louse-born disease of typhus that killed Julius Boldt, Alon Rachamimov, *POWs and the Great War: Captivity on the Eastern Front* (New York: Berg, 2002), 97–99, 104.

149. Bessel, 226.

150. Kathy Peiss, *Cheap Amusements: Working Women and Leisure in Turn-of-the-Century New York* (Philadelphia: Temple University Press, 1986), 8–9, provides a useful discussion of defining the working class.

151. Eine Hauptmanns Witwe, "Was leistet das Reich für die Kriegsbeschädigten und Kriegerhinterbliebenen?" *Neue Lebensfahrt: Mitteilungen für kriegerhinterbliebene, Beilage*

zum Reichsbund, 3 no. 21 (November 1, 1920), n.p.; Gertrud Buetz, "Der Kampf um die weibliche Fortbildungsschule, *Die Frau* 23, no. 3 (December 1915): 159–70.

152. Alice Salomon, "Die Kriegerwitwe auf dem Lande," *Die Frau* 24, no. 3 (December 1916):149–54; Minna Cauer, "Die Landfrau und ihre Aufgaben," *Die Frauenbewegung* 22, no. 3 (February 1, 1916): 1–10; Helene Hurwitz-Stranz, "Stadtkinder aufs Land," *Die Frau* 24, no. 10 (July 1917): 601–5; Anonymous, "Soziale Aufgaben: Hinterbliebenenfürsorge auf dem Land," *Die Frau* 24, no. 10 (July 1917): 629–30; Anonymous, "Darf ich auch aufs Land?" *Die Kriegerwitwe* 5/6 (1920): 3–4.

153. Bessel, 30; a private's widow received 33 marks per month, a corporal's 41 and a sergeant's 50; but a skilled worker brought home about 120 to 150 per month in 1916, Whalen, 76.

154. Hurwitz-Stranz, ed., *Kriegerwitwen*, throughout, but especially 64, 70, 87.

155. Sklar, Schüler, and Strasser, 348; Anna Lindemann, *Die Zukunft der Kriegswitwe* (Berlin: Arthur Collignon, 1915), 12.

156. Lindemann, 12.

157. Ibid., 14–15.

158. Ibid., 17, 29.

159. For a condemnation of this type of industrial labor, see Käthe Gaebel, "Das Hausarbeitgesetzt," in Käthe Gaebel and Magistratsrat von Schulz, *Die Heimarbeit im Kriege* (Berlin: Verlag von Franz Bahlen, 1917), 25–47.

160. Lindemann, 25.

161. Davis, *Home Fires*, 174; Quataert, 211; Domansky, 440.

162. American Consul General (signature unclear) to Hon. Secretary of State, January 2, 1917, Microfilm 336, roll 81, Disasters and Calamities, RG 59, Records of the Department of State Relating to the Internal Affairs of Germany, 1910–1929, National Archives and Records Administration II, College Park, Maryland; Domansky, 440.

163. Rouette, "Mothers and Citizens," 53–54.

164. Ibid., 58–59.

165. Josephine Levy-Rathenau, "Berufsberatung und Kriegshinterbliebene," 1–3; Schlusstagung des Hauptausschusses, *Stand und Künftige Entwicklung der Kriegerwitwen und Kriegswaisenfürsorge* (Berlin: Carl Heymanns, 1918), 8.

166. Hausen, "German Nation's Obligation," 134.

167. Henriette Brey, "Warum brauchen wir Kriegshinterbliebene einen eigenen Verband und eine eigene Zeitung?," *Die Kriegerwitwe* 4 (1920): 1–3.

168. Lagorio, 186–87.

169. Hurwitz-Stranz, ed., *Kriegerwitwen*, 63, 83.

170. Whalen, 110–11, 124–25, 107.

171. Ibid., 128.

172. Hausen, "The German Nation's Obligation," 134.

173. Whalen, 143.

174. Davis, *Home Fires*, 33–35.

175. Anonymous, "Heimatchronik," *Die Frau* 22, no. 1 (October 1914): 56.

176. Helene Simon, "Kriegswitwen und Beruf," *Die Frau* 22, no. 7 (April 1915): 417–21.

177. A. T., "Unsere erste Generalversammlung," *Die Kriegerwitwe* 9/10 (1920): 2–3.

178. Ulrich and Ziemann, eds., *German Soldiers*, 31; Jason Crouthamel, "War Neurosis versus Savings Psychosis: Working-class Politics nd Psychological Trauma in Weimar Germany," *Journal of Contemporary History* 37, no. 2 (2002): 170–71.

179. Hurwitz-Stranz, ed., *Kriegerwitwen*, 91–92.

180. Hurwitz-Stranz, "8 Jahre Beisitzerin an Reichsversorgungsgericht," *Die Frau* 38 (1930/31): 264–71.

181. Kuhlman, *Reconstructing Patriarchy*, 148; quoted in Bessel, 278; letter from the Reichsbund, Ortsgruppe Landberg am Werther to the Oberpräsident der Provinz Brandenburg, December 18, 1918, Reichsarbeitsministerium R 3901, film #36072, BA, Berlin.

182. Brey, 2. Brey's main point, however, is that men's and women's interests are completely different from one another, reflecting the "separate spheres" ideology that merely reinforced women's isolation from activism.

3. THE WAR WIDOWS' ROMANCE:
VICTORY AND LOSS IN THE UNITED STATES

1. August Macke and Franz Marc, *August Macke, Franz Marc: Briefwechsel* (Köln: M. Dumont Schauberg, 1964), 216.

2. Erika Kuhlman, *Petticoats and White Feathers: Gender Conformity, Race, the Progressive Peace Movement and the Debate Over War, 1895–1919* (Westport, CT: Greenwood Press, 1997), 2; David M. Kennedy, *Over Here: The First World War and American Society* (New York: Oxford University Press, 1980), 31.

3. On U.S. government and business support for the Allied cause, see Kathleen Burk, *Britain, America and the Sinews of War, 1914–1918* (London: G. Allen & Unwin, 1984), 208–14; for U.S. popular opinion, see Leslie Midkiff Debauche, *Reel Patriotism: The Movies and World War I* (Madison: University of Wisconsin Press, 1997).

4. Leonard V. Smith, Stéphane Audoin-Rouzeau, and Annette Becker, *France and the Great War, 1914–1918*, trans. Helen McPhail (Cambridge: Cambridge University Press, 2003), 69.

5. Ethel Thurston, "'The Romance of the War Widow," *Syracuse Herald*, February 18, 1917, 160.

6. Joseph F. Keller to Victory Hall Association, September 10, 1920, William S. Keller dossier, dossier files, reel #7, Victory Hall Association records, 1920–1921 (hereafter VHA), MssCol 3165, Manuscripts and Archives Division (hereafter MAD), New York Public Library (hereafter NYPL). The VHA records are arranged alphabetically by soldier's last name.

7. Carrie Brown, *Rosie's Mom: Forgotten Women Workers of the First World War* (Boston: Northeastern University Press, 2002), 153; Benedict Crowell, *America's Munitions, 1917–1918* (Washington: GPS, 1919), 426.

8. Kristin Ramsdell, *Romance Fiction: A Guide to the Genre* (Englewood, CO: Libraries Unlimited, 1999), 7; Pamela Regis, *A Natural History of the Romance Novel* (Philadelphia: University of Pennsylvania Press, 2003), 116–17.

9. Northrop Frye, *The Secular Scripture: A Study of the Structure of Romance* (Cambridge, MA: Harvard University Press, 1976), 50.

10. A copy of the article appears in David Davidson's dossier, dossier files, reel #4, VHA records, MssCol 3165, MAD, NYPL.

11. Thurston, 160.

12. J. M. Winter, "Communities of Mourning," in Frans Coetzee and Marilyn Shevin-Coetzee, eds., *Authority, Identity and the Social History of the Great War* (Providence, RI: Berghahn Books, 1995), 345. For German war widows' economic situation, see chapter 2

of this volume; for war widows in Great Britain, see Janis Lomas, "'Delicate Duties': Issues of Class and Respectability in Government Policy Towards the Wives and Widows of British Soldiers in the Era of the Great War," *Women's History Review* 9, no. 1 (2000): 127–36.

13. Statistics on Great War casualties vary. Brigadier General Frank T. Hines submitted the numbers quoted here in U.S. Congress, *Pensions—World War widows: Pensions to widows and children of World War veterans: Hearings before the Committee on Pensions, House of Representatives, Seventy-fifth Congress, third session, on H.R. 8690 (now known as H.R. 9285) a bill granting a pension to widows and dependent children of World War veterans. January 25 and 28, 1938* (Washington: GPO, 1938), 37; Lisa M. Budreau, *Bodies of War: World War I and the Politics of Commemoration in America, 1919–1933* (New York: New York University Press, 2009), 376, records figures from the American Battle Monuments Commission.

14. Kennedy, 193–94.

15. Godfrey Hodgson, *The Myth of American Exceptionalism* (New Haven, CT: Yale University Press, 2008), 21–24; Irmgard Steinisch, "A Different Path to War: A Comparative Study of Militarism and Imperialism in the United States and Imperial Germany, 1871–1914," in Roger Chickering, Manfred Boemeke, and Stig Förster, eds., *Anticipating Total War: The German and American Experiences, 1871–1914* (Cambridge: Cambridge University Press, 1999), 31; Suzanne Evans, *Mothers of Heroes, Mothers of Martyrs: World War I and the Politics of Grief* (Montreal: McGill-Queen's University Press, 2007), 67, notes that British people also understood their soldiers as crusaders.

16. Budreau, *Bodies of War*, 233.

17. Margaret Dennis to War Department, October 3, 1930, burial file for Ewing W. Dennis, Graves Registration Service (hereafter GRS) files, Records of the Office of the Quartermaster General (hereafter QMG), RG 92, National Archives II (hereafter NA II), College Park, Maryland. GRS burial files are arranged alphabetically by soldier's last name.

18. "Star Mothers Asked to Be in Parade," *Eau Claire Leader*, November 10, 1923, 9; G. Kurt Piehler, *Remembering War the American Way* (Washington: Smithsonian Institution Press, 1995), 114; Budreau, *Bodies of War*, 98.

19. Jennifer D. Keene, *Doughboys, the Great War, and the Remaking of America* (Baltimore: Johns Hopkins University Press, 2001), 179–204.

20. I am indebted to Adam R. Seipp's *The Ordeal of Peace: Demobilitzation and the Urban Experience in Britain and Germany, 1917–1921* (Burlington, VT: Ashgate, 2009), 15–16, for his ideas on reciprocity and citizenship.

21. Archibald Alexander, "A New Mien of Grief," *The Literary Digest* 52, no. 5 (February 1916): 292. See Phillip A. Gibbs, "Self-Control and Male Sexuality in the Advice Literature of Nineteenth Century America, 1930–1860," *Journal of American Culture* 9, no. 2 (1986): 37–41 for more on self-control and popular American culture.

22. Alexander, "A New Mien of Grief"; Piehler, 117.

23. M. Trapp, "Delegation of War Widows, War Orphans, and Maimed War Heroes at the White House, Washington, D.C., 1916" broadside; publisher unknown, located at the Wisconsin Historical Society, Madison, Wisconsin; I am merely suggesting that M. Trapp may have been a woman; I do not have any information about the artist. John Dewey, *Characters and Events: Popular Essays in Social and Political Philosophy, Volume II* (New York: Henry Holt and Company, 1929), 577.

24. Woodrow Wilson, *President Wilson's Foreign Policy: Messages, Addresses, Papers*, ed. James Brown Scott (New York: Oxford University Press, 1918), 389.

25. Brown, 110; for similar problems in Britain, see Seipp, 73–76.

26. Elizabeth Grimm to Rebekah Crawford, July 9, 1916, Rebekah Crawford Papers, MS 0308, Rare Book and Manuscripts Library, Columbia University, New York City, emphasis Grimm's.

27. Lawrence Taylor, "Symbolic Death: An Anthropological View of Mourning in the Nineteenth Century," in *A Time to Mourn*, 46.

28. Theresa Johnson to George W. Wingate, undated, William Rudolph Johnson dossier, dossier files, reel #7, VHA records, MssCol 3165, MAD, NYPL.

29. Piehler, 101.

30. *Stars and Stripes*, November 22, 1918, 4.

31. Advertisement appeared in *Outlook*, 120 (November 27, 1918): 511.

32. Nancy K. Bristow, *Making Men Moral: Social Engineering During the Great War* (New York: New York University Press, 1996), 18–19.

33. Cynthia J. Mills, "The Adams Memorial and American Funerary Sculpture, 1891–1927" (Ph.D. diss., University of Maryland, College Park, 1996), 289. By contrast, Stéphane Audoin-Rouzeau and Annette Becker describe a shift during the war in Europe, where suddenly in 1917 Victorian mourning etiquette ground to a halt, *14–18: Understanding the Great War*, trans. Catherine Temerson (New York: Hill and Wang, 2002), 179.

34. Nevins to Wingate, August 9, 1920, J. B. Nevins dossier, dossier files, reel #11, VHA records, MssCol 3165, MAD, NYPL.

35. Edna Mae Beatty to George W. Wingate, Arthur Beatty dossier, dossier files, reel #1, VHA records, MssCol 3165, MAD, NYPL; Elizabeth Dunne to Wingate, June 17, 1920, John J. Dunne file, dossier files, reel #4, ibid.; Mrs. Katherine Discher to Wingate, June 9, 1920, Frank Discher file, dossier files, reel #4, ibid.

36. "Star Mothers Asked to Be in Parade," *Eau Claire Leader*, November 10, 1923, 9; for a description of the pomp and circumstance accompanying the Gold Star pilgrimage to France in 1930, see "National Affairs: Gold Star Sailing," *Time Magazine* (May 19, 1930), 13.

37. Harriet Pierson to QMG, September 24, 1938, burial file of Ward Wright Pierson, GRS burial files, Office of the QMG, RG 92, NA II.

38. Geertje van Os, "The Disappearance of Mourning Dress among Dutch Widows in the Twentieth Century," in Jan Bremmer and Lourens van den Bosch, eds., *Between Poverty and the Pyre: Moments in the History of Widowhood* (New York: Routledge, 1995), 232–33.

39. James P. Daughton, "Sketches of the *Poilu*'s World: Trench Cartoons from the Great War," in Douglas Peter Mackaman and Michael Mays, eds., *World War I and the Cultures of Modernity* (Jackson: University Press of Mississippi, 2000), 60; Barbara Dodd Hillerman, "Chrysallis of Gloom: Nineteenth Century American Mourning Costume" in Pike and Armstrong, eds., 104.

40. "President Approves War Mourning Bands," *New York Times*, May 26, 1918, 18.

41. "Spirit of French Thrift," *Syracuse Herald*, June 3, 1917, 106.

42. "Bad Effect of Mourning," *New York Times*, November 18, 1917, E2. Sullivan appears to have taken his trip in March 1917.

43. See, for example, Josef Wackerle's painting in this book's introduction; Helene Hurwtiz-Stranz, *Kriegerwitwen gestalten ihr Schicksal* (Berlin: Heymanns, 1931), 30, 116; see chapter 2 for discussion of Johanna Boldt in mourning; J. S., "Etwas über Kleidung," *Frauen-Rundschau* 6, no. 15 (April 15, 1905): 440.

44. Hillerman, 95–96; van Os discusses the colors of mourning, 235–36.

45. "Gold Star as Mourning," *New York Times*, November 13, 1917, 7; "'Mourning' Is Harmful in Wartime," *New York Times*, November 14, 1917, 14.

46. Evans, 93.

47. "Put Ban on Mourning Garb During the War!" *Syracuse Herald*, September 30, 1917, 47.

48. David E. Stannard, "Where all our steps are tending: Death in the American Context," in Pike and Armstrong, eds., 26.

49. Edmund Lindop, *America in the 1920s* (New York: 21st Century, 2004), 21, includes a photograph of President Coolidge wearing the armband; the *Herald* writer may have a point, though. Henry Adams tore off his black crepe armband one evening during dinner, according to his relatives; he refused to continue the tradition of wearing black while mourning his wife's death in 1885, Mills, 21.

50. Barbara Dodd Hillerman, "Chrysallis of Gloom," in Pike and Armstrong, eds., 104.

51. Budreau, *Bodies of War*, 97.

52. Else Lüders, "Das Doppelgesicht des Krieges," *Die Frauenbewegung* 21, no. 4 (February 15, 1915): 1, 14.

53. Belinda Brewster, "War Makes Change in Clothes Worn by Women of America," *Indianapolis Star*, November 11, 1917, 37.

54. Frank Crane, "Mourning in War Time," *The Syracuse Herald*, December 17, 1917, 16.

55. "Announcing Blackshire Mourning Apparel" *Fort Wayne Journal-Gazette*, November 4, 1917, 23.

56. Crane, 16.

57. U.S. Employment Bureau advertisement, *Bridgeport Telegraph*, September 21, 1918, 18.

58. "Hints for the Woman who Wears Morning [sic]," *Chicago Sunday Press and the Women's Press* 2, no. 46 (1919), 7; evidence of this can be found in GRS burial files, Records of the Office of the QMG, Record Group 92, NA II, and the Victory Hall Association records, 1920–21, dossier files, reels 1–17, NYPL.

59. "President Approves War Mourning Bands," *New York Times*, May 26, 1918, 18.

60. Woodrow Wilson, *The Papers of Woodrow Wilson, Volume 48* (Princeton, NJ: Princeton University Press, 1986), 28, 46.

61. Pamphlet, "Reasons Why the Dead Bodies of Our Beloved Martyrs Should Remain in France, by Mabel Fonda Gareisson, A Gold Star Mother Who Served Overseas with the AEF," December 1919, p. 6, dossier files, reel #9, VHA records, MssCol 3165, MAD, NYPL.

62. Piehler, 122.

63. Budreau, *Bodies of War*, 96; "President Approves War Mourning Bands," *New York Times*, May 26, 1918, 18.

64. Charles C. Pierce to Mrs. Gansloser, date unclear, Frank A. Gansloser file, Box 385, World War I Bonus Applications from Veterans and Beneficiaries (hereafter BAVB), RS 503.001, Illinois State Archives (hereafter ISA), Springfield, Illinois. A fire at the State Arsenal partially destroyed the records in 1934, leaving many names and dates unclear.

65. Budreau, *Bodies of War*, 97; Joy Damousi, *The Labour of Loss: Mourning, Memory, and Wartime Bereavement in Australia* (New York: Cambridge University Press, 1999), 54; Suzanne Evans, *Mothers of Heroes, Mothers of Martyrs: World War I and the Politics of Grief* (Montreal: McGill–Queen's University Press), 11; James Diehl, "Victors or Victims? Disabled Veterans in the Third Reich," *The Journal of Modern History* 59, no. 4 (December 1987): 721–22 and corresponding footnotes.

66. Piehler, 105. Pilgrims' expenses during the trip were paid for, but they had to be able to transport themselves to New York to board the steamer bound for France. During the Great Depression, this requirement undoubtedly prevented some women from making the journey.

67. "17 Gold Star Mothers Pray at Graves of Sons Buried on Slopes of Mont Valerien Near Paris," *New York Times*, May 19, 1930, 1.

68. "Armistice Day 1918" cartoon, *Chicago Tribune*, November 11, 1929, 14.

69. See Gold Star Wives of America, "Records, 1933," Mss5, F10, Wisconsin Veterans Museum, Madison, Wisconsin, for materials relating to the pilgrimages.

70. Lisa M. Budreau, "The Politics of Remembrance: The Gold Star Mothers' Pilgrimage and America's Fading Memory of the Great War," *The Journal of Military History* 72, no. 2 (2008): 372.

71. Piehler, 98.

72. Budreau, *Bodies of War*, 203.

73. Piehler, 97.

74. Quoted in Kennedy, 368; "Capital Rebuffs Gold Star Negroes," *New York Times*, May 30, 1930, 12.

75. Sarah Ets-Hokin to QMG, November 6, 1929, Samuel Ets-Hokin burial file, GRS burial files, Records of the Office of the QMG, Record Group 92, NA II.

76. Volker Depkat, "Remembering the War the Transnational Way: The U.S.-American Memory of World War I," in Udo J. Hebel, ed., *Transnational American Memories* (Berlin/New York: Walter de Gruyter, 2009), 187–88.

77. William David Seitz, "'Let Him Remain Until the Judgment in France,'" in ibid., 232; Seitz provides many other examples of families' explanations of their decisions to either repatriate or leave their loved ones' remains in France. The grisly work of removing soldiers' remains from overseas graves was accomplished primarily by African American troops.

78. "Writers Disagree on Soldier Dead," *New York Times*, April 17, 1921, 20; Mabel Fonda Gareisson, 7.

79. Budreau, *Bodies of War*, 75, 80.

80. Grace Brooks to Newton Baker, October 25, 1919, Floyd B. Brooks burial file, GRS burial files, Office of the QMG, RG 92, NA II; Lisa M. Budreau, "Politics of Remembrance," 377.

81. Depkat, 188.

82. Quoted in Bernd Ulrich and Benjamin Ziemann, eds., *German Soldiers in the Great War: Letters and Eyewitness Accounts*, trans. Christine Brocks (South Yorkshire: Pen & Sword Books, 2010), 184.

83. Budreau, *Bodies of War*, 194; Budreau, "Politics of Remembrance," 381, 385.

84. Elizabeth Creevey Hamm, *In White Armor: The Life of Captain Arthur Ellis Hamm, 326th Infantry, United States Army* (New York: Knickerbocker Press, 1919); Elizabeth Hamm to Captain Charles W. Dietz, Office of QMG, August 6, 1932, Arthur Ellis Hamm burial file, GRS burial files, Records of the QMG, RG 92, NAII.

85. Damousi, 71.

86. Quoted in Budreau, *Bodies of War*, 201; ibid., 205; Mathilda Burling testimony recorded in *To Authorize Mothers and Unmarried Widows of Deceased World War Veterans Buried in Europe to Visit the Graves, Hearing Before a Subcommittee of the Committee on Military Affairs, U.S. Senate, 70th Congress, May 14, 1928, Part 1* (Washington: GPO, 1928), 5, 26.

87. Rebecca Jo Plant, "The Repeal of Mother Love: Momism and the Reconstruction of Motherhood in Philip Wylie's America" (Ph.D. diss., Johns Hopkins University, 2001), 118.

88. Linda Kerber, "The Republican Mother: Women and the Enlightenment—An American Perspective," *American Quarterly* 28, no. 2 (Summer 1976): 187–205.

89. "To Authorize Mothers and Unmarried Widows of Deceased World War Veterans," throughout; Damousi, 26; S. Wronsky, "Die Kreigshinterbliebenenfürsorge als Wegbereiter für die moderne Wohlfahrtspflege," in Helene Hurwitz-Stranz, ed., 103.

90. Edward J. Bok, "Let the Soldier Be a Soldier," *Ladies' Home Journal* 35 (May 1918): 1.

91. Constance Potter, "World War I Gold Star Mothers Pilgrimages, Part I," *Prologue Magazine* 31, no. 2 (Summer 1999) http://www.archives.gov/publications/prologue/1999/summer/gold-star-mothers-1.html (accessed March 25, 2010); the fact that wives who had chosen to bring their husbands' bodies homes were not eligible for a trip to visit soldiers' graves overseas was not obvious to all. Mrs. Laura E. Sorenson to Secretary of War Hon. Mr. Patrick J. Hurley, January 7, 1930, Soren C. Sorenson burial file, GRS burial files, Records of the Office of the QMG, Record Group 92, NA II.

92. Excerpt from liaison report, June 8, 1933, Arthur H. Marsh burial file, GRS burial files, Office of the QMG, RG 92, NA II.

93. Nancy Marsh to P. C. Harris, Adjutant General's Office, ibid.

94. Budreau, *Bodies of War*, 235, 227–28.

95. Piehler, 97; Laura Evelyn Sorenson to Adjutant General, September 5, 1919, Soren C. Sorenson burial file, GRS burial files, Records of the QMG, RG 92, NAII.

96. Elsie MacKenzie to Wingate, June 20, 1920, Kenneth MacKenzie dossier, dossier files, reel #9, VHA records, MssCol 3165, MAD, NYPL.

97. "To Relatives and Friends of New York City's War Dead," example of a VHA newspaper advertisement, dossier files, reel #6, ibid.

98. Wingate to Mrs. Angelina Appignani, July 2, 1920, Albert Assenzo dossier, dossier files, reel #1, VHA records, MssCol 3165, MAD, NYPL.

99. This letter appears in nearly all VHA dossier files.

100. Edna Mae Beatty to Dear Sirs, July 6, 1920, Arthur Beatty dossier, dossier files, reel #1, VHA records, MssCol 3165, MAD, NYPL.

101. Edward Guckenheimer to VHA, June 26, 1920, Edgar R. Guckenheimer dossier, dossier files, reel #6, VHA records, MssCol 3165, MAD, NYPL.

102. Budreau, *Bodies of War*, 378.

103. Mrs. Margaret Belfry to Mr. Wingate, January 21, 1920, Earl Belfry dossier, dossier files, reel #1, VHA records, MssCol 3165, MAD, NYPL; Mrs. Margaret Davitt refused to comply with Wingate's request because she could not afford to (Wingate assured her that he did not expect widows to donate to the VHA), Mrs. Margaret Davitt to Mr. Wingate, April 16, 1920, Davitt dossier, dossier files, reel #4, ibid.; Nevins to Wingate, August 9, 1920, J. B. Nevins dossier, dossier files, reel #11, ibid.

104. James Watson Kephart burial file, GRS burial files, Records of the Office of the QMG, RG 92, NA II; in the case of Roy B. Martin, the parents convinced the widow and Martin's body was repatriated; Roy B. Martin burial file, ibid.

105. Depkat, 191.

106. Letter from Carl A. Swallow to Hon. Hanford MacNider, April 23, 1927. Frank Downer burial file, GRS burial files, Records of the Office of the QMG, RG 92, NA II; Robert L. Anderson's widow, Ella Anderson, communicated her displeasure at American Legion interference in the handling of deceased soldiers' bodies, Robert L. Anderson burial file, ibid.

107. Thomas C. Dooner to Illinois Service Recognition Board (hereafter SRB), July 5, 1923, William Howard Bratten file, Box 123, World War I BAVB, RS 503.001, ISA.

108. For France, see Martha Hanna, *Your Death Would Be Mine: Paul and Marie Pireaud in the Great War* (Cambridge, MA: Harvard University Press, 2006), 53–57; for Great Britain, see Janis Lomas, "'Delicate Duties': Issues of Class and Respectability in Government Policy Towards the Wives and Widows of British Soldiers in the Era of the Great War," *Women's History Review* 9, no. 1 (2000): 123–47.

109. K. Walter Hickel, "War, Region, and Social Welfare: Federal Aid to Servicemen's Dependents in the South, 1917–1921," *The Journal of American History* 87, no. 4 (March 2001): 1373; *Congressional Record*, House, 55, Pt. 7, 65th Congress first session (August 30–October 1, 1917), 6754–55.

110. Walter B. Drebelbis burial file, GRS burial files, Records of the Office of the QMG, RG 92, NA II.

111. *Annual Report of the Director of the Bureau of War Risk Insurance for the Fiscal Year Ended June 30, 1920* (Washington: GPO, 1920), 12.

112. Thomas B. Love, "The Social Significance of War Risk Insurance," *The ANNALS of the American Academy of Political and Social* Science (*1918*): 51, emphasis mine.

113. Hickel, "War, Region, and Social Welfare," 1375, 1365.

114. *Congressional Record*, House, 55, Pt. 7, 65th Congress first session (August 30–October 1, 1917), 6752.

115. Ibid., 6752, 6754.

116. *Annual Report of the Director of the Bureau of War Risk Insurance*, 49.

117. S. J. Kleinberg, *Widows and Orphans First: The Family Economy and Social Welfare Policy, 1880–1939* (Urbana: University of Illinois Press, 2006), 23.

118. Samuel McCune Lindsay, "Purpose and Scope of War Risk Insurance," *Annals of the American Academy of Political and Social Science*, 79 (September 1918): 62.

119. Love, 48.

120. Lindsay, 60, 61.

121. Rose Falls Bres, *Maids, Wives, and Widows: The Law of the Land and of the Various States as It Affects Women* (New York: Dutton, 1918), 83.

122. U.S. Congress, House Committee on Pensions, *Pensions—World War widows: pensions to widows and children of World War veterans: hearings before the Committee on Pensions, House of Representatives, Seventy-fifth Congress, third session, on H.R. 8690 (now known as H.R. 9285) a bill granting a pension to widows and dependent children of World War veterans. January 25 and 28, 1938* (Washington: G.P.O., 1938), 14.

123. S. H. Wolfe, "Eight Months of War-Risk Insurance Work," *Annals of the American Academy of Political and Social Science*, 79 (September 1918): 63, 75.

124. Hickel, "War, Region, and Social Welfare," 1364, 1368; ibid., 1377–78.

125. K. Walter Hickel, "Entitling Citizens: World War I, Progressivism, and the Origins of the American Welfare State, 1917–1928" (Ph.D. diss., Columbia University, 1999), 76.

126. "Soldiers' Families Victims of Red Tape," *New York Times*, June 8, 1918, 18; BWRI merged with Federal Board for Vocational Education to create the Veterans Bureau in 1921. Its first director, Charles R. Forbes, proved to be corrupt; in 1924, he was convicted of conspiracy to defraud the U.S. government.

127. Mrs. Rose Hassett Brassell to SRB, October 12, 1924, John Robert Brassell file, Box 123, World War I BAVB, RS 503.001, ISA.

128. "Soldiers' Families Victims of Red Tape," *New York Times*, June 8, 1918, 18.

129. Hickel, "War, Region, and Social Welfare," 1364.

130. Natalia Greensfelder, "An Inquiry into the Problem of Relief for Families of Deceased World War Veterans in Illinois" (M.A. Thesis, University of Chicago, 1931), 1–3. The list of states offering bonuses to veterans but not to survivors includes Michigan, Minnesota, Oregon, Wisconsin (offered orphans educational vouchers), and New York.

131. Ibid., 44.

132. Ibid., 30.

133. Ibid., 64.

134. Ibid., 63, 65.

135. Ibid., 44.

136. Kleinberg, 112.

137. Agnes C. Dolan to Victory Hall Association, undated, William J. Courter dossier, dossier files, reel #3, VHA records, MssCol 3165, MAD, NYPL.

138. Letter from Eva R. Finn to Office of the QMG, August 27, 1932, Richard E. Cook burial file, GRS burial files, Records of the Office of the QMG, RG 92, NA II.

139. These letters from the Illinois Service Recognition Board appear in nearly all of the files. World War I BAVB, RS 503.001, ISA, emphasis SRB's.

140. "Mrs. Glick Will Make Visit to Her Son's Grave," *Constitution Tribune*, Chillicothe, Missouri, January 6, 1930, 1.

141. Greensfelder, 29–30.

142. U.S. Congress, *Pensions—World War widows: Pensions to widows and children of World War veterans: Hearings before the Committee on Pensions, House of Representatives, Seventy-fifth Congress, third session, on H.R. 8690 (now known as H.R. 9285) a bill granting a pension to widows and dependent children of World War veterans. January 25 and 28, 1938* (Washington: GPO, 1938), 22–33.

143. Greensfelder, 59–61.

144. Kleinberg, 3.

145. Karl Nau, *Die Wirtschaftliche und soziale Lage von Kriegshinterbliebenen: Eine Studie auf Grund von Erhebungen über die auswirkung der versorgung von Kriegshinterbliebenen in Darmstadt* (Leipzig: Lühe and Co., Kommissionsverlag, 1930), 48; Hurwitz-Stranz, ed., *Kriegerwitwen*, 64, 70, 87 (in this last example, the husband had earned 650 marks per month before the war; after he died, her pension was 155 marks per month; in a further example, a husband who earned 200 marks per month left a widow with only 72 marks).

146. Greensfelder, 72–73.

147. "Education for Soldiers' Widows," *Salt Lake Tribune*, March 22, 1921, 6.

148. "Labor Senses Plot in Reorganization Plan," Fort Wayne *Journal-Gazette*, May 22, 1921, 13.

149. "Legion Will Push Four Bills," *Ogden Standard Examiner*, April 26, 1921, 26.

150. Great Britain, Ministry of Pensions, *Instructions on the Training of Widows* (London: V.S., 1918) Australian War Memorial, Campbell, ACT, Australia.

151. Kleinberg, 23.

152. U.S. Congress, *Pensions—World War widows*, 5, 7, 5, 24, 8.

4. THE TRANSNATIONALIZATION OF
SOLDIERS, WIDOWS, AND WAR RELIEF

1. William Faulkner, *Soldiers' Pay* (New York: Liveright Publishing Corporation, 1926).

2. John H. Marrow Jr., "Knights of the Sky: The Rise of Military Aviation," in Frans Coetzee and Marilyn Shevin-Coetzee, eds., *Authority, Identity and the Social History of the Great War* (Providence, RI: Berghahn Books, 1995), 305–21.

3. J. L. Carr's novella *A Month in the Country* (Brighton, England: Harvester Press, 1980) includes a conversation between two emotionally scarred veterans. One admits that he wishes he had some physical manifestation of his battle wounds, not because he wants to be a hero but because he finds his nonphysical scars difficult to explain to others.

4. Michael Zeitlin, "The Passion of Margaret Powers: A Psychoanalytic Reading of *Soldiers' Pay*," *Mississippi Quarterly* 46 (1993): 355–57.

5. Faulkner, 36.

6. Ibid., 44.

7. Zeitlin, 359–60.

8. David A. Davis, "The Modernist Death of Donald Mahon," Modern Language Association, Philadelphia, Pennsylvania, November 2006, faulknersociety.com/mla06davis. doc. July 2011

9. "AHR Conversation: On Transnational History," *American Historical Review* 111 no. 5 (December 2006): 1441–64; Kimberly Jensen and Erika Kuhlman, "Introduction," in Jensen and Kuhlman, eds., *Women and Transnational Activism in Historical Perspective* (Dordrecht, Netherlands: Republic of Letters Publishing, 2010), 1.

10. Elisabeth Macke to Maria Marc, September 5, 1914, in *August Macke, Franz Marc: Briefwechsel* (Köln: Verlag M. Dumont Schauberg, 1964), 189–90; Elisabeth to Franz, December 22, 1914, ibid., 201.

11. Leonhard Frank, *Der Mensch ist Gut* (Zürich: M. Rascher, 1918), 24; translation of Frank in Robert Weldon Whalen, *Bitter Wounds*, 69.

12. Marcus Gräser, "World History in a Nation-State: The Transnational Disposition in Historical Writing in the United States," *Journal of American History* 95 no. 4 (March 2009): 1046–47.

13. Eugen Weber, *The Hollow Years: France in the 1930s* (New York: Norton, 1993), 38.

14. Davis, 5.

15. Ernest Hemingway, *A Farewell to Arms* (1929; reprint New York: Charles Scribner's Sons, 1993).

16. Davis, 5.

17. Paul Fussell, *The Great War and Modern Memory* (New York: Oxford University Press, 1975), 21–22; Stefan Goebel, *The Great War and Medieval Memory: War, Remembrance and Medievalism in Britain and Germany, 1914–1940* (Cambridge: Cambridge University Press, 2007), compares medievalism in Great Britain and Germany; for a discussion of gender and the U.S. war declaration, see Erika Kuhlman, *Petticoats and White Feathers: Gender Conformity, Race, the Progressive Peace Movement and the Debate over War, 1895–1919* (Westport, CT: Greenwood Press, 1997), 1–20.

18. Michèle Barrett, *Casualty Figures: How Five Men Survived the First World War* (New York: Verso, 2007), 3, 66–91, features Skirth.

19. Mona Siegel, "'History Is the Opposite of Forgetting': The Limits of Memory and the Lessons of History in Interwar France," *The Journal of Modern History* 74, 4 (December 2002): 775, 784–85.

20. L. L. Farrar Jr., "Nationalism in Wartime: Critiquing the Conventional Wisdom," in Frans Coetzee and Marilyn Shevin-Coetzee, eds., 133–47; see C. Paul Vincent's *The Politics of Hunger: The Allied Blockade of Germany, 1915–1919* (Athens: Ohio University Press, 1985), 2–3, for the traditional account of the enthusiastic response of Europeans at the outbreak of war; see also chapter 2, note 9. But it is difficult to untangle myth from reality. When war appeared imminent in late July, in Hamburg's coffee houses "no one wanted to hear anything of the possibility of a peaceful outcome" to the conflict according to Edith Hagener, *Es Lief so sicher an Deinem Arm: Briefe einer Soldatenfrau, 1914* (Weinheim: Beltz, 1986), 27; Robert Weldon Whalen cites as evidence photographs of young women cheering departing soldiers in Whalen, *Bitter Wounds: German Victims of the Great War* (Ithaca, NY: Cornell University Press, 1984), 71; Elizabeth A. Marsland, *The Nation's Cause: French, English and German Poetry of the First World War* (New York: Routledge, 1991), says that "young men thanking God for making them alive at this time was universal among warring powers," 76.

21. Alexander Watson, *Enduring the Great War: Combat, Morale, and Collapse in the German and British Armies, 1914–1918* (Cambridge: Cambridge University Press, 2008), 82; Aribert Reimann, *Der grosse Krieg der Sprachen: Untersuchungen zur historischen Semantik in Deutschland und England zur Zeit des Ersten Weltkriegs* (Essen: Klartext Verlag, 2000), 129.

22. Kuhlman, *Petticoats and White Feathers*, 1; J. M. Winter describes a war widow who had goaded her husband into enlisting in "Communities in Mourning," in Coetzee and Shevin-Coetzee, eds., 344. See also Harold Frederic's Civil War novel *Marsena, and Other Stories of the War Time* (1894; reprint Freeport, NY: Books for Libraries Press).

23. Henry F. May, *The End of American Innocence: A Study of the First Years of Our Own Time, 1912–1917* (New York: Knopf, 1959), 393–94, pictures the postwar years as divided between the rejection of moralism and a defense of tradition; Kuhlman, *Reconstructing Patriarchy*, 21–25, uses evidence from the U.S. military newspapers *Stars and Stripes* and the *Amaroc* to document the desire among U.S. soldiers for a return to traditional gender norms.

24. Coetzee and Shevin-Coetzee, eds., "Introduction," xix.

25. Fussell, *The Great War and Modern Memory*; Eric J. Leed, *No Man's Land: Combat and Identity in World War I* (Cambridge: Cambridge University Press, 1981).

26. Jay Winter, *Remembering War: The Great War Between Memory and History in the Twentieth Century* (New Haven, CT: Yale University Press, 2006), 4.

27. Ibid., 18–19.

28. Advertisement by the American Telephone & Telegraph Company and U.S. Committee on Public Information. *The Outlook* Vol. 120 (27 November 1918): 511.

29. Fussell, *The Great War and Modern Memory*, 29–35.

30. Winter, 6–7; see Tammy M. Proctor, *Civilians in a World at War, 1914–1918* (New York: New York University Press, 2010).

31. C. Paul Vincent, *The Politics of Hunger*, 50, emphasizes the blockade's importance to the Allies.

32. Tricia Cusack and Síghle Bhreathnach-Lynch, eds., *Art, Nation, and Gender: Ethnic Landscapes, Myths, and Mother-Figures* (Burlington, VT: Ashgate, 2003), especially Part I, "Women as Allegories of the Nation," 8–14.

33. Volker Depkat, "Remembering War the Transnational Way: The U.S.–American Memory of World War I," in Udo J. Hebel, ed., *Transnational American Memories* (Berlin/New York: Walter de Gruyter, 2009), 185; Edward Said, "Invention, Memory, and Place," *Critical Inquiry* 26 (Winter 2000): 177–79.

34. The first phrase was popularized by H. G. Wells in August 1914; the second was used in Germany when soldiers died in battle (see chapter 1 of this volume); Woodrow Wilson used the last in his war declaration against Germany on April 2, 1917.

35. Coetzee and Shevin-Coetzee, eds., "Introduction," x.

36. Katherine Anne Porter, "Pale Horse, Pale Rider," in *Pale Horse, Pale Rider: Three Short Novels*, Afterword by Mark Schorer (New York: Signet Modern Classics, 1962), 140.

37. Ibid., 141.

38. Eric Hobsbawm, "Introduction," in Eric Hobsbawm and Terence Ranger, eds., *The Invention of Tradition* (Cambridge: Cambridge University Press, 1983), 1.

39. "American Pilgrimage Gold Star Mothers and Widows in Europe," itinerary, Gold Star Wives of America, "Records, 1933," WVM Mss 181, Wisconsin Veterans Museum (hereafter WVM), Madison, Wisconsin.

40. Goebel, *The Great War and Medieval Memory*; George L. Mosse, *Fallen Soldiers: Reshaping the Memories of the World Wars* (New York: Oxford University Press, 1990), 101–2; Siegel, 777.

41. Mosse, 70–106; Jay Winter, *Sites of Memory, Sites of Mourning: The Great War in European Cultural History* (Cambridge: Cambridge University Press, 1995), 27–28.

42. Kimberly Jensen, *Mobilizing Minerva: American Women in the First World War* (Urbana: University of Illinois Press, 2008), 123–41.

43. Benedict Anderson, *Imagined Communities: Reflections on the Origin and Spread of Nationalism* (London: Verso, 1991).

44. Quoted in Morris Engelman, *Four Years of Relief and War Work by the Jews of America, 1914–1918: A Chronological Review* (New York: M. Engelman, 1918), 57, emphasis mine.

45. Kenneth Allinson, *The Architects and Architecture of London* (Oxford: Architectural Press, 2008), 243; K. S. Inglis, *Sacred Places: War Memorials in the Australian Landscape* (Melbourne: The Miegunyah Press, 2008), 150.

46. Depkat, 185–86.

47. Suzanne Evans, *Mothers of Heroes, Mothers of Martyrs: World War I and the Politics of Grief* (Montreal: McGill–Queen's University Press, 2007), 123–25.

48. Ibid., 142–43; Siegel, 784.

49. Peter Barton, *The Battlefields of the First World War: The Unseen Panoramas of the Western Front* (London: Constable in Association with the Imperial War Museum, 2005), 279.

50. Anonymous, "Kriegergräberstätten und Kriegergräberpflege im Feindesland," *Die Kriegerwitwe* 3, no. 1 (January 1921): 2.

51. Gold Star Wives of America, "Records, 1933" WVM Mss 181, WVM.

52. Randolph Bourne, "Trans-national America," *Atlantic Monthly* 118 (July 1916): 86–97; Israel Zangwill, *The Melting-pot, Drama in Four Acts* (New York: Macmillan, 1909), coined the phrase several years before U.S. intervention.

53. Jonathan D. Sarna and Jonathan Golden, "The American Jewish Experience in the Twentieth Century: Antisemitism and Assimilation" (Triangle Park, NC: National Humanities Center), http://nationalhumanitiescenter.org/tserve/twenty/tkeyinfo/jewish-exp.htm (accessed May 2010). "Jewish Relief Day Crowds Hero Land," *New York Times*, November 29, 1917, 13.

54. Sarna and Golden, "The American Jewish Experience."

55. Engelman, 52, 24, 57, 13.

56. Nancy G. Ford, *Americans All! Foreign-born Soldiers in World War I* (College Station: Texas A & M University Press, 2001), 17–18.

57. Coetzee and Shevin-Coetzee, eds., "Introduction," xiii–xiv; in contrast Vincent, 2–4, argues that nationalism successfully united populations in the belligerent European countries.

58. Amy Bentley, *Eating for Victory: Food Rationing and the Politics of Domesticity* (Urbana: University of Illinois Press, 1998), 20–21; Belinda J. Davis, *Home Fires Burning: Food, Politics, and Everyday Life in World War I Berlin* (Chapel Hill: University of North Carolina Press, 2000), 130, 191–92; Vincent, 8, 14; see also Adam R. Seipp's *The Ordeal of Peace: Demobilization and the Urban Experience in Britain and Germany, 1917–1921* (Burlington, VT: Ashgate, 2009) for comparisons between citizens' negative relationship with their governments in Britain and Germany.

59. Heather Jones, "International or Transnational? Humanitarian Action during the First World War," *European Review of History* 16, no. 5 (2009): 708.

60. Kuhlman, *Reconstructing Patriarchy*, 27; David G. Williamson, *The British in Germany, 1918–1933: The Reluctant Occupiers* (New York: Berg, 1991), 211; Weber, 87; Lisa M. Budreau, "The Politics of Remembrance: The Gold Star Mothers' Pilgrimage and America's Fading Memory of the Great War," *Journal of Military History* 72, no. 2 (2008): 404.

61. Philomene Maas to QMG, no date, Alfred Maas burial file, GSR burial files, Office of the Quartermaster General, RG 92, NA II.

62. "17 Gold Star Mothers Pray at Graves of Sons Buried on Slopes of Mont Valerien Near Paris," *New York Times*, May 19, 1930, 1.

63. Alice Hamilton, "At the War Capitals," *Survey* (August 7, 1915): 418.

64. Matthew Stibbe, "Elisabeth Rotten and the 'Auskunfts- und Hilfsstelle für Deutsche im Ausland und Ausländer in Deutschland,' 1914–1919," in Alison S. Fell and Ingrid Sharp, eds., *The Women's Movement in Wartime: International Perspectives, 1914–19* (Basingstoke: Palgrave Macmillan, 2007), 196.

65. Gold Star Wives of America, "Records, 1933" WVM Mss 181, WVM.

66. "17 Gold Star Mothers Pray at Graves of Sons Buried on Slopes of Mont Valerien Near Paris," *New York Times*, May 19, 1930, 1.

67. Great Britain Ministry of Pensions, "Instructions on the Training of War Widows" (London: V. S., 1918), 2. Australian War Memorial, Campbell, ACT, Australia.

68. Quoted in J. M. Winter, "Communities of Mourning," 347.

69. Ingrid Sharp, "Blaming the Women: Women's 'Responsibility' for the First World War," in Ingrid Sharp and Alison S. Fell, eds., *The Women's Movement in Wartime: International Perspectives, 1914–19* (Basingstoke: Palgrave Macmillan, 2007), 81–82.

70. Essentialist feminists believe that there are fundamental and innate differences between the sexes.

71. Jacobs's speech was reproduced in two issues of *Die Frauenbewegung*: "Aus Holland," *Die Frauenbewegung* 21, no. 15 (August 1, 1915): 58–59, and "Aufruf der Amerikanischen Frauen in Deutschland: Appell an die Frauen in den Vereinigten Staaten," *Die Frauenbewegung* 21, no. 14 (July 15, 1915): 54.

72. Quoted in Barrett, 130.

73. Dora Apel, "Cultural Battlegrounds: Weimar Photographic Narratives of War," *New German Critique* No. 76, Special Issue on Weimar Visual Culture (Winter, 1999), 49–50.

74. Matthew Stanley, "'An Expedition to Heal the Wounds of War': The 1919 Eclipse and Eddington as Quaker Adventurer," *Isis* 94 no. 1 (March 2003): 64.

75. Quoted in Dora Apel, "'Heroes' and 'Whores': The Politics of Gender in Wieimar Antiwar Imagery," *Art Bulletin* LXXIX, no. 3 (September 1997): 378.

76. Apel, "Cultural Battlegrounds," 49–50.

77. Anonymous, "Das sehr wichtige Moment der Kameradschaft von Leidensgenossen unter Ausschaltung aller sozialen Einengungen möchte ich noch besonders hervorheben," in Helene Hurwitz-Stranz, ed., *Kriegerwitwen gestalten ihr Schicksal: Lebenskämpfe deutscher Kriegerwitwen nach eigenen Darstellungen* (Berlin: Carl Heymanns Verlag, 1931), 43.

78. See Epilogue to this volume.

79. Karl Ruetti, *Die Entwicklung der Militär-hinterbliebenen-Versorgung in Deutschland* (Berlin: Carl Heymanns Verlag, 1920), 84–85.

80. Hurwitz-Stranz, 64, 84.

81. Weber, 17.

82. Winter, *Sites of Memory*, 227.

83. Siegel, 784.

84. Leonard V. Smith, Stéphane Audoin-Rouzeau, and Annette Becker, *France and the Great War, 1914–1918* (Cambridge: Cambridge University Press, 2002), 73–74, describes the situation in France.

85. Capt. David E. Williams to Harriot [*sic*], January 3, 1918, Pierson Family Papers, Collection 3040, Historical Society of Pennsylvania, Philadelphia, Pennsylvania.

86. Depkat, 192; Winter, "Communities of Mourning," 349.

87. David William Seitz, "'Let Him Remain Until the Judgment in France,'" in Udo J. Hebel, ed., 229.

88. Winter, "Communities of Mourning," 345. Janis Lomas has written extensively about British war widows in "'Delicate Duties': Issues of Class and Respectability in Government Policy Towards the Wives and Widows of British Soldiers in the Era of the Great War," *Women's History Review* 9, no. 1 (2000): 123–47.

89. Francesca Lagorio, "Italian Widows of the First World War," in Coetzee and Shevin-Coetzee, eds., 178–81; Karin Hausen, "The German Nation's Obligation to the Heroes' Widows of World War I," in Margaret Randolph Higonnet, Jane Jenson, Sonya Michel, Margaret Collins Weitz, eds., *Behind the Lines: Gender and the Two World Wars* (New Haven, CT: Yale University Press, 1987), 126–53; Janis Lomas, "'Delicate Duties,'" 123–47.

90. Depkat, 186.

91. These include *International Woman Suffrage News* (also published under the title *Jus Suffragii*) and the *International Women's News*; Dr. Gertraud Wolf, "Der Frauenerwerb in den Hauptkulturstaaten," *Die Frau* 23, no. 11 (August 1916): 647–57; Anonymous, "Frauenarbeit in Frankreich," *Die Frauenbewegung* 22, no. 23 (December 1, 1916): 92a; Anonymous, "Frauenstimmrecht im In- und Ausland," *Die Frauenbewegung* 21, no. 15 (August 1, 1915): 60b.

92. Else Lüders, "Das Doppelgesicht des Krieges," *Die Frauenbewegung* 21, no. 4 (February 15, 1915): 1.

93. Dr. Lübbering (probably Heinrich Lübbering), "Mode, Politik und Volkswirtschaft," *Frauenwirtschaft: Zeitschrift für den Unterricht und die Fortbildung in Hauswirtschaft und Handarbeit, Landwirtschaft und Gartenbau* 7, no. 4 (July 1916): 73–83.

94. David P. Forsythe and Barbara Ann J. Rieffer-Flanagan, *The International Committee of the Red Cross: A Neutral Humanitarian Actor* (New York: Routledge, 2007), xii.

95. Jones, 698; Philip Gourevitch, "Alms Dealers," *The New Yorker* (October 11, 2010): 106, writes about Red Cross service at Nazi death camps that "impartiality in the face of atrocity can be indistinguishable from complicity."

96. Jones, 697–99, 707; Tammy M. Proctor, *Civilians in a World at War, 1914–1918* (New York: New York University Press, 2010), 174; for information about the relationship between the German Red Cross and the German government, see Paul Weindling, "Social Hygiene and the Birth Rate in Wartime Germany," in Jay Winter and Richard Wall, eds., *The Upheaval of War: Family, Work and Welfare in Europe, 1914–1918* (Cambridge: Cambridge University Press, 1988), 419, 428.

97. Anderson, *Imagined Communities*; Matthew Stibbe, "The Internment of Civilians by Belligerent States during the First World War and the Response of the International Committee of the Red Cross," *Journal of Contemporary History* 41 (January 2006):18.

98. Vincent, 77–116.

99. Ibid., 79. American Red Cross Secretary W.W. Husband to American chargé d'affaires Mr. Grant-Smith, November 30, 1918, Calamites and Disasters, roll 81, M336, Records of the Department of State Relating to the Internal Affairs of Germany, 1910–1929 (hereafter SDR), RG 59, National Archives and Records Administration (hereafter NA), Washington, D.C. These microfilmed records are arranged chronologically by date of correspondence.

100. Vincent, 72; U.S. officials relied on expert opinions on conditions in Germany obtained from a variety of sources, including W. W. Husband of the Red Cross, but also Germans themselves, including Wilhelm Solf, Dr. Siegfried Heckscher, Count Scherr-Thoss, and a report filed by the Kaiser Wilhelm Institute for Labor Physiology, no date, roll 81, M336, SDR, RG 59, NA.

101. W. W. Husband, American Red Cross, to Mr. Grant-Smith, November 30, 1918, roll 81, M336, SDR, RG 59, NA.

102. There were exceptions to the notion that only German men constituted the "enemy." For example, during the occupation of Germany after the war, British soldiers warned one another that if they were to marry a German *Fräulein*, their child might shout "*Gott strafe England!*" as it emerged from her womb. Kuhlman, *Reconstructing Patriarchy*, 22.

103. Vincent's title is *The Politics of Hunger*.

104. Belinda J. Davis, 22–23; Elizabeth Domansky, "Militarization and Reproduction in World War I Germany," in G. Eley, ed., *Society, Culture and the State in Germany 1870–1930* (Ann Arbor: University of Michigan Press, 1996), 441; for more evidence of this, see Bernd Ulrich and Benjamin Ziemann, eds., *German Soldiers in the Great War: Letters and Eyewitness Accounts*, trans. Christine Brocks (South Yorkshire: Pen & Sword Books, 2010), 105–6.

105. Jones, 708.

106. Richard Bessel, "The Great War in German Memory: The Soldiers of the First World War, Demobilization, and Weimar Political Culture," *German History* 6, no. 1 (1988): 21.

107. Kuhlman, *Reconstructing Patriarchy*, 127.

108. Elizabeth D. Heinemann, *What Difference Does a Husband Make? Women and Marital Status in Nazi and Postwar Germany* (Berkeley: University of California Press, 1999), 7; Gerda Szepansky, *Blitzmädel, Heldenmutter, Kriegerwitwe: Frauenleben im Zweiten Weltkrieg* (Frankfurt: Fischer Taschenbuch Verlag, 1986), 12, quotes *Mein Kampf*, in which Adolf Hitler declared that the only proper education for women is in motherhood.

109. Karen Hagemann, "Home/Front: The Military, Violence and Gender Relations in the Age of the World Wars," in Karen Hagemann and Stefanie Schüler-Springorum, eds., *Home/Front: The Military, War and Gender in Twentieth-Century Germany* (New York: Berg, 2002), 18–24; Claudia Koonz, *Mothers in the Fatherland: Women, the Family, and Nazi Politics* (New York: St. Martin's Press, 1987), 387–89; Helen Boak, "The Female Nazi Voter," in Anthony McElligott and Tim Kirk, eds., *Working Towards Hitler* (Manchester: Manchester University Press, 2003), 82, maintains that Hitler encouraged married women to stay at home and not "double earn" (that is, work for wages).

110. William H. McMasters to Secretary of State Hon. Robert Lansing, December 20, 1915, roll 81, M336, SDR, RG 59, NA; Johnson Hagood's account of Gerard disputes this point, see Larry Grant, ed., *Caissons Go Rolling Along: A Memoir of America in Post–World War I Germany* (Columbia: University of South Carolina Press, 2010), 59–60; Stibbe, "Internment of Civilians," 12.

111. Vincent, 77–78, 81; Hoover claimed that he had been responsible for the provisions clause for Germany within the armistice agreement, but there is no evidence to verify that claim; see George H. Nash, *The Life of Herbert Hoover: Master of Emergencies, 1917–1918* (New York: Norton, 1996), 636, note 89.

112. Quoted in Vincent, 95.

113. W. W. Husband to Mr. Grant-Smith, November 30, 1918, 2, roll 81, M336, SDR, RG 59, NA.

114. Vincent, 43–49.

115. Quoted in ibid., 70.

116. Vincent, 109–13, 117.

117. Jane Addams and Alice Hamilton, *Report to the American Friends Service Committee on the Situation in Germany*, AFSC Bulletin 25 (Philadelphia: AFSC, 1919), available from AFSC, 1501 Cherry Street, Philadelphia, Pennsylvania, 19101.

118. Addams, *Peace and Bread*, 199–201; for more on the politics of care, see Joan C. Tronto, *Moral Boundaries: A Political Argument for an Ethic of Care* (New York: Routledge, 1993).

119. Addams, *Peace and Bread*, 172–73, 208.

120. Jones, 703.

121. Matthew Stibbe, "Anti-Feminism, Nationalism and the German Right, 1914–1920: A Reappraisal," *German History* 20 no. 2 (2002): 186–87; Hamilton, "At the War Capitals," 418.

122. Letters to Julia Wickham Porcher Wickham from French widows H. Rebardy and Mme. Ollivon, series 12, box 28, Wickham Family Papers, 1766–1945, Mss1W6326aFA2, Virginia Historical Society, Richmond, Virginia, translated by Pamela Park.

123. A. F. Stoeger to Hon. Robert H. Lansing, February 5, 1917, roll 81, M336, SDR, RG 59, NA; Stoeger identifies his wife as president in his letter.

124. "European War Notes," in Robert M. Green, George G. Smith, and Walter L. Brundage, eds., *The Boston Medical and Surgical Journal*, CLXXV, no. 3 (July 20, 1916):106–7.

125. Charles S. Macfarland, *Library of Christian Cooperation, Volume 2* (New York: The Federal Council of the Churches of Christ in America, 1917), 111.

126. Gail Bederman, "'The Women Have Had Charge of the Church Work Long Enough': The Men and Religion Forward Movement of 1911–1912 and the Masculinization of Middle-class Protestantism," *American Quarterly* 41, no. 3 (September 1989): 432–65.

127. American Relief Committee pamphlet, undated, roll 81, M336, SDR, RG 59, NA.

128. Ludwig Grosse to John D. Crimmins, July 26, 1916, ibid.

129. "Gerard Banquetted by Notable Germans," *Ogden Examiner*, January 6, 1917, 1; Gerard left his Berlin post in February 1917 after President Wilson severed diplomatic ties with Germany a month earlier, Stibbe, "The Internment of Civilians," 12.

130. Ulysses Grant-Smith to Secretary of State, December 11, 1918, roll 81, M336, SDR, RG 59, NA.

131. Frank L. Polk to Gerard, November 5, 1916, ibid.

132. Second Assistant Secretary A. Adee to Mr. E. Fischer, Star Electric Company, December 11, 1916, ibid.

133. Jones, 703.

134. Telegram from Joseph C. Grew, aide to Ambassador in Berlin, et al., to Secretary of State, November 28, 1916, roll 81, M336, SDR, RG 59, NA.

135. Telegram from Grew to Secretary of State, November 14, 1916, ibid.; W. Phillips to Mr. Hengstler, State Department, November 27, 1916, ibid. Phillips and Gerard may have had Elizabeth Grimm in mind when they penned those words, for Grimm was bitterly opposed to any actions by the U.S. government that were, as she put it, "un-neutral."

136. W. W. Husband to Grant-Smith, December 7, 1918, roll 81, M336, SDR, RG 59, NA.

137. Letter from F. N. Stevens to Hon. Secretary of State Lansing, March 19, 1917, ibid.

138. Vincent, 41.

139. Mayer to Lansing, December 3, 1919, roll 81, M336, SDR, RG 59, NA; Phillips to Mayer, December 15, 1919, ibid.; Mayer to Phillips, December 17, 1919, ibid.

140. Stibbe, "Elisabeth Rotten," 194; the organization's name was the Information and Assistance Bureau for Germans Abroad and for Foreigners in Germany.

141. Letter from J. J. Hammel to the Assistant Secretary of State, date unclear but received November 24, 1919 (emphasis Hammel's), roll 81, M336, SDR, RG 59, NA; Lansing to Welfare Committee for Prisoners of War, December 1, 1919, ibid.; Carl Boschwitz to Department of State, December 9, 1919, ibid.; Dr. H. Gerhard to Hon. Robert Lansing, December 12, 1919, ibid.

142. Charles Osner to Edgar N. Gott, November 4, 1919, ibid.; Gott to Osner, November 17, 1919, ibid.; Osner to Gott, November 13, 1919, ibid.; Gott to Secretary of State, December 11, 1919, ibid.; Long to Gott, January 6, 1920, ibid.

143. Assistant director Owsley to Hon. Charles E. Hughes, April 20, 1921, ibid.

5. "THE OTHER TRENCH": REMARRIAGE, PRO-NATALISM, AND THE REBIRTHING OF THE NATION

1. I am borrowing my title from Marie-Monique Huss, "Pronatalism and the Popular Ideology of the Child in Wartime France: The Evidence of the Picture Postcard," in Jay Winter and Richard Wall, eds., *The Upheaval of War: Family, Work and Welfare in Europe, 1914–1918* (Cambridge: Cambridge University Press, 1988), 329; William Zimmermann,

A Popular History of Germany from the Earliest Period to the Present Day, Volume 2 (New York: Henry J. Johnson, 1878), 721; Thomas Kaufmann, "'Our Lord God's Chancery' in Magdeburg and Its Fight Against the Interim," *Church History* 73 no. 3 (September 2004): 574–75.

2. Ibid., 568, 572–73.

3. Roland H. Bainton, *Here I Stand: A Life of Martin Luther* (Nashville: Abingdon Press, 1950), 287–93; Herbert David Rix, *Martin Luther: The Man and the Image* (New York: Irvington Publishers, 1984), 313.

4. Adam Seipp, *The Ordeal of Peace: Demobilization and Urban Experience in Germany and Britain, 1917–1921* (Burlington, VT: Ashgate, 2009), 189, 212; Erika Kuhlman, *Reconstructing Patriarchy after the Great War: Women, Gender, and Postwar Reconciliation between Nations* (New York: Palgrave Macmillan, 2008), 145; Susanne Rouette, *Sozialpolitik als Geschlechterpolitik: Die Regulierung der Frauenarbeit nach dem Ersten Weltkrieg* (Frankfurt: Campus Verlag, 1993), 35–36.

5. Hans Harmsen, *Der Einfluß der versorgungsgesetzlichen Regelung auf die wirtschaftliche und soziale Lage der Kriegerwitwen: eine soziologische und bevölkerungspolitische Untersuchung, zugleich der Versuch einer sozialhygienischen Beurteilung und Kritik unserer heutigen Versorgungsgesetzgebung* (Berlin: Schoetz, 1926), 60–62, 52; see Helene Hurwitz-Stranz, ed., *Kriegerwitwen gestalten Ihr Schicksal: Lebenskämpfe deutscher Kriegerwitwen nach eigenen Darstellung* (Berlin: Carl Heymanns Verlag, 1931), 94–95, for an example of a farmer who did run her husband's business during his absence.

6. "Männer auf Lager für Frauen Gefallener," *Vorwärts*, April 8, 1915, 2; Karin Hausen, "The German Nation's Obligations to the Heroes' Widows of World War I," in Margaret Randolph Higonnet, Jane Jenson, Sonya Michel, and Margaret Collins Weitz, eds., *Behind the Lines: Gender and the Two World Wars* (New Haven, CT: Yale University Press, 1987), 129; Harmsen, 35.

7. Robert Weldon Whalen, *Bitter Wounds: German Victims of the Great War, 1914–1939* (Ithaca, NY: Cornell University Press, 1984), 70.

8. Karl Nau, *Die Wirtschaftliche und soziale Lage von Kriegshinterbliebenen: Eine Studie auf Grund von Erhebungen über die auswirkung der versorgung von Kriegshinterbliebenen in Darmstadt* (Leipzig: Lühe & Co., Kommissionsverlag, 1930), 70.

9. For Italy's pro-natalism, see Patrizia Albanese, *Mothers of the Nation: Women, Families, and Nationalism in Twentieth-Century Europe* (Toronto: University of Toronto Press, 2006), 48–55.

10. Marie-Monique Huss provides a brief but interesting comparison between French, German, and British campaigns, 355–56; Belinda J. Davis, *Home Fires Burning: Food, Politics, and Everyday Life in World War I Berlin* (Chapel Hill: University of North Carolina Press, 2000), 165–66, notes that in Germany, women were urged to perform war work rather than become pregnant. The sight of pregnant women led lurid newspapers to hint at women's supposed infidelity and fraternization with the enemy.

11. Elisa Camiscioli, "Producing Citizens, Reproducing the 'French Race': Immigration, Demography, and Pronatalism in Early Twentieth-Century France," *Gender & History* 13, no. 3 (November 2001): 596; Jill Stephenson, "'Reichsbund der Kinderreichen': The League of Large Families in the Population Policy of Nazi Germany," in *European Studies Review* 9 no. 3 (July 1979): 352–53; Richard A. Soloway, "Eugenics and Pronatalism in Wartime Britain," in Wall and Winter, eds., 375–76.

12. Richard A. Soloway, *Demography and Degeneration: Eugenics and the Declining Birth Rate in Twentieth-Century Britain* (Chapel Hill: University of North Carolina Press, 1995), 138–93; Stefan Kühl, "The Cooperation of German Racial Hygienists and American Eugenicists before and after 1933," in Michael Berenbaum and Andrew J. Peck, eds., *The Holocaust and History: The Known, the Unknown, the Disputed and the Re-examined* (Bloomington: Indiana University Press, 1998), 134–39; quote is on 139.

13. Wilson H. Grabill, "Effect of the War on the Birth Rate and Postwar Fertility Prospects," *American Journal of Sociology* 50, no. 2 (September 1944): 107–11; Louis I. Dublin, "War and the Birth Rate—A Brief Historical Summary," *American Journal of Public Health* 35 (April 1945): 315–20; John C. Hunter, "The Problem of the French Birth Rate on the Eve of World War I," *French Historical Studies* 2, no. 4 (Autumn, 1962): 490–503; J. M. Winter, "The Fear of Population Decline in Western Europe, 1870–1940," in R. W. Hiorns, ed., *Demographic Patterns in Developed Societies* (London: Taylor and Francis, 1980), 171–98. Studies of the relationship between war and national birth rates suggested reasons for the continuation of low birth rates following the war, but those written before the advent of women's history—all of those listed above—rarely took women's behavior into consideration.

14. Michael Lanthier, "Women Alone: Widows in Third Republic France, 1870–1940" (Ph.D. diss., Simon Fraser University, Burnaby, BC, Canada, 2004), 6.

15. Karl Reutti, "Zahlenergebnis," in *Kriegshinterbliebenenfürsorge in Preussen: Ergebnis einer Umfrage bei den Fürsorgestellen* (Berlin: Carl Heymanns Verlag, 1919), 9.

16. Michael Geyer, "The Stigma of Violence, Nationalism, and War in Twentieth-Century Germany," *German Studies Review* special issue (Winter 1992): 88; Eugen Weber, *The Hollow Years: France in the 1930s* (New York: Norton, 1994), 15–25; Regina Braker, "Helene Stöcker's Pacifism in the Weimar Republic: Between Ideal and Reality," *Journal of Women's History* 13.3 (2001): 89, writes that the German peace movement had shut down by the late 1920s.

17. Gertrud Bäumer, "Geleitwort," in Hurwitz-Stranz, ed., 9.

18. "Toten-Ehrentag für die Gefallenen Münchener," *Die Kriegerwitwe* Nr. 19/20 (October 1920): 1; A. Sch., "Unseren Fernen Heldengräbern," *Die Kriegerwitwe* Nr. 21/22 (November 1920): 1; on Gold Star women see this volume, chapter 3; on Anzac Day see this volume, chapter 4.

19. Mona Siegel, "'History Is the Opposite of Forgetting': The Limits of Memory and the Lessons of History in Interwar France," *The Journal of Modern History* 7, no. 4 (December 2002): 770–75.

20. Elizabeth Domansky offers the best analysis of the perpetual militarized state and society in Germany after the war in Domansky, "Militarization and Reproduction in World War I Germany," in Geoff Eley, ed., *Society, Culture, and the State in Germany, 1870–1930* (Ann Arbor: University of Michigan Press, 1996), 427–63.

21. Detlev J. K. Peukert, *The Weimar Republic: The Crisis of Classical Modernity*, trans. Richard Deveson (New York: Hill and Wang, 1987), 227; Regina Schulte, "The Sick Warrior's Sister: Nursing During the First World War," in Lynn Abrams and Elizabeth Harvey, eds., *Gender Relations in German History*, 121–41 (Durham, NC: Duke University Press, 1997), 135–36.

22. Karen Hagemann, "Men's Demonstrations and Women's Protest: Gender in Collective Action in the Urban Working-Class Milieu during the Weimar Republic," *Gender & History* 5, no. 1 (Spring 1993): 101–2; Matthew Stibbe, "Anti-Feminism, Nationalism and the German Right, 1914–1920," *German History* 20 no. 2 (2002): 193–208.

23. As Mona Siegel points out, this participation was largely passive, as opposed to active veterans and government officials, 787. The Gold Star Mothers and Widows pilgrimages were an exception; see chapter 4 of this volume.

24. Mary Louise Roberts, *Civilization without Sexes: Reconstructing Gender in Postwar France, 1917–1927* (Chicago: University of Chicago Press, 1994), 128; Ingrid Sharp, "Women's Responsibility for the First World War," in Sharp and Fell, eds., *Women's Movement in Wartime, 1914–19* (Basingstoke: Palgrave Macmillan, 2007), 70–71; see chapter 3 for attitudes toward U.S. war widows who had remarried.

25. Helene Hurwitz-Stranz, ed., *Kriegerwitwen*, 13–17.

26. Hermann Geib, "Einführung," in Hurwitz-Stranz, ed., *Kriegerwitwen*, 6; ibid., 54; ibid., 57; Anna Lindemann. *Die Zukunft der Kriegswitwe* (Berlin: Arthur Collignon, 1915); Helene Hurwitz-Stranz, "8 Jahre Beisitzerin an Reichsversorgungsgericht" *Die Frau* 38 (1930/31): 264–71.

27. Braker, 79; Susan Pedersen, *Family, Dependence, and the Origins of the Welfare State: Britain and France, 1914–1945* (Cambridge: Cambridge University Press, 1993), 176, quotes feminist Ellen Wilkinson's speech to the British House of Commons regarding the relationship between motherhood and the state.

28. Atina Grossmann, *Reforming Sex: The German Movement for Birth Control and Abortion Reform, 1920–1950* (New York: Oxford University Press, 1995), 4, argues that war and defeat in Germany exacerbated anxieties about low birth rates and quality of children being born.

29. See Kuhlman, *Reconstructing Patriarchy*, 118–21, for feminist pacifist arguments in favor of arms reduction and U.S. congressmen's negative responses, which made it clear that the United States would not compromise its military superiority. The context was the 1921 congressional hearings on universal arms reduction and the 1923 Senate hearing on the War Department appropriations bill.

30. Grossmann, 5; Mary Nolan, *Visions of Modernity: American Business and the Modernization of Germany* (New York: Oxford University Press, 1994), 206–11; Tammy M. Proctor, *Civilians in a World at War, 1914–1918* (New York: New York University Press, 2010), 177.

31. Joy Damousi, *The Labour of Loss: Mourning, Memory, and Wartime Bereavement in Australia* (Cambridge: Cambridge University Press), 74; for British examples see Janis Lomas, "'Delicate Duties': Issues of Class and Respectability in Government Policy Towards the Wives and Widows of British Soldiers in the Era of the Great War," *Women's History Review* 9 no. 1 (2000): 136.

32. "Die Wiederverheiratung der Kriegerwitwen," Part II, *Die Kriegerwitwe* 3, no. 5 (May 1921): 2.

33. Francesca Lagorio, "Italian Widows of the First World War," in Frans Coetzee and Marilyn Shevin-Coetzee, eds., *Authority, Identity and the Social History of the Great War* (New York: Berg, 1997), 176–77.

34. Damousi, *Labour of Loss*, 77.

35. Cornelie Usborne, "Pregnancy Is the Woman's Active Service: Pro-natalism in Germany during the First World War," in JayWinter and Richard Wall, eds., 395.

36. Anonymous, "Das sehr wichtige Moment der Kameradschaft von Leidensgenossen unter Ausschaltung aller Sozialen Einengungen möchte ich noch besonders hervorheben," in *Kriegerwitwen*, 39–43; Geertje van Os, "Hidden from View: The Disappearance

of Mourning Dress among Dutch Widows in the Twentieth Century," in Jan Bremmer and Lourens van den Bosch, eds., *Between Poverty and the Pyre: Moments in the History of Widowhood* (New York: Routledge, 1995), 235, notes that some historians feel that the disappearance of mourning dress during and after the First World War was due to the sense that it was no longer realistic for widows to indicate the end of their emotional and sexual lives by wearing mourning garb.

37. Helene Simon, "Erinnerungsblatt," in Hurwitz-Stranz, ed., 11; ibid., 49, 54.

38. Ibid., 92, 114; "Die Wiederverheiratung der Kriegerwitwen," Part I, *Die Kriegerwitwe* 3, no. 4 (April 1921): 2; Hurwitz-Stranz, ed., *Kriegerwitwen*, 28.

39. Grete Meisel-Hess, *Krieg und Ehe* (Berlin: Oesterheld, 1916), 1–2.

40. Stefan Berger, review of Ilse Fischer's *Versöhnung von Nation und Sozialismus? Lothar Erdmann (1888–1939)*, in *English Historical Review* CXXIV (June 2009): 761–63.

41. Katharine Anthony, *Feminism in Germany and Scandinavia* (New York: Henry Holt and Co., 1915), 85; Richard Soloway, "Eugenics and Pronatalism in Wartime Britain," in Winter and Wall, eds., 379; Grossmann, 6; Virginia Nicholson, *Singled Out: How Two Million British Women Survived without Men after the First World War* (New York: Oxford University Press, 2008).

42. "Many War Widows Are Remarried," *Portsmouth Herald*, April 23, 1926, 2.

43. "War Widows as Brides," *London Daily Mail*, August 28, 1920, 5.

44. Whalen, 109; Hans Harmsen places the rate of remarriage for German widows at 33 percent in 1924, 32; Colin Dyer, *Population and Society in Twentieth-Century France* (New York: Holmes and Meier Publishers, 1978), 44.

45. Anthony, 200, 186.

46. Harmsen, 35–38.

47. "Zur Frage der Heiratsabfindungen," *Die Kriegerwitwe*, nr. 17/18 (September 1920): 1–2.

48. Lomas, "So I Married Again," 226; Lomas, "'Delicate Duties,'" 138; "War-Widows Wed," *Daily Mail*, August 30, 1920, 4; Damousi, *Labour of Loss*, 72; Lanthier, "Women Alone," 6.

49. See Dudley Kirk's *Europe's Population in the Interwar Years* (Geneva: League of Nations, 1946), 65–66, for statistics on First World War losses; the figures quoted here do not include deaths due to influenza. Exact figures are impossible to reconstruct because of numbers of people missing and deaths unaccounted for.

50. Jason Crouthamel, "Male Sexuality and Psychological Trauma: Soldiers and Sexual Disorder in World War I and Weimar Germany," *Journal of the History of Sexuality* 17.1 (2008): 60–84; Joanna Bourke, *Dismembering the Male: Men's Bodies, Britain, and the Great War* (Chicago: University of Chicago Press, 1996).

51. Camiscioli, 594.

52. Bessel, 141; Ethel M. Smith, "'Surplus Women': England's Struggle with a European Problem," *National Business Woman* 8, no. 9 (1924): 7–8.

53. Grossmann, 8, 15.

54. Laura E. Nym Mayhall, *The Militant Suffrage Movement: Citizenship and Resistance in Britain, 1860–1930* (New York: Oxford University Press, 2003); Christl Wickert, Silke Hanschke, und Bärbel Clemens, *Heraus mit dem Frauenwahlrecht: die Kämpfe der Frauen in Deutschland und England um die politische Gleichberechtigung* (Pfaffenweiler: Centaurus-Verlagsgesellschaft, 1990); Eleanor Flexner, *Century of Struggle: The Woman's Rights Movement in the United States* (Cambridge, MA: Harvard University Press, 1975).

55. J. M. Winter, "Fear of Population Decline," 176–77; A. B. Wolfe noted the same for declining marriage rates—that is, that France's lower marriage rate translated into its loss in the Franco-Prussian War, A. B. Wolfe, "Economic Conditions and the Birth-Rate After the War," *The Journal of Political Economy* 25, No. 6 (June 1917): 525.

56. Richard Bessel, *Germany after the First World War* (Oxford: Oxford University Press, 1993), table on 229; Albanese, 26.

57. Dyer, 80; Bessel, 228 (for divorce rate, see 232); Anonymous, "Birth Rate Falls as Marriages Increase," *Equal Rights* 1, no. 20 (1923): 154.

58. Grossmann, 4.

59. Foderich von Ungern-Sternberg, "The Causes of the Decline in Birth-Rate within the European Sphere of Civilization," *Eugenics Research Association* (Cold Spring Harbor, NY: 1931), 2.

60. Roberts, 123.

61. Gudrun Hamelmann, *Helene Stöcker, der "Bund für Mutterschutz" und "Die Neue Generation"* (Frankfurt: Haag und Herchen Verlag, 1992), 8.

62. Nancy Woloch, *Women and the American Experience* (New York: Knopf, 1984), 541.

63. Paul Weindling, "Social Hygiene and the Birth Rate in Wartime Germany," in Winter and Wall, eds., 422–24.

64. Margaret Vining and Barton C. Hacker, "From Camp Follower to Lady in Uniform: Women, Social Class, and Military Institutions Before 1920," *Contemporary European History* 10, no. 3 (November 2001): 353–73; Cynthia Enloe, *Maneuvers: The International Politics of Militarizing Women's Lives* (Berkeley: University of California Press, 2000), 37–43; Huss, 339.

65. Huss, 342–43.

66. Usborne, 391.

67. Domansky, 432, 449.

68. Dora Apel, "'Heroes' and 'Whores': The Politics of Gender in Weimar Antiwar Imagery," *The Art Bulletin* 79, no. 3 (1997): 379.

69. Grossmann, 16, 37–40, 50–57.

70. Quoted in ibid., 46.

71. Quoted in Usborne, 399.

72. Gertrud Bäumer, "Der Seelische Hintergrund der Bevölkerungsfrage," *Die Frau* 23, no. 3 (December 1915): 132–33.

73. Usborne, 391, 393.

74. Ibid., 406.

75. Stephenson, 353.

76. Albanese, 28.

77. Weber, 77; Roberts, 93–94.

78. Grossmann, 9–10.

79. Weindling, 428.

80. Bäumer, "Seelische," 129–30; Roberts, 119, 123.

81. Weindling, 429.

82. Bäumer, "Seelische,"132.

83. Mathilde Planck, "Unsere Zukunft," *Die Frauenbewegung* 23, no. 5/6 (March 15, 1917): 18.

84. Max Reuscher, *Der Kampf gegen den Geburtenrückgang in Deutschland, früher und heute* (Stettin: Ostsee-druckerei und- Verlag 1937), 38, 23; See also A. B. Wolfe's review of James Marchant, *The Declining Birth Rate: Its Causes and Effects,* in *The American Economic Review* 8, no. 1 (March 1918): 159.

85. Quoted in Usborne, 397; Camiscioli, 606. For differing attitudes toward working women during wartime see Josephine Levy-Rathenau, "Berufsberatung und Kriegshinterbliebene," in *Tagung des Hauptausschusses der Kriegerwitwen- und -Waisenfürsorge, Frauenerwerb und Kriegswitwe: Referate erstattet auf der 2. Tagung des Hauptausschusses der Kriegerwitwen- und -Waisenfürsorge am 27. November 1915 im Reichstagsgebäude in Berlin* (Berlin: Carl Heymanns Verlag, 1916), 1–3, and Camiscioli, 606, where the author quotes pro-natalist Louis Duval-Arnould as saying that nonwhite immigrant workers in France are the equivalent of women workers: Both, in his opinion, were docile and weak.

86. Huss, 330–31, lists French pro-natalists' professions as doctor, lawyer, politician, economist, and journalist; Roberts, 128.

87. Grossmann, 3.

88. Anonymous, *Der Geburtenrückgang: seine Ursachen und seine Bekämpfung* (Leipzig: Volger, 1928), 25.Available at the Stiftung Archiv der deutschen Frauenbewegung, Kassel, Germany.

89. Anthony, 122, 124.

90. Minna Cauer, "Zur Dienstpflict der Frau," *Die Frauenbewegung* 22, no. 5 (March 1, 1916): 17.

91. A. B. Wolfe, "Review," *The American Economic Review* 8, no. 1 (March 1918): 157–58.

92. Usborne, 400.

93. Irvine Loudon, *Death in Childbirth: An International Study of Maternal Care and Maternal Mortality, 1800–1950* (Oxford: Clarendon Press, 1992), 235, 451. For more on the acceptance or rejection of antisepsis see Judith Walzer Leavitt, *Brought to Bed: Childbearing in America, 1750–1950* (New York: Oxford University Press, 1986), 157–70. Loudon provides a chart showing German, French, English, and U.S. maternal mortality in 1920: Germany's rate was 51.5, England and Wales's was 43.3; France's was 66.4, the United States' was 79.9, all per 10,000 live births, 153.

94. Loudon, 453–54.

95. Usborne, 406.

96. Secretary of State of the Imperial Food Office to Secretary of State of Foreign Affairs (U.S.), November 21, 1918, 5, roll 81, M336, SDR, RG 59, NA.

97. Quoted in C. Paul Vincent, *The Politics of Hunger: The Allied Blockade of Germany, 1915–1919* (Athens: Ohio University Press, 1985), 68; ibid., 80–81; Belinda J. Davis, "Home Front: Food, Politics, and Everyday Life during the First World War," in Karen Hagemann and Stefanie Schüler-Springorum, eds., *Home/Front: The Military, War and Gender in Twentieth-Century Germany* (New York: Berg, 2002), 127.

98. Paul Weindling, "The Medical Profession, Social Hygiene and the Birth Rate in Germany, 1914–18," in Winter and Wall, eds., 421.

99. Roberts, 114.

100. Anonymous, Review of *Essays in War Time, International Woman Suffrage News* 11, no. 5 (1917): 77.

101. Anonymous, "Zum Bevölkerungs Problem," *Die Frauenbewegung* 10 (June 1, 1917): 40–41. The author quoted from *Bulletin der Studiengesellschaft für soziale folgen des Krieges*, published by the Kopenhagen Studiengesellschaft für soziale folgen des Krieges, 1917 issue.

102. Anonymous, *Der Geburtenrückgang: Seine Ursachen und seine Bekämpfung*, 5.

103. Hagemann, "Men's Demonstrations," 102.

104. Usborne, 389–90.

105. J. M. Winter, "The Fear of Population Decline in Western Europe, 1870–1940" in R. W. Hiorns, ed., *Demographic Patterns in Developed Societies* (London: Taylor and Francis, 1980), 181–82.

106. Bäumer, "Seelische," 129–33.

107. Helene Lange, "Zur Wiederaufnahme der Bevölkerungspolitik," *Die Frau* 23, no. 2 (November 1915): 100.

108. Huss, 332 and 360, note 15.

109. Usborne, 407; Weindling, 428.

110. Huss, 339, 352.

111. Kuhlman, *Petticoats and White Feathers*, 86–91.

112. Kuhlman, *Reconstructing Patriarchy*, 135–36.

113. Siegel, 776–81.

114. Huss, 342; Roberts, 131.

115. Lange, 101; Domansky has argued that male domination in the home did not recur after 1918; instead, the state continued to play a powerful role in shaping German family life, 435–37; Camiscioli, 602.

116. *Die Kriegerwitwe* 3, no. 4 (April 1921): 2–3; a stateless person is one with no citizenship or nationality, making that person effectively a refugee.

117. Camiscioli, 595–96.

118. Winter, "Fear of Population Decline," 173, 175.

119. Ibid., 177; Quoted in ibid., 179.

120. Kuhlman, *Reconstructing Patriarchy*, 39–69.

121. Vicki L. Ruiz, *Cannery Women, Cannery Lives: Mexican Women, Unionization, and the California Food Processing Industry, 1930–1950* (Albuquerque: University of New Mexico Press, 1987), 8–9.

122. Honoré Willsie, "American Race-Control," *Woman's Journal* 7, no. 1 (1922): 15.

123. Usborne, 394.

124. Weindling, 429, 430, 432.

125. Huss, 330.

126. Gesine Nordbeck, "Zwischen zwei Gesetzen?" *Die Frau* 23, no. 4 (January 1916): 216–21(Bäumer responded to Nordbeck in the same issue, 221–22); Rosa Schwann-Schneider, "Bemerkungen zu Mathilde Plancks Artikel," *Die Frauenbewegung* 23 no. 9 (May 1, 1917): 35–36 (this article included a rebuttal from Planck); Mathilde Planck's original article, "Unsere Zukunft," *Die Frauenbewegung* 23, no. 4/5 (March 1917): 17–18.

127. Huss, 336.

128. Quoted in Richard David Sonn, "'Your Body Is Yours': Anarchism, Birth Control, and Eugenics in Interwar France," *Journal of the History of Sexuality* 14, no. 4 (2005): 425.

129. Weber, 77–78.

130. Kuhlman, *Reconstructing Patriarchy*, 123–24.

131. Apel, 379.

132. Rosa Schwann-Schneider, 35.

133. Quoted in Bernd Ulrich and Benjamin Ziemann, eds., *German Soldiers in the Great War: Letters and Eyewitness Accounts*, trans. Christine Brocks (South Yorkshire: Pen & Sword Books, 2010), 99–100.

134. Bessel, 260.

135. Elizabeth Harvery, "Visions of the *Volk*: German Women and the Far Right from *Kaiserreich* to Third Reich," *Journal of Women's History* 16, no. 3 (2004): 156–58; Raffael Scheck, *Mothers of the Nation: Right-Wing Women in Weimar Germany* (New York: Berg, 2004), 23–39.

136. Elizabeth Harvey, "The Failure of Feminism? Young Women and the Bourgeois Feminist Movement in Weimar Germany, 1918–1933," *Central European History* 28 (1995): 2.

137. Kuhlman, *Reconstructing Patriarchy*, 111.

138. Usborne, 398–99.

139. Gesine Nordbeck, "Zwischen zwei Gesetzen?" *Die Frau* 23, no. 4 (January 1916): 220.

140. Braker, 79.

141. Gudrun Hamelmann, *Helene Stöcker, der "Bund für Mutterschutz" und "Die neue Generation"* (Frankfurt: Haag and Herchen Verlag, 2003), 121–23.

142. Quoted in Braker, 78.

143. Braker, 79, 81, 83.

144. Albanese, 11–15, 17.

145. Weber, 76.

146. Louis James, *The Victorian Novel* (Malden, MA: Blackwell Publishing, 2006), 204, notes that the phrase was coined in 1894.

147. Schwann-Schneider, 35; Helene Stöcker, *Moderne Bevölkerungspolitik* (Berlin: Oesterheld, 1916), 4; Stöcker herself attributed the phrase to the Gospel.

148. Anonymous, "Review of *Fecundity Versus Civilisation*," *International Woman Suffrage News* 11, no. 5 (1917): 77 (this review may have been written by Mary Sheepshanks, editor of the journal); Adelyne More, *Uncontrolled Breeding, or Fecundity Versus Civilization* (New York: Critic and Guide Company, 1917), 108. Adelyne More was the pen name of British author C. K. Ogden; *Uncontrolled Breeding* was first published by Allen & Unwin, a London publisher, in 1916.

EPILOGUE

1. Elizabeth D. Heinemann, *What Difference Does a Husband Make? Women and Marital Status in Nazi and Postwar Germany* (Berkeley: University of California Press, 1999), 40.

2. G. Kurt Piehler, *Remembering War the American Way* (Washington: Smithsonian Institution Press, 1995), 129; Melissa Dabakis, "Gendered Labor: Norman Rockwell's *Rosie the Riveter* and the Discourses of Wartime Womanhood," in Barbara Melosh, ed., *Gender and American History Since 1890* (New York: Routledge, 1993), 185.

3. For example, see Redd Evans and John Jacob Loeb, "Rosie the Riveter" musical score and lyrics (New York: Paramount Music, 1942); hear the song in Connie Field, *Life and Times of Rosie the Riveter*, VHS (Los Angeles: Direct Cinema, Ltd., 1987).

4. I thank Sion Harrington at the North Carolina State Archives for sharing this letter with me. Mrs. Abe C. Webb to Dear Sir, July 20, 1945, and note from Ben L. Rose, Army Chaplain, to North Carolina State Archives, September 1, 1999, Ben L. Rose Papers, Box 6, Private Collection, World War II Papers, Military Collection, North Carolina State Archives, Raleigh, North Carolina.

5. Piehler, 128–32.

6. Lilian Rixey, "Shall I Remarry?" *Life* (April 1946): 106–16.

7. Heinemann, 1–3.

8. Gerda Szepansky, *Blitzmädel, Heldenmutter, Kriegerwitwen: Frauenleben im Zweiten Weltkrieg* (Frankfurt: Fischer Taschenbuch Verlag, 1986), 12–13, notes the discrepancy between Nazi propaganda of the ideal woman and the reality of women's lives as munitions makers during the Second World War.

9. Quoted in Heinemann, 125.

10. Heinemann, 169; Anna Schnädelbach, *Kriegerwitwen: Lebenswältigung zwischen Arbeit und Familie in Westdeutschland nach 1945* (Frankfurt: Campus Verlag, 2009), 7–15.

11. Heinemann, 162, 164, 189–91.

12. Hubertus Thiel, "Hubertus Thiel," in Wolfgang W. E. Samuel, ed., *The War of Our Childhood: Memories of World War II* (Jackson: University Press of Mississippi, 2002), 26–33.

13. Cynthia J. Mills, "The Adams Memorial and American Funerary Sculpture, 1891–1927" (Ph.D. diss., University of Maryland at College Park, 1996), 270.

14. Geertje van Os, "Hidden from View: The Disappearance of Mourning Dress among Dutch Widows in the Twentieth Century," in Jan Bremmer and Lourens van den Bosch, eds., *Between Poverty and the Pyre: Moments in the History of Widowhood* (New York: Routledge, 1995), 239–40.

15. Rixey, 106–7.

16. Anonymous, "The Family: Second Life for War Widows," *Time* (July 25, 1969): 55–56.

17. Janis Lomas, "'So I Married Again': Letters from British Widows of the First and Second World Wars," *History Workshop Journal* 38, no. 1 (1994): 218–19.

18. Rachel L. Swarns, "Commanding a Role for Women in the Military," *New York Times*, June 30, 2008, http://www.nytimes.com/2008/06/30/washington/30general.html?emc=eta1 (accessed October 2010).

19. Julie A. Mertus, *Bait and Switch: Human Rights and U.S. Foreign Policy* (New York: Routledge, 2004), 111–12; Philip Gourevitch, "Alms Dealers: Can You Provide Humanitarian Aid without Facilitating Conflicts?" *The New Yorker* (October 11, 2010): 106.

20. Quoted in Donald E. Pease, *The New American Exceptionalism* (Minneapolis: University of Minnesota Press, 2009), 196.

21. Lauren Collins, "Cherie Amour," *The New Yorker* (July 5, 2010): 20–21.

22. Campaign for Innocent Victims of Conflict, http://www.civicworldwide.org/index.php (accessed October 2010).

23. Barbara Sonneborn, Director, *Regret to Inform*, DVD (New York: Docurama, 1998); Ed Martini, "Exhibition Review," *Journal of American History* 87 no. 3 (December 2000): 987–91; Widows of War Living Memorial, http://archive.ideum.com/portfolio/widows_war (accessed October 2010). Quoted in Martini, p. 990.

24. Gourevitch, 106; Peter Schjeldahl, "Turning Away," *The New Yorker* (October 25, 2010): 91.

25. Sheryl Gay Stolberg, "Senate Backs Ban on Photos of G.I. Coffins," *New York Times*, June 22, 2004, http://www.nytimes.com/2004/06/22/us/senate-backs-ban-on-photos-of-gi-coffins.html?emc=eta1 (accessed November 2010).

26. "Aus eiserner Zeit für eiserne Zeit," *Die Frau* 21 no. 12 (September 1914): 737; Else Lüders, "Das Doppelgesicht des Krieges," *Die Frauenbewegung* 21 no. 4 (February 15, 1915): 13–14; Else Lüders, "Die Stellung der Frauen zu Krieg und Frieden," *Die Frauenbewegung* 25 no. 18 (December 15, 1919): 122.

27. *Die Kriegerwitwe* was published from 1920 to 1921. It is available at the *Staatsbibliothek* (National Library) in Berlin.

28. Jean H. Quataert, *Reluctant Feminists in German Social Democracy, 1885–1917* (Princeton, NJ: Princeton University Press, 1979); Matthew Stibbe, "Anti-Feminism, Nationalism and the German Right, 1914–1920," *German History* 20 no. 2 (2002): 193–208, notes that despite confirming traditional roles for women at the beginning of the war, by 1917 the Reich began to encourage the employment of women in wartime industries and in patriotic organizations.

Selected Bibliography

ARCHIVES

American Friends Service Committee Archives, Philadelphia, Pennsylvania, USA
  Report to the American Friends Service Committee on the Situation in Germany, AFSC
    Bulletin 25
Australian War Memorial, Campbell, ACT, Australia
  Instructions on the Training of Widows / Ministry of Pensions, 355.115 I43
Bundesarchiv, Berlin, Germany
  Reichskanzlei, R 43
Columbia University, Rare Book and Manuscript Library, New York, New York, USA
  Rebekah Crawford Papers, 1910–1925, MS #0308
Gerritsen Collection of Aletta H. Jacobs, Ann Arbor, Michigan, USA
  Periodical Series
Historical Society of Pennsylvania, Philadelphia, Pennsylvania, USA
  Pierson Family Papers, 1917–1928, Collection 3040
Illinois State Archives, Springfield, Illinois, USA
  World War I Bonus Applications from Veterans and Beneficiaries, RS 503.001
National Archives and Records Administration, Washington, D.C., USA
  Records of the Department of State Relating to the Internal Affairs of Germany,
    1910–1929, RG 59
National Archives II, College Park, Maryland, USA
  Records of the Office of the Quartermaster General, RG92
New York Public Library, Manuscripts and Archives Division, New York, New York, USA
  Victory Hall Association Records, 1920–1921, MssCol 3165
North Carolina State Archives, Raleigh, North Carolina, USA
  World War II Collection, 1939–1947, Ben L. Rose Papers
Staatsbibliothek, Berlin, Germany
  Die Kriegerwitwe, 1920–1921
Stiftung Archiv der deutschen Frauenbewegung, Kassel, Germany
  Zeitschriftenbestand
Virginia Historical Society, Richmond, Virginia, USA
  Wickham Family Papers, 1766–1945, Mss1W6326aFA2
Wisconsin Historical Society, Madison, Wisconsin, USA
  Broadsides Collection
Wisconsin Veterans Museum, Madison, Wisconsin, USA
  Gold Star Wives of America Records, 1933, Mss5

NEWSPAPERS

Bridgeport (Connecticut) *Telegraph*
Chicago Sunday Press and *The Women's Press*
Eau Claire (Wisconsin) *Leader*
Fort Wayne (Indiana) *Journal-Gazette*
Indianapolis (Indiana) *Star*
London Daily Mail
New York Times
Ogden (Utah) *Standard Examiner*
Portsmouth (New Hampshire) *Herald*
Salt Lake (Utah) *Tribune*
Schwäbische Frauenzeitung
Syracuse (New York) *Herald*
Vorwärts

PUBLISHED SOURCES

Addams, Jane. *Peace and Bread in Time of War.* New York: Macmillan, 1922.
Albanese, Patricia. *Mothers of the Nation: Women, Families, and Nationalism in Twentieth-Century Europe.* Toronto: University of Toronto Press, 2006.
Alexander, Archibald. "A New Mien of Grief." *The Literary Digest* 52, no. 5 (1916): 292.
Alonso, Harriet Hyman. *Peace as a Woman's Issue: A History of the U.S. Women's Movement for World Peace and Human Rights.* Syracuse, NY: Syracuse University Press, 1993.
Andersen, Kristi. *After Suffrage: Women in Partisan and Electoral Politics Before the New Deal.* Chicago: University of Chicago Press, 1996.
Anderson, Benedict. *Imagined Communities: Reflections on the Origins and Spread of Nationalism.* London: Verso, 1990.
Anonymous. *"Aus eiserner Zeit für eiserne Zeit." Die Frau* 21 no. 12 (September 1914): 737.
Anonymous, "The Family: Second Life for War Widows," *Time* (July 25, 1969): 55–56.
Anonymous. *"Die Fürsorge für unsere Krieger-Witwen und -Waisen als soziales Problem." Die Frauenbewegung* 21, no. 9 (1915): 33.
Anonymous. *Der Geburtenrückgang: Seine Ursachen und seine Bekämpfung.* Leipzig: Volger, 1928.
Anonymous. "Was leistet das Reich für die Kriegsbeschädigten und Kriegerhinterbliebenen?" *Neue Lebensfahrt: Mitteilungen für Kriegerhinterbliebene, Beilage zum Reichsbund* 3, no. 21 (1920): n.p.
Anthony, Katharine. *Feminism in Germany and Scandinavia.* New York: Henry Holt, 1915.
Apel, Dora. "Cultural Battlegrounds: Weimar Photographic Narratives of War." *New German Critique* 76 (Winter 1999): 49–84.
Apel, Dora. "'Heroes' and 'Whores': The Politics of Gender in Weimar Antiwar Imagery." *The Art Bulletin* 79, no. 3 (1997): 366–84.
Ashenburg, Katherine. *The Mourner's Dance: What We Do When People Die.* New York: North Point Press, 2002.
Bainton, Roland H. *Here I Stand: A Life of Martin Luther.* Nashville: Abingdon Press, 1950.

Barrett, Michéle. *Casualty Figures: How Five Men Survived the First World War*. New York: Verso, 2007.

Bauer, Hans. "Standrecht." *Simplicissimus* 24, no. 3 (1919): 45.

Bäumer, Gertrud. "Der Seelische Hintergrund der Bevölkerungsfrage." *Die Frau* 23, no. 3 (1915): 129–33.

Bäumer, Gertrud and Helene Lange. "Rechtsfrieden?" *Die Frau* 26, no. 2 (1918): 37–40.

Belkin, Samuel. "Levirate and Agnate Marriage in Rabbinic and Cognate Literature." *The Jewish Quarterly Review* 60, no. 4 (1970): 275–329.

Berry, Paul, and Mark Bostridge. *Vera Brittain: A Life*. London: Chatto & Windus, 1995.

Bessel, Richard. *Germany after the First World War*. New York: Oxford University Press, 1993.

Braker, Regina. "Helene Stöcker's Pacifism in the Weimar Republic: Between Ideal and Reality." *Journal of Women's History* 13, no. 3 (2001): 70–97.

Bridgwater, Patrick. *The German Poets of the First World War*. New York: St. Martin's Press, 1985.

Bristow, Nancy K. *Making Men Moral: Social Engineering During the Great War*. New York: New York University Press, 1996.

Brittain, Vera. *Testament of Youth: An Autobiographical Study of the Years 1900–1925*. New York: Macmillan, 1933.

Bromme, Moritz. "Stumme Märtyrerinnen." *Die Frau* 21, no. 4 (1914): 229–33.

Brown, Carrie. *Rosie's Mom: Forgotten Women Workers of the First World War*. Boston: Northeastern University Press, 2002.

Budreau, Lisa M. *Bodies of War: World War I and the Politics of Commemoration in America, 1919–1933*. New York: New York University Press, 2009.

———. "The Politics of Remembrance: The Gold Star Mothers' Pilgrimage and America's Fading Memory of the Great War." *Journal of Military History* 72, no. 2 (2008): 371–411.

Buitelaar, Marjo. "Widows' Worlds: Representations and Realities." In Jane Bremmer and Lourens vanBosch, eds., *Between Poverty and the Pyre: Moments in the History of Widowhood*. New York: Routledge, 1995.

Burk, Kathleen. *Britain, America and the Sinews of War, 1914–1918*. London: G. Allen & Unwin, 1984.

Camiscioli, Elisa. "Producing Citizens, Reproducing the 'French Race': Immigration, Demography, and Pronatalism in Early Twentieth-Century France." *Gender and History* 13, no. 3 (2001): 593–621.

Cannadine, David. "War and Death, Grief and Mourning in Modern Britain." In Joachim Whaley, ed., *Mirrors of Mortality: Studies in the Social History of Death*. New York: St. Martin's Press, 1981.

Cauer, Minna. "Die Landfrau und ihre Aufgaben." *Die Frauenbewegung* 22, no. 3 (1916): 1–10.

———. "Zur Dienstpflicht der Frau." *Die Frauenbewegung* 22, no. 5 (1916): 18.

Cavallo, Sandra, and Lyndan Warner, eds. *Widowhood in Medieval and Early Modern Europe*. New York: Longman, 1999.

Chickering, Roger, Manfred Boemeke, and Stig Förster, eds. *Anticipating Total War: The German and American Experiences, 1871–1914*. New York: Cambridge University Press, 1999.

Chickering, Roger, and Stig Förster, eds. *Great War, Total War: Combat and Mobilization on the Western Front, 1914–1918*. Washington: German Historical Institute, 2000.

Code, Lorraine. *What Can She Know? Feminist Theory and the Construction of Knowledge.* Ithaca, NY: Cornell University Press, 1991.

Coetzee, Frans. and Marilyn Shevin-Coetzee. "Introduction." In Frans Coetzee and Marilyn Shevin-Coetzee, eds., *Authority, Identity and the Social History of the Great War.* Providence, RI: Berghahn Books, 1995.

Crouthamel, Jason. "Male Sexuality and Psychological Trauma: Soldiers and Sexual Disorder in World War I and Weimar Germany." *Journal of the History of Sexuality* 17, no. 1 (2008): 60–84.

———. "War Neurosis versus Savings Psychosis: Working-class Politics and Psychological Trauma in Weimar Germany." *Journal of Contemporary History* 37.2 (2002): 170–71.

Crowell, Benedict. *America's Munitions, 1917–1918*. Washington: GPO, 1919.

Dabakis, Melissa. "Gendered Labor: Norman Rockwell's Rosie the Riveter and the Discourses of Wartime Womanhood." In Barbara Melosh, ed., *Gender and American History Since 1890*. New York: Routledge, 1993.

Damousi, Joy. *The Labour of Loss: Mourning, Memory, and Wartime Bereavement in Australia*. New York: Cambridge University Press, 1999.

Daniel, Ute. *The War from Within: German Working-Class Women in the First World War.* Translated by Margaret Ries. New York: Berg, 1997.

Daughton, James P. "Sketches of the *Poilu*'s World: Trench Cartoons from the Great War." In Douglas Peter Mackaman and Michael Mays, eds., *World War I and the Cultures of Modernity*. Jackson: University Press of Mississippi, 2000.

Davis, Belinda J. *Home Fires Burning: Food, Politics, and Everyday Life in World War I Berlin*. Chapel Hill: University of North Carolina Press, 2000.

———. "Homefront: Food Politics and Women's Everyday Life during the First World War." In Karen Hagemann and Stefanie Schüler-Springorum, eds., *Home/Front: The Military, War and Gender in Twentieth-Century Germany*. New York: Berg, 2002.

Davy, Jennifer Anne. "Pacifist Thought and Gender Ideology in the Political Biographies of Women Peace Activists in Germany, 1899–1970." *Journal of Women's History* 13, no. 3 (2001): 34–45.

Dean, Carolyn Janice. *The Fragility of Empathy after the Holocaust*. Ithaca, NY: Cornell University Press, 2004.

DeBauche, Leslie Midkiff. *Reel Patriotism: The Movies and World War I*. Madison: University of Wisconsin Press, 1997.

Depkat, Volker. "Remembering War the Transnational Way: The U.S.-American Memory of World War I." In Udo J. Hebel, ed., *Transnational American Memories*. Berlin/New York: Walter de Gruyter, 2009.

Deutscher Verein für Armenpflege und Wohltätigkeit. Soziale Fürsorge für Kriegerwitwen und Kriegerwaisen. Munich and Leipzig: Duncker und Humboldt, 1915.

Diehl, James. "Victors or Victims? Disabled Veterans in the Third Reich." *The Journal of Modern History* 59, no. 4 (1987): 705–36.

Domansky, Elisabeth. "Militarization and Reproduction in World War I Germany." In Geoff Eley, ed., *Society, Culture, and the State in Germany, 1870–1930*. Ann Arbor: University of Michigan Press, 1996.

Dublin, Louis I. "War and the Birth Rate—A Brief Historical Summary." *American Journal of Public Health* 35 (1945): 315–20.

Dubois, Ellen Carol. "Harriot Stanton Blatch and the Transformation of Class Relations among Women Suffragists." In Noralee Frankel and Nancy S. Dye, eds., *Gender, Class, Race and Reform in the Progressive Era*. Lexington: University Press of Kentucky, 1992.

Dyer, Colin. *Population and Society in Twentieth-Century France*. New York: Holmes and Meier Publishers, 1978.

Eksteins, Modris. *Rites of Spring: The Great War and the Birth of the Modern Age*. London: Black Swan, 1990.

Engelman, Morris. *Four Years of Relief and War Work by the Jews of America, 1914–1918: A Chronological Review*. New York: M. Engelman, 1918.

Enloe, Cynthia. *Maneuvers: The International Politics of Militarizing Women's Lives*. Berkeley: University of California Press, 2000.

Erdmann-Macke, Elisabeth. *Erinnerung an August Macke*. Stuttgart. W. Kohlhammer, 1962.

Evans, Richard J. *Death in Hamburg: Society and Politics in the Cholera Years, 1830–1910*. New York: Oxford University Press, 1987.

———. *The Feminist Movement in Germany, 1984–1933*. London: SAGE Publications, 1976.

Evans, Suzanne. *Mothers of Heroes, Mothers of Martyrs: World War I and the Politics of Grief*. Montreal: McGill–Queen's University Press, 2007.

Falls-Bres, Rose. *Maids, Wives, and Widows: The Law of the Land and of the Various States as It Affects Women*. New York: Dutton, 1918.

Farrar, L. L. Jr. "Nationalism in Wartime: Critiquing the Conventional Wisdom." In Frans Coetzee and Marilyn Shevin-Coetzee, eds., *Authority, Identity and the Social History of the Great War*. Providence, RI: Berghahn Books, 1995.

Faulkner, William. *Soldier's Pay*. New York: Liveright Publishing Corporation, 1926.

Faust, Drew Gilpin. *Mothers of Invention: Women of the Slaveholding South during the American Civil War*. Chapel Hill: University of North Carolina Press, 1996.

———. *This Republic of Suffering: Death and the American Civil War*. New York: Knopf, 2008.

Fischer, Fritz. *Germany's Aims in the First World War*. New York: Norton, 1967.

Frank, Leonhard. *Der Mensch ist Gut*. Zurich: Max Rascher, 1918.

Frazer, James George. *The Golden Bough: A Study in Magic and Religion*. New York: Macmillan, 1958.

Frese, Werner, and Ernst-Gerhard Güse. *August Macke: Briefe an Elisabeth und die Freunde*. München: Bruckmann, 1987.

Freud, Sigmund. *The Standard Edition of the Complete Psychological Works, XIV*. Translated by James Strachey. London: Hogarth Press, 1957.

Fritzsche, Peter. *Germans into Nazis*. Cambridge, MA: Harvard University Press, 1998.

Frye, Northrop. *The Secular Scripture: A Study of the Structure of Romance*. Cambridge, MA: Harvard University Press, 1978.

Fussell, Paul. *The Great War and Modern Memory*. New York: Oxford University Press, 1975.

Gaebel, Käthe, and Max von Schulz. *Die Heimarbeit im Kriege*. Berlin: F. Vahlen, 1917.

Gerhard, Ute. "National oder International: Die internationalen Beziehungen der deutschen bürgerlichen Frauenbewegung." *Feministische Studien* 3 (1994): 34–52.

Geyer, Michael. "The Stigma of Violence, Nationalism, and War in Twentieth-Century Germany." *German Studies Review* (Winter 1992): 75–110.

Gibbs, Phillip A. "Self-Control and Male Sexuality in the Advice Literature of Nineteenth-Century America, 1930–1860." *Journal of American Culture* 9, no. 2 (1986): 37–41.

Goebel, Stefan. *The Great War and Medieval Memory: War, Remembrance and Medievalism in Britain and Germany, 1914–1940.* Cambridge: Cambridge University Press, 2007.

Gourevitch, Philip. "Alms Dealers: Can You Provide Humanitarian Aid without Facilitating Conflicts?" *The New Yorker* (October 11, 2010): 102–9.

Grabill, Wilson H. "Effect of the War on the Birth Rate and Postwar Fertility Prospects." *American Journal of Sociology* 50, no. 2 (1944): 107–11.

Gräser, Marcus. "World History in a Nation-State: The Transnational Disposition in Historical Writing in the United States." *Journal of American History* 95, no. 4 (March 2009): 1038–52.

Grayzel, Susan. *Women and the First World War.* New York: Longman, 2002.

Grossmann, Atina. *Reforming Sex: The German Movement for Birth Control and Abortion Reform, 1920–1950.* New York: Oxford University Press, 1995.

Hagemann, Karen. "Home/Front: The Military, Violence and Gender Relations in the Age of the World Wars." In Hagemann and Stefanie Schüler-Springorum, eds., *Home/Front: The Military, War and Gender in Twentieth-Century Germany.* New York: Berg, 2002.

———. "Men's Demonstrations and Women's Protest: Gender in Collective Action in the Urban Working-Class Milieu during the Weimar Republic." *Gender & History* 5, no. 1 (1993): 101–19.

Hagener, Edith, Johanna Boldt, and Julius Boldt. *Es Lief so sicher an Deinem Arm: Briefe einer Soldatenfrau, 1914.* Weinheim: Beltz, 1986.

Hamelmann, Gudrun. "Helene Stöcker, der 'Bund für Mutterschutz' und 'Die neue Generation.'" Frankfurt: Haag and Herchen Verlag, 2003.

Hamilton, Alice. "At the War Capitals." *Survey* (August 7, 1915): 417–22.

Hamm, Elizabeth Creevey. *In White Armor: The Life of Captain Arthur Ellis Hamm, 326th Infantry, United States Army.* New York: Knickerbocker Press, 1919.

Hanna, Martha, *Your Death Would Be Mine: Paul and Marie Pireaud in the Great War.* Cambridge, MA: Harvard University Press, 2006.

Harmsen, Hans. *Der Einfluß der versorgungsgesetzlichen Regelung auf die Wirtschaftliche und soziale Lage der Kriegerwitwen: eine soziologische und bevölkerungspolitische Untersuchung, zugleich der Versuch einer sozialhygienischen Beurteilung und Kritik unserer heutigen Versorgungsgesetzgebung.* Berlin: Schoetz, 1926.

Harvey, Elizabeth. "Visions of the Volk: German Women and the Far Right from Kaiserreich to Third Reich." *Journal of Women's History* 16, no. 3 (2004): 152–67.

———. "The Failure of Feminism? Young Women and the Bourgeois Feminist Movement in Weimar Germany, 1918–1933." *Central European History* 28 (1995): 2–28.

Hausen, Karin. "The 'Day of National Mourning' in Germany." In Gerald Sider and Gavin Smith, eds., *Between History and Histories: The Making of Silences and Commemorations.* Toronto: University of Toronto Press, 1997.

———. "The German Nation's Obligation to the Heroes' Widows of World War I." In Margaret Randolph Higonnet, Jane Jenson, Sonya Michel, and Margaret Collins Weitz, eds., *Behind the Lines: Gender and the Two World Wars.* New Haven, CT: Yale University Press, 1987.

————."Die Sorge der Nation für ihre 'Kriegsopfer': Ein Bereich der Geschlechterpolitik während der Weimarer Republik." In Jürgen Kocka and Gerhard Ritter, eds., *Von der Arbeiterbewegung zum modernen Sozialstaat*. Munich: Saur Verlag, 1994.

Heinemann, Elizabeth D. *What Difference Does a Husband Make? Women and Marital Status in Nazi and Postwar Germany*. Berkeley: University of California Press, 1999.

Helmar, Anica. "*Einsame Frauen.*" *Frauen-Rundschau* 7, no. 7 (April 1, 1906): 183–88.

Hemingway, Ernest. *A Farewell to Arms*. 1929. Reprint, New York: Charles Scribner's Sons, 1993.

Herbert, David Rix. *Martin Luther: The Man and the Image*. New York: Irvington Publishers, 1984.

Hickel, K. Walter. "War, Region, and Social Welfare: Federal Aid to Servicemen's Dependents in the South, 1917-1921." *The Journal of American History* 87, no. 4 (March 2001): 1362–96.

Hillerman, Barbara Dodd. "Chrysalis of Gloom: Nineteenth-Century American Mourning Costume." In Martha V. Pike and Janice Gray Armstrong, eds., *A Time to Mourn: Expressions of Grief in Nineteenth-Century America*. Stony Brook: Museums at Stony Brook, 1980.

Hobsbawm, Eric. "Introduction." In Eric Hobsbawm and Terence Ranger, eds., *The Invention of Tradition*. Cambridge: Cambridge University Press, 1983.

Hodgson, Godfrey. *The Myth of American Exceptionalism*. New Haven, CT: Yale University Press, 2008.

Homer. *The Odyssey*. Translated by Rodney Merrill. Ann Arbor: University of Michigan Press, 2002.

Hunter, John C. "The Problem of the French Birth Rate on the Eve of World War I." *French Historical Studies 2, no. 4 (1962): 490–503.*

Hurwitz-Stranz, Helene. "8 Jahre Beisitzerin an Reichsversorgungsgericht." *Die Frau* 38 (1930/31): 264–71.

————. "Stadtkinder aufs Land." *Die Frau* 24, no. 10 (July 1917): 601–5.

Hurwitz-Stranz, Helene, ed. *Kriegerwitwen gestalten ihr Schicksal: Lebenskämpfe deutscher Kriegerwitwen nach eigenen Darstellungen*. Berlin: Heymann, 1931.

Huss, Marie-Monique. "Pronatalism and the Popular Ideology of the Child in Wartime France." In Jay Winter and Richard Walls, eds., *The Upheaval of War: Family, Work, and Welfare in Europe, 1914–1918*. Cambridge: Cambridge University Press, 1988.

Jackson, Frank, "What Mary Didn't Know." In Paul K. Moser and J. D. Trout, eds., *Contemporary Materialism: A Reader*. London: Routledge, 1993.

Jaggar, Alison M. *Feminist Politics and Human Nature*. New York: Rowman and Littlefield, 1988.

Jensen, Kimberly. *Mobilizing Minerva: American Women in the First World War*. Urbana: University of Illinois Press, 2008.

Jensen, Kimberly, and Erika Kuhlman, "Introduction." In Jensen and Kuhlman, eds., *Women and Transnational Activism in Historical Perspective*. Dordrecht, Netherlands: Republic of Letters Publishing, 2010.

Jones, Heather. "International or Transnational? Humanitarian Action during the First World War." *European Review of History* 16, no. 5 (2009): 697–713.

Jünger, Karl. *Deutschlands Frauen und Deutschlands Krieg; Ein Rat-, Tat- u. Trostbuch*. Stuttgart: Lutz, 1916.

Kaufmann, Thomas. "'Our Lord God's Chancery' in Madgeburg and Its Fight Against the Interim." *Church History* 73 no. 3 (September 2004): 566–82.

Keith, Jeanette. *Rich Man's War, Poor Man's Fight: Race, Class, and Power in the Rural South during the First World War.* Chapel Hill: University of North Carolina Press, 2004.

Kennedy, David M. *Over Here: The First World War and American Society.* 1980. Reprint, New York: Oxford, 2004.

Kevles, David J. *In the Name of Eugenics: Genetics and the Uses of Heredity.* New York: Knopf, 1985.

Kirk, Dudley. *Europe's Population in the Interwar Years.* Geneva: League of Nations, 1946.

Kleinberg, S. J. *Widows and Orphans First: The Family Economy and Social Welfare Policy, 1880–1939.* Urbana: University of Illinois Press, 2006.

Kuhlman, Erika. *Petticoats and White Feathers: Gender Conformity, Race, the Progressive Peace Movement, and the Debate over War, 1895–1919.* Westport, CT: Greenwood Press, 1997.

———. *Reconstructing Patriarchy after the Great War: Women, Gender, and Postwar Reconciliation between Nations.* New York: Palgrave Macmillan, 2008.

Kundrus, Birthe. "Gender Wars: The First World War and the Construction of Gender Relations in the Weimar Republic." In Karen Hagemann and Stefanie Schüler-Springorum, eds., *Home/Front: The Military, War and Gender in Twentieth-Century Germany.* New York: Berg, 2002.

Lagorio, Francesca. "Italian Widows of the First World War." In Frans Coetzee and Marilyn Shevin-Coetzee, eds., *Authority, Identity, and the Social History of the Great War.* Providence, RI: Berghahn Books, 1995.

Lange, Helene. "Zur Wiederaufnahme der Bevölkerungspolitik." *Die Frau* 23, no. 2 (1915): 100.

Lanthier, Michael. "War Widows and the Expansion of the French Welfare State." *Proceedings of the Western Society for French History* 31 (2003): 255–70.

Leavitt, Judith Walzer. *Brought to Bed: Childbearing in America, 1750–1950.* New York: Oxford University Press, 1986.

Leed, Eric J. "Class and Disillusionment in World War I." *Journal of Modern History* 50, no. 4 (1978): 680–99.

———. *No Man's Land: Combat and Identity in World War I.* Cambridge: Cambridge University Press, 1981.

Lerner, Gerda. *The Creation of Patriarchy.* New York: Oxford University Press, 1986.

Levy-Rathenau, Josephine. "Berufsberatung und Kriegshinterbliebene." In *Tagung des Hauptausschusses der Kriegerwitwen und Waisenfürsorgung, Frauenerwerb und Kriegswitwe Referate entstattet auf der 2. Tagung des Hauptasschusses der Kreigerwitwen und Waisenfürsorge am 27. November 1915 im Reichstagsgebäude in Berlin.* Berlin: Carl Heymann, 1916.

Lewis, David. "Postscript to 'Mad Pain and Martian Pain.'" *Philosophical Papers,* Volume 1. Oxford: Oxford University Press, 1983.

Lindemann, Anna. *Die Zukunft der Kriegswitwe.* Berlin: Arthur Collignon, 1915.

Lomas, Janis. "'Delicate Duties': Issues of Class and Respectability in Government Policy Towards the Wives and Widows of British Soldiers in the Era of the Great War." *Women's History Review* 9, no. 1 (2000): 123–47.

———. "'So I Married Again': Letters from British Widows of the First and Second World Wars." *History Workshop Journal* 38 no. 1 (1994): 218–27.

Loudon, Irvine. *Death in Childbirth: An International Study of Maternal Care and Maternal Mortality, 1800–1850*. Oxford: Clarendon Press, 1992.

Love, Thomas B. "The Social Significance of War Risk Insurance." *The Annals of the American Academy of Political and Social Science* (1918): 51.

Lübbering, Heinrich. "Mode, Politik und Volkswirtschaft." *Frauenwirtschaft: Zeitschrift für den Unterricht und die Fortbildung in Hauswirtschaft und Handarbeit, Landwirtschaft und Gartenbau* 7, no. 4 (July 1916): 73–83.

Lüders, Else. "Die Dankesschuld gegen die Mutter." *Die Frauenbewegung* 21, no. 19 (October 1, 1915): 1–2.

———. "Das Doppelgesicht des Krieges." *Die Frauenbewegung* 21, no. 4 (February 15, 1915): 1.

———. "Die Stellung der Frauen zu Krieg und Frieden." *Die Frauenbewegung* 25 no. 18 (December 15, 1919): 122.

Luebke, Frederick C. *Bonds of Loyalty: German Americans and World War I*. DeKalb: Northern Illinois University Press, 1974.

Mackaman, Douglas Peter, and Michael Mays, eds., *World War I and the Cultures of Modernity*. Jackson: University Press of Mississippi, 2000.

Macke, August, and Franz Marc. *August Macke, Franz Marc: Briefwechsel*. Köln: M. Dumont Schauberg, 1964.

Marrow, John H. Jr. "Knights of the Sky: The Rise of Military Aviation." In Frans Coetzee and Marilyn Shevin-Coetzee, eds., *Authority, Identity and the Social History of the Great War*. Providence, RI: Berghahn Books, 1995.

Marsland, Elizabeth. *The Nation's Cause: French, English, and German Poetry in the First World War*. New York: Routledge, 1991.

Martini, Ed. "Exhibition Review." *Journal of American History* 87 no. 3 (December 2000): 987–91.

May, Henry F. *The End of American Innocence: A Study of the First Years of Our Own Time, 1912–1917*. New York: Knopf, 1959.

Mayer, Tamar. "Gender Ironies of Nationalism: Setting the Stage." In Tamar Mayer, ed., *Gender Ironies of Nationalism: Sexing the Nation*. New York: Routledge, 2000.

McCartney, Helen B. *Citizen Soldiers: The Liverpool Territorials in the First World War*. Cambridge: Cambridge University Press, 2005.

McCune Lindsay, Samuel. "Purpose and Scope of War Risk Insurance." *Annals of the American Academy of Political and Social Science* 79 (September 1918): 52–68.

Meisel-Hess, Grete. *Krieg und Ehe*. Berlin: Oesterheld, 1916.

Meseure, Anna. *August Macke, 1887–1914*. Köln: Taschen, 1993.

Meyer, Jessica. *Men of War: Masculinity and the First World War in Britain*. Basingstoke: Palgrave Macmillan, 2009.

More, Adelyne. *Uncontrolled Breeding, or Fecundity Versus Civilization*. New York: Critic and Guide Company, 1917.

Mosse, George. *Fallen Soldiers: Reshaping the Memory of the World War*. New York: Oxford University Press, 1990.

Nagel, Thomas. "What Is It Like to Be a Bat?" *Philosophical Review* 83 (1974): 435–50.

Nau, Karl. *Die wirtschaftliche und soziale Lage von Kriegshinterbliebenen: Eine Studie auf grund von Erhebungen über die Auswirkung der Versorgung von Kriegshinterbliebenen in Darmstadt*. Leipzig: Lühe & Company, 1930.

Nelson, Robert L. "German Comrades/Slavic Whores: Gender Images in the German Soldier Newspapers of the First World War." In Karen Hagemann and Stefanie Schüler-Springorum, eds., *Home/Front: The Military, War and Gender in Twentieth-Century Germany*. New York: Berg, 2002.

Nolan, Mary. *Visions of Modernity: American Business and the Modernization of Germany*. New York: Oxford University Press, 1994.

Nordbeck, Gesine. "Zwischen zwei Gesetzen?" *Die Frau* 23.4 (1916): 216–21.

Pagels, Elaine. *Adam, Eve, and the Serpent*. New York: Vintage Books, 1989.

Pease, Donald E. *The New American Exceptionalism*. Minneapolis: University of Minnesota Press, 2009.

Pedersen, Susan. *Family, Dependence, and the Origins of the Welfare State: Britain and France, 1914–1945*. Cambridge: Cambridge University Press, 1993.

Peiss, Kathy. *Cheap Amusements: Working Women and Leisure in Turn-of-the-Century New York*. Philadelphia: Temple University Press, 1986.

Peukert, Detlev J.K. *The Weimar Republic: The Crisis of Classical Modernity*. Translated by Richard Deveson. New York: Hill and Wang, 1987.

Piehler, G. Kurt. *Remembering War the American Way*. Washington: Smithsonian Institution Press, 1995.

Pike, Martha V., and Janice Gray Armstrong, eds. *A Time to Mourn: Expressions of Grief in Nineteenth-Century America*. New York: The Museums at Stony Brook, 1980.

Planck, Mathilde. "Unsere Zukunft." *Die Frauenbewegung* 23, no. 5/6 (1917): 17–19.

Porter, Kathrine Anne. *Pale Horse, Pale Rider: Three Short Novels*. New York: Harcourt, Brace and Co., 1939.

Potter, Constance. "World War I Gold Star Mothers Pilgrimages, Part I." *Prologue* 31, no. 2 (1999): 140–45.

———. "World War I Gold Star Mothers Pilgrimages Part II." *Prologue* 31, no. 3 (1999): 210–15.

Proctor, Tammy M. *Civilians in a World at War, 1914–1918*. New York: New York University Press, 2010.

Quataert, Jean H. *Reluctant Feminists in German Social Democracy, 1885–1917*. Princeton, NJ: Princeton University Press, 1979.

Rachamimov, Alon. *POWs and the Great War: Captivity on the Eastern Front*. New York: Berg, 2002.

Reimann, Aribert. *Der grosse Krieg der Sprachen: Untersuchungen zur historischen Semantik in Deutschland und England zur Zeit des Ersten Weltkriegs*. Essen: Klartext Verlag, 2000.

Reuscher, Max. *Der Kampf Gegen den Geburtenrückgang in Deutschland, früher und heute*. Stettin: Ostsee-druckerei und- Verlag, 1937.

Reutti, Karl. "Zahlenergebnis." In *Kriegshinterbliebenenfürsorge in Preussen: Ergebnis einer Umfrage bei den Fürsorgestellen*. Berlin: Heymann, 1919.

Rich, Norman. *The Age of Nationalism and Reform, 1850–1890*. New York: Norton, 1970.

Rimbaud, Arthur. *Arthur Rimbaud Collected Poems*. Translated by Martin Sorrell. New York: Oxford University Press, 2001.

Rixey, Lilian. "Shall I Remarry?" *Life* (April 1946): 106–16.

Roberts, Mary Louise. *Civilization without Sexes: Reconstructing Gender in Postwar France, 1917–1927*. Chicago: University of Chicago Press, 1994.

Rollet, Catherine. "The Home and Family Life." In Jay Winter and Jean-Louis Robert, eds., *Capital Cities at War: Paris, London, and Berlin, 1914–1919, Volume 2*. Cambridge: Cambridge University Press. 2007.

Rouette, Susanne. "Mothers and Citizens: Gender and Social Policy in Germany after the First World War." *Central European History* 30 (1997): 48–66.

———. *Sozialpolitik als Geschlechterpolitik: die Regulierung der Frauenarbeit nach dem Ersten Weltkrieg*. Frankfurt: Campus, 1996.

Rybczynski, Witold. *Home: A Short History of an Idea*. New York: Penguin, 1986.

Said, Edward. "Invention, Memory, and Place." *Critical Inquiry* 26 (Winter 2000): 177–79.

Salomon, Alice. "*Die Fürsorge für die Hinterbliebenen der gefallenen Krieger*." *Die Frau* 22, no.7 (April 1915): 385.

Scheck, Raffael. "German Conservatism and Female Political Activism in the Early Weimar Republic." *German History* 15, no. 1 (1997): 34–55.

———. *Mothers of the Nation: Right-Wing Women in Weimar Germany*. New York: Berg, 2004.

———. "Women against Versailles: Maternalism and Nationalism of Female Bourgeois Politicians in the Early Weimar Republic." *German Studies Review* 22 no. 1 (1999): 21–42.

Schjeldahl, Peter. "Turning Away." *The New Yorker* (October 25, 2010): 91–92.

Schlusstagung des Hauptausschusses. *Stand und Künftige Entwicklung der Kriegerwitwen und Kriegswaisenfürsorge*. Berlin: Heymann, 1918.

Schnädelbach, Anna. *Kriegerwitwen: Lebenswältigung zwischen Arbeit und Familie in Westdeutschland nach 1945*. Frankfurt: Campus Verlag, 2009.

Schüler, Paul. "Die Frau im Recht—Der Lezte Wille." *Die Frau* 2, no. 8 (May 1895): 453–57.

Schwann-Schneider, Rosa. "Bemerkungen zu Mathilde Plancks Artikel." *Die Frauenbewegung* 23, no. 9 (1917): 35–36.

Scott, James Brown, and Woodrow Wilson. *President Wilson's Foreign Policy: Messages, Addresses, Papers*. New York: Oxford University Press, 1918.

Seipp, Adam R. *The Ordeal of Peace: Demobilization and the Urban Experience in Britain and Germany, 1917–1921*. Burlington, VT: Ashgate, 2009.

Seitz, David William. "'Let Him Remain Until the Judgment in France': Family Letters and the Overseas Burying of U.S. World War I Soldiers." In Udo J. Hebel, ed., *Transnational American Memories*. Berlin/New York: Walter de Gruyter, 2009.

Seraphim, Franziska. *War Memory and Social Politics in Japan, 1945–2005*. Cambridge, MA: Harvard University Asia Center, 2006.

Sharp, Ingrid. "Blaming the Women: Women's 'Responsibility' for the First World War." In Ingrid Sharp and Alison S. Fell, eds., *The Women's Movement in Wartime: International Perspectives, 1914–19*. Basingstoke: Palgrave Macmillan, 2007.

Shenk, Gerald E. *Work or Fight! Race, Gender and the Draft in World War I*. New York: Palgrave Macmillan, 2005.

Showalter, Dennis. "Mass Warfare and the Impact of Technology." In Roger Chickering and Stig Förster, eds., *Great War, Total War: Combat and Mobilization on the Western Front, 1914–1918*. Washington: German Historical Institute, 2000.

Siegel, Mona. "'History Is the Opposite of Forgetting': The Limits of Memory and the Lessons of History in Interwar France." *The Journal of Modern History* 7, no. 4 (2002): 770–800.

Simon, Helene. "Kriegswitwen und Beruf." *Die Frau* 22, no. 7 (April 1915): 417.

Sklar, Kathryn Kish, Anja Schüler, and Susan Strasser, eds., *Social Justice Feminists in the United States and Germany: A Dialogue in Documents, 1885–1933*. Ithaca, NY: Cornell University Press, 1998.

Smith, Ethel M. "'Surplus Women': England's Struggle with a European Problem." *National Business Woman* 8, no. 9 (1924): 7–8.

Smith, Leonard V., Stéphane Audoin-Rouzeau, and Annette Becker. *France and the Great War, 1914–1918*. Cambridge: Cambridge University Press, 2003.

Soloway, Richard A. *Demography and Degeneration: Eugenics and the Declining Birth Rate in Twentieth-Century Britain*. Chapel Hill: University of North Carolina Press, 1995.

———. "Eugenics and Pronatalism in Wartime Britain." In Richard Wall and Jay Winter, eds., *The Upheaval of War: Family, Work and Welfare in Europe, 1914–1918*. New York: Cambridge University Press, 1988.

Sonn, Richard David. "'Your Body Is Yours': Anarchism, Birth Control, and Eugenics in Interwar France." *Journal of the History of Sexuality* 14, no. 4 (2005): 415–32.

Sonneborn, Barbara, director. *Regret to Inform*. DVD. New York: Docurama, 1998.

Stanley, Matthew. "'An Expedition to Heal the Wounds of War': The 1919 Eclipse and Eddington as Quaker Adventurer," *Isis* 94 no. 1 (March 2003): 57–89.

Stannard, David E. "Where All Our Steps Are Tending: Death in the American Context." In Martha V. Pike and Janice Gray Armstrong, eds., *A Time to Mourn: Expressions of Grief in Nineteenth-Century America*. Stony Brook, NY: Museums at Stony Brook, 1980.

Stephenson, Jill. "'Reichsbund der Kinderreichen': The League of Large Families in the Population Policy of Nazi Germany." *European Studies Review* 9, no. 3 (1979): 351–75.

Steinisch, Irmgard, "A Different Path to War: A Comparative Study of Militarism and Imperialism in the United States and Imperial Germany, 1871–1914." In Roger Chickering, Manfred Boemeke, and Stig Förster, eds., *Anticipating Total War: The German and American Experiences, 1871–1914*. Cambridge: Cambridge University Press, 1999.

Stibbe, Matthew. "Anti-Feminism, Nationalism and the German Right, 1914–1920." *German History* 20 no. 2 (2002): 193–208.

———. "Elisabeth Rotten and the 'Auskunfts- und Hilfsstelle für Deutsche im Ausland und Ausländer in Deutschland,' 1914–1919," in Alison S. Fell and Ingrid Sharp, eds., *The Women's Movement in Wartime: International Perspectives, 1914–19*. Basingstoke: Palgrave Macmillan, 2007.

———. "The Internment of Civilians by Belligerent States during the First World War and the Response of the International Committee of the Red Cross." *Journal of Contemporary History* 41 (January 2006): 5–19.

Stöcker, Helene. *Moderne Bevölkerungspolitik*. Berlin: Oesterheld, 1916.

Stolberg, Sheryl Gay. "Senate Backs Ban on Photos of G.I. Coffins," New York Times, June 22, 2004 http://www.nytimes.com/2004/06/22/us/senate-backs-ban-on-photos-of-gi-coffins.html?emc=eta1

Szepansky, Gerda. *Blitzmädel, Heldenmutter, Kriegerwitwen: Frauenleben im Zweiten Weltkrieg*. Frankfurt: Fischer Taschenbuch Verlag, 1986.

Taylor, Irmgard C. *Das Bild der Witwe in der deutschen Literatur*. Darmstadt: Gesellschaft Hessischer Literaturfreunde, 1980.

Taylor, Lawrence. "Symbolic Death: An Anthropological View of Mourning in the Nineteenth Century." In Martha V. Pike and Janice Gray Armstrong, eds., *A Time to Mourn:*

Expressions of Grief in Nineteenth-Century America. Stony Brook, NY: Museums at Stony Brook, 1980.

Taylor, Lou. *Mourning Dress: A Costume and Social History.* London: George Allen and Unwin, 1983.

Thiel, Hubertus. "Hubertus Thiel." In Wolfgang W. E. Samuel, ed., *The War of our Childhood: Memories of World War II.* Jackson: University Press of Mississippi, 2002.

Travers, Martin. *German Novels on the First World War and Their Ideological Implications, 1918–1933.* Stuttgart: H. D. Heinz, 1982.

Ullrich, Volker. *Kriegsalltag: Hamburg im ersten Weltkrieg.* Köln: Prometh, 1982.

Ulrich, Bernd. *Die Augenzeugen: Deutsche Feldpostbriefe in Kriegs- und Nachkriegszeit, 1914–1933.* Essen: Klartext Verlag, 1997.

Ulrich, Bernd, and Benjamin Ziemann, eds. *German Soldiers in the Great War: Letters and Eyewitness Accounts.* Translated by Christine Brocks. South Yorkshire: Pen & Sword Books, 2010.

Usborne, Cornelie. "Pregnancy Is the Women's Active Service: Pronatalism in Germany During the First World War." In Richard Wall and Jay Winter, eds., *The Upheaval of War: Family, Work, and Welfare in Europe, 1914–1918.* Cambridge: Cambridge University Press, 1988.

van Os, Geertje. "Widows Hidden from View: The Disappearance of Mourning Dress among Dutch Widows in the Twentieth Century." In Jan Bremmer and Lourens van den Bosch, eds., *Between Poverty and the Pyre: Moments in the History of Widowhood.* New York: Routledge, 1995.

Vincent, C. Paul. *The Politics of Hunger: The Allied Blockade of Germany, 1915–1919.* Athens: Ohio University Press, 1985.

Vining, Margaret, and Barton C. Hacker. "From Camp Follower to Lady in Uniform: Women, Social Class, and Military Institutions Before 1920." *Contemporary European History* 10, no. 3 (2001): 353–73.

Wall, Richard, and Jay Winter, eds. *The Upheaval of War: Family, Work and Welfare in Europe, 1914–1918.* Cambridge: Cambridge University Press, 1988.

Watson, Alexander. *Enduring the Great War: Combat, Morale and Collapse in the German and British Armies, 1914–1918.* Cambridge: Cambridge University Press, 2008.

Weber, Eugen. *The Hollow Years: France in the 1930s.* New York: Norton, 1994.

Weindling, Paul. "The Medical Profession, Social Hygiene and the Birth Rate in Wartime Germany." In Richard Wall and Jay Winter, eds., *The Upheaval of War: Family, Work, and Welfare in Europe, 1914–1918.* Cambridge: Cambridge University Press, 1988.

Whalen, Robert Weldon. *Bitter Wounds: German Victims of the Great War, 1914–1939.* Ithaca, NY: Cornell University Press, 1984.

Willsie, Honoré. "American Race-Control." *Woman's Journal* 7, no. 1 (1922): 15.

Winter, Jay M. "Communities in Mourning." In Frans Coetzee and Marilyn Shevin-Coetzee, eds., *Authority, Identity and the Social History of the Great War.* Providence, RI: Berghahn Books, 1995.

———. "The Fear of Population Decline in Western Europe, 1870–1940." In R. W. Hiorns, ed., *Demographic Patterns in Developed Societies.* London: Taylor and Francis, 1980.

———. *Remembering War: The Great War Between Memory and History in the Twentieth Century.* New Haven, CT: Yale University Press, 2006.

———. *Sites of Memory, Sites of Mourning: The Great War in European Cultural History.* Cambridge: Cambridge University Press, 1995.

Wolfe, A. B. "Economic Conditions and the Birth-Rate After the War." *The Journal of Political Economy* 25, no. 6 (June 1917): 521–41.

Wolfe, S. H. "Eight Months of War-Risk Insurance Work." *Annals of the American Academy of Political and Social Science* 79 (September 1918): 68–79.

Woloch, Nancy. *Women and the American Experience.* New York: Knopf, 1984.

Zeiger, Susan. *In Uncle Sam's Service: Women Workers with the American Expeditionary Force, 1917–1919.* Philadelphia: University of Pennsylvania Press, 2004.

Zeitlin, Michael. "The Passion of Margaret Powers: A Psychoanalytic Reading of Soldiers' Pay." *Mississippi Quarterly* 46 (1993): 351–72.

Zimmerman, William. *A Popular History of Germany from the Earliest Period to the Present Day, Volume 2.* New York: Henry J. Johnson, 1878.

UNPUBLISHED MANUSCRIPT

Davis, David A. "The Modernist Death of Donald Mahon." Modern Language Association, Philadelphia, Pennsylvania, November 2006. faulknersociety.com/mla06davis. doc. July 2011

THESIS

Greensfelder, Natalia. "An Inquiry into the Problem of Relief for Families of Deceased World War Veterans in Illinois." M.A. thesis, University of Chicago, 1931.

DISSERTATIONS

Hickel, K. Walter. "Entitling Citizens: World War I, Progressivism, and the Origins of the American Welfare State, 1917–1928," Ph.D. dissertation, Columbia University, 1999.

Lanthier, Michael. "Women Alone: Widows in Third Republic France, 1870–1940." Ph.D. dissertation. Simon Fraser University, 2004.

Mills, Cynthia J. "The Adams Memorial and American Funerary Sculpture, 1891–1927." Ph.D. dissertation. University of Maryland at College Park, 1996.

Plant, Rebecca Jo. "The Repeal of Mother Love: Momism and the Reconstruction of Motherhood in Philip Wylie's America." Ph.D. dissertation. Johns Hopkins University, 2001.

Index

Kenyon-Fess bill. *See under* Female labor-
ers, job training programs for widows
Knowledge, versus experience, 27, 171n40
Die Kriegerwitwe, 50, 127

Lange, Helene, 36, 141–142
Lansing, Robert, U.S. Secretary of State,
112, 118–119
League for the Protection of Motherhood
(BfM), 147, 148
Leed, Eric J., 26, 29, 45
Letter-writing, 18, 25, 26, 27, 36, 68, 147
Lindemann, Anna, 46–47
Literature, prescriptive, 18, 56
Lüders, Else, 37, 43, 66, 108, 161

Macke, August, 25, 27, 53, 99; bequeath-
ment of his wife and children, 35, 42;
death of, 32; as soldier, 28, 33, 131
Macke, Elisabeth Erdmann, 10, 25, 32–37,
53, 99, 108, 131, 162; marriages of, 31, 35,
125; as mother, 28, 43, 125; as war widow,
18–19, 27, 71, 92–93, 107
Magdeburg, Germany, 123–125, 129, 130
Maginot Line, 127, 141
Marc, Franz, 31, 33–34, 37
Marc, Maria, 31, 33
Marriage, 3, 10–11,102–103, 133–138; com-
panionate, 4–5; in Germany, 22, 42, 45,
50, 112, 123–125
Marsh, Nancy Payne, 19, 74–75, 93–94
Maternal mortality rate, 139–140, 199n93
Militarization, 5, 13, 16, 24, 70, 74, 88,
93–94, 142, 136. *See also* Remilitarization
Miscegenation, 143–144
A Month in the Country, 29, 172n51, 186n3
Modernity. *See under* Nations and
nationalism
Monuments, to WWI, 98–99
Motherhood, in Germany, 22, 25, 31, 43,
136, 145–148; in the United States, 73
Mourning, 5, 7–8, 13–14, 91, 97–98, 108,
130, 142; in Germany, 23, 25, 39, 160
Mourning attire, 8, 11, 13, 41, 56, 155–156,
160–161, 180n33, 181n49; in the U.S., 57,
64–70

Munitions factories. *See under* Female
laborers, in armaments factories

National Socialism (Nazis), 35, 42, 112,
155–156
Nations and nationalism, 9–11, 13–20,
92–99, 104–108, 124–130, 132–136,
142–145, 149; as modernizing force,
148–149; in the U.S., 57, 63, 66–67, 69–71,
73, 75, 88
Neutrality (U.S.), 59–61, 88
New Woman, 4–5, 6–7, 42, 54–55, 67, 149
Nordbeck, Gesine, 145, 147

Pacifism, 15, 53, 88, 96, 107, 108, 129, 145–148
Peace movements, 7, 107, 126–127, 129
Pensions, 11, 14, 103–104, 122, 131–132; in
Germany, 26, 43, 45–50, 129–132, 143,
155–156, 177n153, 185n145; in the U.S.,
72–73, 78–88, 154
Phillips, William, 117–120
Piehler, G. Kurt, 17, 62
Pierce, Major Charles C., 62, 60
Pierson, Harriet, 57, 62–63, 75, 107, 130
Pierson, Major Ward Wright, 62–63
Pilgrimages, Gold Star, 57, 61, 69–75, 78, 85
Pireaud, Paul, and Marie Pireaud, 26–27
Planck, Mathilde, 138, 145
Postcards, French. *See under* Visual arts
Postwar, 25, 43, 95, 113–115, 130–131, 133–134;
surplus of females, 131
Progressive era, U.S., 53, 62, 81
Pronatalism, 19, 135–149
Propaganda, 29, 95–97, 110, 112; anti-
natalist, 145; pronatalist, 125–126, 139,
142, 144–145

Quartermaster General (U.S.), 63, 69–71, 85

Race, 16, 105; and Allotments and Allowances (U.S.), 79; and eugenics, 126, 128,
141, 143–144. *See also* Rhineland horror
campaign
Red Cross 28, 97, 109–110, 115, 120. *See also*
Humanitarian organizations
Regret to Inform (film), 159, 173n69

About the Author

ERIKA KUHLMAN is Associate Professor of History at Idaho State University. She is the author of *Petticoats and White Feathers, Reconstructing Patriarchy after the Great War*, and a volume coedited with Kimberly Jensen titled *Women and Transnational Activism in Historical Perspective*. She is the editor of *Peace & Change: A Journal of Peace Research*.